Hot Showers! *Maine Coast Lodgings for Kayakers and Sailors* will help you experience that special part of Maine right at the water's edge. It will guide you to some of the unique places on Maine's magnificent coast. You'll discover:

- Great oceanfront lodgings, everything from snug bed and breakfasts to grand resorts
- Campgrounds providing access to sheltered waters or rocky shores
- Wonderful boating destinations
- Coastal hiking and biking opportunities
- Nautical museums and shops of special interest to boaters

"Here is a useful guide for those cruising in kayaks, small boats, and yachts who want to inject a bit of shoreside comfort – or even a touch of luxury – into their travels. Lee has 'been there' and it shows in this well-researched book."

Dave Getchell, Sr., editor of the *Outboard Boater's Handbook*

"Lee has provided a very helpful and detailed guide for anyone wanting to stay in land-side comfort while enjoying the wind and waves of the Maine coast by small boat. Definitely add this one to your kayaking library."

Tamsin Venn, author of *Sea Kayaking Along the New England Coast* and editor of *Atlantic Coastal Kayaker*

HOT SHOWERS!

MAINE COAST LODGINGS FOR KAYAKERS AND SAILORS

BY LEE BUMSTED

AUDENREED PRESS
BRUNSWICK, MAINE

Library of Congress Catalog Card Number: 97-72064

Publisher's Cataloging-in-Publication Data
Hot Showers! Maine Coast Lodgings for Kayakers and Sailors /
    by Lee Bumsted – 1st ed.
Includes bibliographical references and indexes.
ISBN 1-879418-81-9

1. Sea kayaking – Maine. 2. Sailing – Maine. 3. Bed and breakfast accommodations – Maine. 4. Campsites, facilities, etc. – Maine. I. Bumsted, Lee. II. Title.

Published by Audenreed Press
P.O. Box 1305 #103
Brunswick, Maine 04011
207-833-5016

Book design: Laurie Downey, West Baldwin, Maine
Regional maps: Jane Crosen, Penobscot, Maine, maps © 1985, 1986, 1989, 1995
Illustrations: Jane O'Conor, Portland, Maine
Printed by J. S. McCarthy Printers, Augusta, Maine, on chlorine-free recycled
    paper with 20% post-consumer content

To all those who help preserve
Maine's wild islands.

CONTENTS

197 PART III

ACKNOWLEDGMENTS

Many people provided encouragement, guidance, and technical support as I researched and produced this guidebook. I couldn't begin to note all the friends whose suggestions are incorporated in the book, but I thank them just the same.

For their encouragement in the early stages of this project, I'd like to thank Karen Stimpson, Tamsin Venn, and Bill Legge. I owe a particular debt of gratitude to Karen, who has taught me a great deal about writing, editing, and island conservation issues over the last five years at the Maine Island Trail Association's Union Wharf office.

As I researched the lodgings and campgrounds described here, I found their owners and hosts to be almost invariably friendly and helpful. I thank them for graciously dropping what they were doing to show me around their properties and field my questions.

I'd like to thank those who shared their knowledge of the Maine coast and reviewed the sections on Maine islands: Cate Cronin, Charlie Jacobi, Bruce Kidman, Annette Naegel, Steve Spencer, and Stan Skutek. I appreciate Forrest Dillon's insights into the Mount Desert Island area, and I thank Bob Hicks for locating the 1880 shadow-canoe story for me. Several people read and commented on early drafts of my book; I appreciate the time and suggestions of Wayne Curtis, Dave Getchell, Sr., Curtis Rindlaub, Jane Yurko, Jerry Yurko, and my parents.

It was a pleasure to work with the individuals who helped produce this book. I appreciate the guidance of Julie Zimmerman, of Audenreed Press. Proofreader Joan Terry taught me a few things I missed in English 101. I thank Jane O'Conor for her delightful illustrations, and Jane Crosen for permission to include her wonderful maps. I appreciate book designer Laurie Downey's sense of humor, flexibility, and creativity. Special thanks go to Mark Daniele, for producing the chart scans and for his support throughout the project.

ABOUT THE AUTHOR

Lee Bumsted has lived in Maine for 15 years, and continues to enjoy exploring the coast of her adopted home state. She often goes sea kayaking in Casco, Muscongus, and Penobscot Bays, and currently serves as president of the Southern Maine Sea Kayaking Network. Four years on the Maine Island Trail Association's board of trustees enhanced her understanding of island conservation and boating safety issues. She contributes as a writer, photographer, and editor to Maine Island Trail Association publications.

Lee has travelled extensively in the United States and abroad, and has kayaked in Alaska, New Zealand, and Australia. During her travels, she stays in all sorts of accommodations, from simple hostels to luxurious hotels. While she enjoys wilderness camping, she has come to appreciate the value of a hot shower!

NOTES TO READERS

Warning and disclaimer

Boating in Maine is a pleasurable but also inherently dangerous activity. The information in this book is meant to aid in your enjoyment and discovery of the Maine coast. It is your responsibility to assess factors such as sea conditions, the weather forecast, your skills, and your equipment's suitability before setting out on the water, or deciding to stay on the water. It is up to you to determine if boating destinations suggested in this book are appropriate for you and all members of your party.

Maps and charts provided in this book are for orientation only and are not to be used for navigation. Readers are urged to equip themselves with appropriate nautical charts.

Every effort has been taken to make this book accurate. However, coastal conditions and the status of accommodations are in constant states of change. Use of the information provided in this book is the sole risk of the reader. The author and publisher disclaim any liability or responsibility for any damage or loss to property or persons caused, or alleged to be caused, directly or indirectly by the information contained in this book, or by the interpretation of this information.

If you do not wish to be bound by the above considerations, you may return this book to the publisher, at the address below, for a full refund.

Reader suggestions

In your travels you may discover a wonderful new place to stay, a convenient boatyard, or an attraction of special interest to boaters. A note to the author, at the address below, would be much appreciated!

Audenreed Press
P.O. Box 1305 #103
Brunswick, Maine 04011

STAYING AT COASTAL LODGINGS

Sea kayakers like to camp on wild islands.

Sailors enjoy anchoring for the night in a quiet cove.

Why would they need a guide to coastal lodgings in

Maine? The reasons are almost as varied as the boats

they use to explore Maine's magnificent waters.

Creature comforts

Kayakers, think back to the last night you spent camping in the rain. Water is dripping through a tent seam and onto your head. You sleep fitfully, and observe that your self-inflating mattress seems to be deflating. The next morning, you give up on coffee when the cook stove acts up again, and settle for some cold cereal. What you'd do for some dry clothes!

Sailors, recall that night you awakened at three in the morning to check your anchor when the wind shifted? You never do get back to sleep as the boat rolls more and more. While trying to fix breakfast, you trip over your companions in the galley. You really wish it hadn't been four days since you last washed your hair.

Now consider what the same night would be like at a cozy waterfront inn. You settle into your down pillow and sleep soundly. In the morning, you indulge in a long hot shower, put on dry clothes, and sit down to a sumptuous breakfast in the dining room overlooking the harbor.

~

Staying in onshore lodgings is the perfect solution for boaters who may be tired of "roughing it" all the time. You can still enjoy self-sufficient boating on some trips; but on others, why not treat yourself to the amenities of coastal bed and breakfasts and inns: great food, comfortable beds, spacious rooms, steamy showers, perhaps even a jacuzzi or a hot tub?

Varied interests

Some of your boating friends may be diehard boaters, while others would like to mix some mountain biking, hiking, sightseeing, or shopping in with their travels. In the past, your group may have tried to find time for these pursuits, but it seemed you'd head for home without enjoying any off-the-water activities. This time you stay right in a coastal village. Most of you go boating every day, but one friend spends time biking, another touring a maritime museum, and everyone's happy.

~

Staying in shorefront lodgings allows those who want to explore Maine's coastal communities and the nearby countryside the option of doing so, while others spend the day on the water. This can be particularly handy for kayakers of varied skill levels, when some of them would rather go for a hike on a windy day, or go for a shorter outing. Crew members feeling cooped up on a sailboat will relish a day left to their own devices in town. In the case of families, one parent can take a turn entertaining the children while the other goes off boating. Or perhaps your favorite travelling companion is not a boater at all (heaven forbid!); staying at a waterfront lodging allows each of you to follow your respective interests during the day and meet up again for dinner.

~

Several islands in Maine, accessible only by boat or airplane, have year-round communities and guest accommodations. If you travel to one of these remarkable destinations, you can begin to get a sense of what it is like to live on a Maine island, while enjoying area boating.

Safety and weather

You have been looking forward to this three-day camping trip for a long time. The day before your scheduled departure, you check the weather forecast. There's a possibility of a storm arriving midway through your trip, when you would be camping far from shore. Instead of worrying about your return journey, you make reservations at a waterfront bed and breakfast (B&B). The storm passes to the south, and you comfortably explore islands and coves on day trips from your cozy B&B.

~

By boating out of a mainland base, you can respond better to changing weather patterns. You're less likely to find yourself in wind and waves beyond your skills, since conditions can change dramatically while you sleep far from the mainland. If the weather turns really nasty while you are on shore, you can simply save boating for another day, and head for a lunch-time lobster or a bit of shopping.

~

Onshore lodgings can extend your boating season beyond your usual summer forays. You can enjoy brisk springtime and fall foliage trips more, knowing you have a snug bed waiting after your day on the water.

Time

It's Thursday, the weather forecast for the weekend is marvelous, and your friend just called to suggest a weekend boating trip. You really don't have time to go grocery shopping and sort out your camping gear. You suggest a stay at a B&B near your favorite launch ramp.

~

Staying in waterfront lodgings or campgrounds can be a time-saver, since you are not packing, unpacking, and repacking food and gear. You may find you have even more time to do the things you came for: gunkholing along the coast, exploring the islands, relaxing on a sunny pocket beach.

Access and parking

You are heading to Penobscot Bay for a few days of sea kayaking and plan to camp on public islands. But you're leaving work on Thursday afternoon and can't get on the water before dark. Plus, you don't know where you can leave your car for a few days. You decide to line up Thursday and Sunday night reservations at a waterfront inn.

~

Many coastal lodgings can provide parking for guests' cars for a few days, while they are off boating. You can arrive after work, enjoy a good night's sleep and a hearty breakfast, and launch your kayak from the innkeeper's shore the next morning. You don't have to worry about finding a launch ramp and a parking space.

Reducing negative impacts to islands and coastal communities

You and seven of your friends plan to spend five days sea kayaking in Casco Bay. You've heard that some of the public wild islands have started to show signs of wear and tear from the number of campers visiting. Your group is large: you'd be setting up four tents, and you would need a place to leave all your cars. You opt to stay in mainland campgrounds, from which there is easy access to the islands you wish to visit.

~

Over the last several years a growing number of campers have come to Maine's wild islands. Even when you camp using low-impact techniques, it is difficult to leave no trace of your visit: vegetation gets trampled, shorelines eroded. Particularly if you are travelling in a large group, the best way to show that you treasure the islands is to limit your use of them. Day visits, with stops on beaches or granite shorelines, are much less likely to cause damage.

~

By staying in shorefront lodgings and campgrounds with their own launching and parking spots, you reduce the impact to local communities of using their limited launching and parking facilities. Many coastal communities have small public launch ramps or docks, for use by those who make their living from the sea as well as local recreational users. Visiting boaters can unintentionally take over the launch area while loading gear, or take parking needed by fishermen and clammers.

Exploring the options

You can stay on shore at night and do day trips, mix in mainland stays with your usual camping or staying aboard plans, or travel inn-to-inn. Besides comfortable beds and hot showers, you'll enjoy great meals that someone else has prepared for you. You can boat *and* have a roof over your head at night.

Staying on shore expands your experience of the Maine coast. You will learn a bit about a region's cultural and natural history, and you will meet some interesting people. And you'll be giving something back, by supporting the economies of local communities.

PICKING YOUR DESTINATION

The coastline of Maine starts off rather straight heading north from the New Hampshire border to Portland. Then things turn into a recreational boater's dream. The coast suddenly becomes irregular, with peninsulas and all manner of beautiful islands coming into view. Maine's shoreline snakes in and out so much that it is estimated to be at least 3500 miles long. Wonderful boating opportunities continue in a generally northeast (or "down east") direction along the coast to Machias, within 20 miles of the Canadian border. After Machias there is a bold, rockbound coast. It is the intriguing stretch of the Maine coast between Portland and Machias that is covered in this book.

Within a few miles of this shoreline is the variety that is Maine: everything from traditional fishing villages to cities with first-rate entertainment and museums, sandy beaches to mountainous hiking trails, restaurants serving lobsters to those featuring ethnic food, general stores to espresso shops. People have been using the water as a means of transportation along the Maine coast for hundreds of years, so boating and visiting coastal communities are easily linked activities.

Guidebook overview

To help you select the section of the coast you'd like to explore on your next trip, this guide divides the waters and neighboring communities into seven regions. It presents them from southwest to northeast, starting with Casco Bay and heading down east. You will find brief descriptions of the coastal villages and towns, with attractions you might wish to visit while you're ashore. Next are overviews of the neighboring waters, with descriptions of islands open to careful visitors. Descriptions of the lodgings and campgrounds follow.

This guide describes 155 of the bed and breakfasts, inns, motels, and hotels conveniently located on or near the water. Twenty-eight waterfront campgrounds are listed as well. Lodging and campground entries include information for kayakers and those with trailered boats on launching opportunities from the property or nearby. For sailors, the availability of guest moorings or rental moorings, slips, or dock space is indicated. Detailed nautical chart excerpts, showing the locations of accommodations, appear in Appendix E.

The bibliography provides reading suggestions to help you become better acquainted with the Maine coast.

Lodging choices

Of the lodgings available on the waterfront, the most commonly found are bed and breakfasts. B&B owners offer not only their hospitality, but sometimes a slice of history as well. Their homes are often stately houses, listed on the National Register of Historic Places, and furnished with antiques that might have been found in the house a hundred years ago. A number of the houses belonged to wealthy 19th-century sea captains. On the Maine coast, B&B's have been created from a former lighthouse keeper's home, a coast guard station, a tavern, lodgings for granite quarry workers, carriage houses, and a number of grand old summer cottages. When you stay in these well-restored structures, you can start to peel back layers of the area's history. It becomes easier to imagine the days of steamships and waterfront boardwalks.

Like the buildings they occupy, B&B's vary tremendously in the types of guest rooms and breakfasts they provide. Some B&B hosts offer two or three simple rooms in their homes and invite guests to share their living room. A stay in a small bed and breakfast can feel more like a stay with newly discovered friends or relatives. Other hosts purchase a large house and convert it to a B&B; they offer several luxurious guest rooms filled with antiques and fine linens. The large B&B's will have separate living rooms and other common spaces designated for guest use.

Some of these large B&B's blur the line between B&B's and inns. Breakfast at a B&B can be anything from muffins and cereal to a three-course meal.

Besides bed and breakfasts, there are also a number of full-scale inns, a few grand old resorts, and some modern motels right on the water.

Since accommodations in B&B's, inns, and resorts vary so, if you have specific requirements it is best to voice them when placing a reservation. If you love clawfoot tubs, ask for one. Conversely, if you want to be sure your bath has a shower, ask for that. Guest rooms range in size, and some have water views. Some guest rooms come with private baths, and others share baths; sometimes private baths are located across the hall from the room. Most lodgings have a choice of bed sizes, so if you want a queen-sized bed, request one. Tall visitors might wish to avoid top-floor rooms, and light sleepers might want to head directly to them. Some rooms offer more privacy than others.

The owners' pets are present in many B&B's. While these pets are unlikely to be allowed in guest rooms, they frequently make appearances in the living and dining spaces. The lodging entries that follow indicate if hosts allow their pets in such common spaces. Those of you allergic to cats or dogs would do well to confirm when making your reservations that a kitten or puppy hasn't joined the household.

The rate for a night's stay depends on the amenities provided as well as the time of year. Within a given facility there can be a wide range of prices linked to the size of the room, the view, and the presence of a private bath. You will find that rates are often lower in June and September than they are in July and August.

Hosts and guests

As I travelled along the coast visiting the hosts whose bed and breakfasts and inns are described in this book, I was struck by how warm and friendly they are. They will work hard to help make your stay a pleasant one. If you have particular lodging or dietary requirements, they are eager to help. They are often experts in what the surrounding communities have to offer in the way of entertainment, hiking trails, and dining, and enjoy sharing this information with guests. A surprising number are boaters themselves and can provide local knowledge of the nearby waters. They can help you find a place to leave a car for a few days while you're out on the water, and many have space on their property.

In return for your hosts' hospitality, a little extra consideration is called for on your part. For instance, guest rooms may be furnished with your hosts' family heirlooms, so if you need a place to drape your damp foul-weather gear, ask for the hosts' recommendation. The 100-year-old walls may not be as soundproof as they'd be in a modern hotel, so as you recount your tales of great seamanship, you'll want to keep your neighbors in mind. Also, if you prefer a level of anonymity, you may be more comfortable in a large B&B or inn instead of a small B&B, where your party might be the only guests.

Campground choices

Waterfront campgrounds range from those on sheltered tidal estuaries to ones with popplestone beaches tumbled by ocean waves. Many are small, family-run operations. Others are larger, with a full range of activities and services. Some cater to tenters; others are designed primarily for those with travel trailers and recreational vehicles (RV's). Since most camping boaters will be using tents, the campground descriptions focus on the information needed by tenters.

Boating options

Just about any kind of boating experience you'd like to have, you can find in Maine. You can spend your time nosing around clusters of wild islands, heading to an inhabited island far off shore, exploring narrow rivers, or seeking out sheltered bays.

If you're arriving at your lodgings by car, think about what type of waters you would like to boat in, and what kind are appropriate to your skills and boat. Some of the lodgings provide easy access to sheltered waters, for instance, while others are near open waters requiring strong skills. Refer to nautical charts and boating guides, then select your lodgings accordingly. (See page 11 for boating guide references.) If you are unfamiliar with Maine waters, err on the side of sheltered waters.

This guide provides specific water access information for kayakers, cruising sailors, and those trailering either sailboats or motorboats. Boaters using other types of watercraft will find some of these accommodations suitable as well, and can refer to the water access details for kayak and trailered boat launching. Those using canoes, rowing shells, or sailboards will find lodgings and campgrounds that meet their needs.

When picking day trip or inn-to-inn routes, sea kayakers with limited experience should plan their routes to take advantage of sheltered waters and not stray far from shore. That way if the weather suddenly turns sour, you have options for getting off the water. Some of Maine's most popular summer tourist destinations, such as Camden and Mount Desert Island, are not ideal kayaking areas for novices because the waters off their shores are exposed to wind. Less exposed waters can be found in parts of Casco, Muscongus, and eastern Penobscot Bays. At any location on the coast though, wind, waves, or fog can prevent boaters from venturing out, or make them wish they hadn't. Because of its higher tides and frequently foggy conditions, the Down East region is not recommended for beginning boaters unless they are accompanied by experienced friends or a guide.

When to visit

Vacationers are fond of Maine in midsummer because the weather is warmer and tends to be more stable. If you can travel off season, you will find that you'll have an easier time getting lodgings and lower rates, and you'll miss the crowds. September days can be warm and sunny, with less risk of fog. As the water temperature is still quite cold, being on the water in June can be a little chilly, but nevertheless delightful. With the promise of a hot shower and comfortable bed, you can enjoy boating in late May and early October as well.

Resources for onshore attraction information

There are a number of excellent guides to mainland points of interest. There are two of particular note. *Maine: An Explorer's Guide,* by Christina Tree and Elizabeth Roundy, provides thorough coverage not only of attractions, but also the gamut of dining choices, from lobster shacks to fine restaurants. *Maine: Off the Beaten Path,* by Wayne Curtis, leads you to some fascinating sights away from Route 1.

The Maine Publicity Bureau can send you visitor information. Request its overview of the state, "Maine Invites You," or one of its lodging or campground guides. Call the bureau at (207) 623-0363, or write to P.O. Box 2300, Hallowell, ME 04347. It operates information centers just off Interstate 95 in Kittery and in Yarmouth.

Driving times

When estimating the driving time to your accommodations, keep in mind that Maine is a big state. With apologies to boaters from Canada, New Hampshire, and Vermont, here are driving time estimates from Portland to the seven regions in this guide: Casco Bay, within an hour; Rivers and Boothbay Harbor, 1.5 hours; Muscongus Bay, 1.5 hours; Western Penobscot Bay, including Rockland and Camden, 2 hours; Eastern Penobscot and Blue Hill Bays, including Deer Isle and Stonington, 3 to 3.5 hours; Mount Desert Island, 3.5 hours, and Down East, 3.5 to

5 hours. (Portland is a 2-hour drive from Boston.)

U.S. Route 1 can become congested in the summer. If you have a destination in Rockport or further north or east, you may find driving north on Interstate 95 to Augusta more to your liking. From Augusta, Routes 17 and 90 will take you to Rockport and Camden, and Route 3 will link to Route 1 at Belfast.

For information on buses and airlines, see Appendix C.

BOATING IN MAINE

Boating safety

If you are unfamiliar with boating in cold water and open ocean conditions, it is critical that you do your homework *before* leaving shore. Maine's icy waters may not give you the opportunity to learn as you go along. Some of the things to keep in mind:

- Tides range from 9 to 14 feet in the region covered by this guide, with tides increasing as you head down east (towards the Canadian border). Tides of this size mean that tidal forces are stronger here than in waters further south. In addition, the currents in rivers with a large volume of water can be quite strong. Tidal currents and river currents can present difficulties to boaters at any time, and particularly midway between high and low tides, when the greatest volume of water is moving. Watch out for situations where water is flowing in one direction and the wind is blowing in the opposite, as you may find yourself dealing with confused and choppy waters.

- Tide height varies over time at any given location. Since the tidal range is large, these tidal variations can also prove significant. When leaving small boats unattended on shore, leave them well above the apparent high tide line, and secure them for good measure.

- The ocean temperature hovers in the 50's (degrees Fahrenheit) much of the boating season, so immersion carries a real risk of hypothermia even in midsummer. The water is especially cold in May and June.

- The weather on the Maine coast can turn from benign to frightening in a matter of minutes when a front passes through. On sunny days the wind will often increase significantly by noon or 1 p.m. and stay strong until a few hours before sunset. In summer, winds will often blow from the southwest, but that too can change suddenly.

- Fog is a likely accompaniment to a Maine boating trip, so strong navigation skills are a necessity. Kayakers should keep in mind that their boats do not register on the radar of larger boats. When visibility is restricted, they should limit their paddling to right along the shore or in coves unlikely to attract larger boats.

• It should go without saying that boaters should be wearing and carrying appropriate safety gear, and know how to use it.

• Know the limits of your equipment. Kayakers, for instance, will want full-length sea kayaks with proper floatation for Maine's open waters. (Full-length singles generally run 16-18 feet long, and doubles are 17-22 feet long.) Shorter kayaks are designed for use on the sheltered waters of rivers and lakes.

• It's wise to give lobster boats and other working boats wide berth. Lobstermen will steer paths that at first glance seem unpredictable, because they move from trap to trap. They often work alone and can miss seeing small boats as they are busy hauling traps from the sides of their boats. Since they're working, and you're playing, give them the right-of-way.

• Large passenger ferries and cargo vessels frequent the major shipping channels, and move deceptively quickly. Large ships are often spotted underway in Portland Harbor and the region just to its south, in the vicinity of Bar Harbor, and in the shipping channel paralleling the western shore of Penobscot Bay. Good-sized ferries and other commercial vessels can be found along many parts of the coast. Kayakers and others in small boats must not move into the paths of ferries and other large vessels. Small boats are difficult to spot from the decks of large vessels, and the captains cannot easily adjust course when they do spot them. Small boats are particularly hard to see in choppy waters.

• Emergency phone numbers for the Coast Guard are listed in Appendix A.

• Sea kayakers will find that there are a number of excellent outfitters here in Maine. If paddlers are fairly new to the sport or to the conditions in Maine, they should consider hiring a Registered Maine Guide to lead a customized trip, or joining a trip already scheduled. Some guides lead inn-to-inn trips. Guides can teach kayakers navigation and other seamanship skills as well as help strengthen their strokes and rescue techniques. Paddlers may wish to take a two or three-day course with a Maine outfitter, then go off on their own with their newly honed skills. Among the larger Maine kayaking outfitters are: Maine Island Kayak Company (800-796-2373), L.L. Bean (800-341-4341, ext. 6666), H2Outfitters (800-205-2925), and Maine Sport Outfitters (800-722-0826). The Maine Publicity Bureau (207-623-0363) maintains a partial list of kayak outfitters.

Nautical charts and road maps
The chart excerpts in Appendix E are meant to be used in conjunction with nautical charts. They will help you

pinpoint lodgings and campgrounds on your charts, and give you a sense of the boating opportunities near the accommodations. *They are not to be used for navigation.* Each lodging and campground listing includes the 1:40,000 scale National Oceanic and Atmospheric Administration (NOAA) chart number where you'd find it. The excerpts are taken from 1:40,000 scale NOAA charts to make it easy for you to match them up with full-sized charts. (NOAA also produces 1:80,000 scale charts to cover longer distances, and 1:20,000 harbor charts.)

Charts can be obtained at many vendors throughout the state. For those travelling from the south, convenient places to pick up NOAA charts in Portland include The Chart Room at Chase Leavitt (10 Dana St., in the Old Port, 207-772-3751), Norumbega Outfitters (58 Fore St., on the waterfront, 207-773-0910), and Hamilton Marine (100 Fore St., 800-639-2715 for phone orders). Heading up Interstate 95 north of Portland, you can jump off at Exit 17 in Yarmouth and visit the DeLorme Map Store (Route 1, 800-452-5931 for phone orders); it's right across from the Tourist Information Center. Any of these stores will ship you a chart if you provide them with the number you need.

The DeLorme Mapping Company produces a valuable resource called *The Maine Atlas and Gazetteer*. The atlas provides very detailed road maps, with a scale of 1/2" equaling one mile. The information on boat launch locations would be reason enough for some boaters to purchase it. In addition, nature preserves, hiking trails, camp-

grounds, beaches, historic sites, and the smallest roads are indicated. (If you check the interior of cars with Maine license plates, you'll frequently spot this tool that keeps us from getting lost while looking for new put-ins or small villages.) Copies can be obtained in bookstores or by calling DeLorme.

When you are on the road and looking for your lodging or campground, keep an eye out for the small blue Department of Transportation signs. Most accommodations have at least one sign on a major road indicating where to turn and the distance to your destination.

Shore access

Many of the lodgings and campgrounds described in this book have spots to launch kayaks on their properties, and some have places to launch a trailered boat. Others have ramps near enough that you can bring your car back after you've unloaded your boat. A surprisingly large number of the lodgings have guest moorings, with docks or beaches for your dinghy. Sometimes you can arrange with your hosts to store your vehicle if you will be off boating for a few days. This would be quite helpful for inn-to-inn trips.

By launching from your accommodation's shore, or by leaving your car at your lodgings while you're out boating, you help reduce the pressure on sometimes crowded launch ramps and parking areas. Some of these ramps are provided by the state government; others were developed primarily for use by local communities. Local working and recreational boaters rely on these facilities to get to the water. They become understandably dismayed when they arrive to find all the parking taken, or their access to the ramp blocked by recreational boating gear.

A courtesy that you can extend to local boaters and other community residents is to use paid parking facilities when you do need to leave your car near a ramp or town dock for more than a few hours. (Be aware that overnight parking is either prohibited or frowned upon at most public ramps. A quick call to the local town office or police station will yield information on particular spots.) Boatyards and marinas are generally happy to provide parking for nominal fees, and they have ramps or floats you can use for launching. Some towns have overnight parking areas designated for boaters. Information on some of the better long-term parking options is included in the "Regional Access" sections of this book.

Since the kayak launching spots on lodging properties are improvised, some will be easier to use than others. Much of the Maine coast is rocky, after all. Often the launching spots are at the edge of a lawn, so walking over uneven terrain is required. Don't expect to drive right to the water's edge and find a graded slope waiting. The lodging entries note where long or difficult carries are required. In cases where the launch strikes you as too difficult, you have the option of using a nearby public ramp. Your host or DeLorme's *Maine Atlas and Gazetteer* can help you locate one. Most launches at campgrounds, on the other hand, are well defined; you simply drive up, drop off your gear, and return your car to your campsite.

Boating guidebooks

While there are some boating tips in this book, they certainly do not substitute for a cruising or paddling guide. *A Cruising Guide to the Maine Coast,* by Hank Taft, Jan Taft and Curtis Rindlaub, and *The Cruising Guide to the New England Coast,* by Roger Duncan et al., are valuable resources for boaters in any size craft. Rindlaub's revision of the Taft guide has highly detailed information on harbor services, navigation, weather, and tides. He also provides great insights into the coastal communities you might visit. Duncan specializes in putting an historical perspective on your trip.

Kayakers will find Tamsin Venn's *Sea Kayaking along the New England Coast* invaluable. Venn maps out several Maine coast paddling routes and gives advice on safety and weather. Earl Brechlin describes six saltwater routes and tips on local conditions in *Paddling the Waters of Mount Desert Island.*

Sailors, powerboaters, and paddlers will find safety recommendations included in the Maine Island Trail Association's annual guidebook (see page 21).

Periodicals of interest are listed in the bibliography.

Besides reading up on where you are heading, seeking local knowledge of the waters you'll be travelling through is time well spent. Fellow boaters and people living on the coast are often invaluable sources of information.

Kayakers will find that the closest put-in may require the use of a dock's float; this will be indicated in the put-in description. Since floats are used seasonally, those travelling early or late in the boating season should verify that the float will be in the water at the time they'll be visiting.

Kayakers who usually carry their boats into the water may find their first experience with a float a bit challenging. Before entering your boat, look for the lowest part of the float, and drop your boat in the water there. Higher floats are more difficult; look for ones no more than 6 inches higher than the deck of your floating boat. Transfer your weight gently from the float to your kayak, keeping your weight low. Some kayakers use their paddle as a brace, holding the shaft to the cockpit coaming behind them with one hand, and placing their other hand on the float. (Avoid putting much weight on your paddle shaft.) They move one leg at a time into the kayak. To exit a kayak onto a float, reverse the procedure. A helping hand is sometimes in order.

INN-TO-INN BOATING

Instead of day tripping from a single lodging, you may wish to plan a trip that includes visits to a few different communities. Inn-to-inn bicycling and inn-to-inn cross-country skiing trips have been popular vacations for years. With careful planning, boaters can enjoy inn-to-inn travel. Many of the older waterfront inns and homes were designed to be reached from the water, and it is still the grandest way to approach them. You will be arriving the way the steamship passengers of a hundred years ago did.

There are many parts of the coast where boaters can link stays at different accommodations. Lodging entries are designed to help you plan your own routes. The following will help you consider some of the logistics of inn-to-inn (including B&B-to-B&B) travel.

Appendix B offers some ideas to help you get started. Sample inn-to-inn itineraries are shown for kayakers. For sailors, many of the lodgings with guest moorings or nearby rental moorings, dock space, or slips are listed, in a southwest to northeast sequence.

Reservations
Waterfront lodgings can be fully booked in the summer, so you'll want to make reservations if you'll be travelling by boat. You don't want to arrive late in the day at a coastal village with two choices of lodgings, only to discover that they are both full, or the guest moorings all taken. When you are selecting your series of lodgings, keep in mind that reservation deposits are

nonrefundable. If you plan too aggressive a trip leg, you can lose your deposit by not arriving on the day of your reservation. (While this may not seem fair to you, remember that the high season is brief in Maine and the innkeepers may not be able to fill your room on short notice. Also, the hosts may not have room for you later in the week.) If the weather forces you to lose a day, you may find you have another problem: where you are staying may be completely booked for the following night.

If you are travelling in high season but prefer to make your plans with knowledge of the day's weather forecast, you can make your reservations before leaving your previous night's accommodations. This still carries the risk that the lodgings closest to the shore, or the ones that most interest you, will be full.

Boaters with room to stay aboard, or those with camping gear, can call from their boats or come ashore to phone lodgings when they're in the mood for a hot shower and a comfortable bed.

Off-season travel (generally before July and after Labor Day) gives inn-to-inn boaters greater flexibility. Hosts may more readily honor a request to shift your reservation forward. Your hosts at the lodging where you are waiting out the weather are more likely to have an extra room.

Contingency planning

If you select inns that are easy to drive between, weather delays will not present as many difficulties. You can arrange to leave your boats with your hosts or at the local boatyard, and catch a taxi or a ride to your next

night's accommodations. By linking inns on the same peninsula, you may only be asking for a 10-mile ride, which innkeepers might be able to help you with. It would be more difficult to arrange for a ride if your next night's lodging is at the tip of another peninsula: it may be 8 miles by boat, but 50 miles by car.

If your plans include a stay on an inhabited island with ferry service, you can fall back on the ferry to help you reach your reserved room. Some ferries will take hand-carried kayaks; others require that they be on top of a vehicle. See the listings in the Regional Access sections for details.

Selecting inn-to-inn combinations

Once you've picked the region you'd like to explore, look through the listings to determine which accommodations provide the type of water access and services you need. Kayakers will need all but their starting point to have direct access to and from the water, unless they have a set of packable wheels. (At their starting point they can stay overnight near the water, and use a ramp with overnight parking provisions to begin their trip.) Sailors will want to check that moorings, dock space, or slips are available at the lodging or a nearby boatyard. Review distances and crossings between lodgings on your nautical chart, keeping in mind that less aggressive distances and crossings improve your chances of arriving on the day of your reservation.

Kayakers and those of you with trailered boats will need to consider parking options at your starting point. Work out

An 1880 inn-to-inn adventure by paddle and sail

In case you thought the idea of inn-to-inn boating was new, the following highlights the adventures of two Massachusetts gentlemen back in 1880, who stowed their portmanteaus and paddled and sailed from Andover to Bar Harbor. Their ocean-front accommodations along the way included hotels and a lighthouse.

A SHADOW-CANOE TRIP.
From Andover, Mass., to Bar Harbor, Me., in Aug., 1880.
By G. W. W. Dove.

The shadow-canoe is a small cedar lap-streak keel boat, thirteen feet long by two and one-half beam, and of about sixty pounds weight; decked over, except where the operator sits, and is propelled by a double paddle, or sails. In the bow and stern are water-tight compartments, which render the canoe very buoyant and safe in rough water. It is yawl-rigged and sails very well before the wind.

On the trip in question some supplies were taken, such as water, pilot-bread, etc., and a good-sized portmanteau carried the necessary clothing. All these were comfortably stowed away, fore and aft, leaving the middle free for the passenger. The journey was begun on the 9th of August by two gentlemen, the writer and Wm. R. Robeson, of Boston, each in his own canoe, with everything carefully stored and made fast, so that, in case of an unlucky upset, nothing would be lost.

Thursday, 12th. ...We did not reach the Point of Rocks off Biddeford Pool until 2:25 P.M., and were rather drearily lunching on a bit of hardtack, when our friend, Mr. Joseph W. Smith, who, from the piazza of his hotel, had espied the two little specks out on the water, as we were passing, drove quickly down to the Point, and hailed us, and we paddled round into the harbor at the Pool, and had the pleasure of dining with him. We intended to go on immediately after, to Cape Elizabeth for the night, but as we had already experience enough for one day, there being no wind, concluded to remain where we were, which decision we did not regret, as we found we had fallen among friends.

Friday, 13th. Started at 8:30 A.M., the water still as a mill-pond, the sun shining brightly, and a gay party giving us a good send-off. At 11:30 passed Richmond Island, when we spread sails and slanted over to Cape Elizabeth, where we dined quite comfortably at the hotel....One charm about this kind of sailing is the delightful freedom from having to retrace one's course in order to get home again before night – often midnight – as we carry our homes with us for the time being.

Saturday, 14th. Started at 8:30 A.M., though it was raining a little. The paddle across Cape Smallpoint was against quite a head sea. Shipped a number of white caps which drenched us, since we could not paddle in overcoats, but the exercise kept us in a glow, and we passed safely over. At 11:30 passed the lonely island of Seguin, with its solitary light-house perched on its high cliff. Then came an hour of rugged work as we paddled across the mouth of the Kennebec, against wind and tide, and waves higher than our heads. If we had known what was in store for us when we started in the morning we should not have left Harpswell so willingly. [After more paddling and a stop to rest] we had to push out into the shower and make the best of our way to Mouse Island, which we reached at dark, and hauling our canoes above high water mark, we sponged out the little water that had stolen in, put on the covers, locked them up, and with our portmanteaus, walked up to the hospitable hotel for Sunday. We changed our wet clothes, had supper, and slept in a closet, which, however, we did not mind a bit. I believe we could have slept on a picket fence, though of course we were thankful that we did not have to try.

Monday, 16th. ...We expected to sleep at Tennant's Harbor, but learned that the only hotel there had been burned. With the tide in our favor it was no hardship to paddle on a while, after losing the breeze with the sun. The last five miles were made under a bright moon, which was a very pleasant novelty. Progress, to-day, thirty-two miles.

Tuesday, 17th. ...We paddled away for the North Fox Island, which we reached at 1 o'clock, and dined upon our pilot bread and milk. At 2:30 our afternoon breeze brisked up again and carried us flying to Eagle Island, where we put up at the lighthouse for the night.

Wednesday, 18th. [As we paddled along Eggemoggin Reach,] the steamer *Lewiston,* from Mt. Desert, gave us a friendly "toot" as she passed us, her passengers craning their necks at us as though we had been the sea serpent.... At quarter past 5, passed Bass Harbor light without accident, which we considered good time. Tried our sails on changing our course a little, but, not making satisfactory progress, clewed up and paddled round to the harbor, not reaching there until past 7, after a hard day's work against the wind all the way. Supper was over at the hotel, but the good-natured deacon had a steak cooked for us, which we immediately swallowed and called for more. Our appetites were not entirely appeased until about 9 o'clock, and then we had to hunt up a bed, every room at the hotels being full. We got through the night somehow. I know we slept soundly and breakfasted heartily. Paid our one dollar each cheerfully, wondering if the good deacon made any money out of his summer boarders, especially canoeists, and at 10 A.M., bore away for Bar Harbor, the end of our journey, which we reached at 2 o'clock, having made two hundred and seventy-five miles in our jolly little boats, in ten working days of about seven hours each. The pleasure of our trip was such that we really felt regret that it was so soon over.

Excerpted from *Gleanings from the Sea: Showing the pleasures, pains and penalties of life afloat, with contingencies ashore.* Edited and published by Joseph W. Smith, Andover, Massachusetts, 1887. A facsimile edition is available from Harding's Bookstore, P.O. Box 184, Wells, ME 04090, (207) 646-8755.

if you'll be doing a loop or arranging to retrieve your car. (See discussions on parking and transportation below.)

Consult the "Breakfast/meals" and "Walk to" entries for any lodging you'll be visiting without a car. If your lodging does not serve dinner, check the "Walk to" entry to see if there are restaurants nearby. Some lodgings can provide dinner by advance arrangement, or allow you to cook your own.

If you are combining your onshore stay with staying aboard your boat or island camping, the "Walk to" section will help you determine if you will be able to pick up groceries or do your laundry while you are in town. It will also point out if there are bicycle rentals, galleries, and shops nearby.

Check the "Rates" section to determine if the lodgings have any minimum stay requirements. If none are listed, they will accept a single night's reservation.

Locating your accommodations from the water

The nautical chart excerpts in Appendix E can help you locate your accommodations from the water. Numbers associated with each facility are placed on the excerpts. The number placements are based on observations by the author and the various hosts.

It should be fairly straightforward to pick out larger inns and hotels from the water, if you have some idea of their appearance. Locating individual B&B's can be trickier, since they may be clustered with homes of similar appearance, or be set in the woods above the water. Whenever you call to reserve your room, ask the innkeepers for a description of their lodging from the water. Ask if there are distinguishing landmarks on or near their property. If it appears that it will be hard to pick out your destination, agree on an identifying marker with your hosts. (You'd like to avoid ambling up the private lawn of the retired couple next door in your drysuit.) Your hosts might place a colorful windsock or flag at the shoreline, or tie a red bandanna to a tree. If they have portable lawn furniture, they might move it closer to shore and put a little welcome sign on it for you.

Keep in mind that fog is quite common and that your visibility can be so restricted that you can see only very close landmarks, or possibly none at all. You should have back-up plans in case you are unable to reach your destination, and sufficient food, water, clothing, and shelter to get you through a cold night if you have to anchor or make an emergency landing. The best plan on a foggy day can be to stay put; don't assume it will clear out before you reach your destination.

If you have a car, and your subsequent lodgings are fairly close to your first night's accommodations, you might consider doing a "scouting trip" before getting on the water. You can drive to each of your destinations to familiarize yourself with the lodging's appearance from the waterfront, and pick out useful landmarks.

Where to leave your kayak or dinghy

When you arrive by water, check with the hosts for suggestions on where to leave your boats. Many will suggest that you leave them anyplace above the high tide line, but some may have a specific location they would like them stored. (When picking a spot, remember that the tides are high and variable, and tie boats to a tree or rock.) The chances of someone taking your boats for a joy ride are slim, except perhaps on the heavily visited waterfronts of larger towns such as Camden and Bar Harbor. You can improve the odds that your boats will be left undisturbed by taking along your paddles or oars, or by using a cable lock. Likewise, when transporting kayaks on a roof rack, the use of a cable lock might be wise in major tourist centers if you are parking on the street or in a large parking lot overnight.

Vehicle parking

For those of you with kayaks and trailered boats, or sailors meeting friends already underway, the question arises of what to do with vehicles while you are travelling to other accommodations. The majority of hosts whose lodgings are listed in this book said they can help their guests find a place to leave a car for a few days, either on or near their property. A request prior to your visit would be appreciated. A smaller number can store a trailer. Hosts' ability to store cars is sometimes dependent on the season; some can do this only during the off season.

Boatyards are a good source of long-term parking spaces and their rates are quite reasonable, except in some large towns. Refer to the Regional Access sections of the book for overnight parking suggestions. Avoid tying up public parking spaces at town docks or launch ramps, since these are used by local working and recreational boaters on a daily basis.

Getting back to your vehicle

A loop trip, with an overnight stay at the same accommodations at the beginning and end of your trip, makes it easy to retrieve your car, especially if the hosts can provide you with a place to store it while you're gone. If you'd prefer a one-way boating trip, you can spot a second car at the terminus of your trip. Other options include using local public transportation, which is more likely to be found in the southern part of the state; see Appendix C.

CAMPGROUND-TO-CAMPGROUND BOATING

Some campground-to-campground combinations are possible, although the distances between them tend to be long. You may find the best camping combinations can be created using established campgrounds along with those public wild islands where camping is permitted. Most campgrounds can help with overnight parking while you're away; some have set fees and at others you can offer to pay for the service.

Those staying in shorefront campgrounds may find that many are full only on summer weekends, except those in the busiest areas such as Mount Desert Island. The logistics of travelling from campground to campground are eased if you are prepared to camp on a public island. You might find that, in an emergency, your campground hosts can find you a spot to pitch a tent even if their designated sites are booked.

COASTAL SAMPLERS

For sea kayakers and those with trailered boats, there is an alternative to boating inn-to-inn that is simpler, yet still allows you to explore both onshore and offshore attractions. You can plan a coastal sampler, day tripping from one lodging for a few days, then driving to a new lodging.

There are a number of advantages to the coastal sampler method of travel. First, you get a better feel for a place, really get to explore it, if you stay a few days instead of just overnight. So many of the towns and villages along the coast offer more than what can be seen in a few hours of touring. Second, weather delays pose no problems in reaching a reserved room. Third, if the weather is mediocre, you can enjoy activities on the mainland instead of pressing onward. Fourth, you will have your car available so you can drive to restaurants and activities beyond walking distance. Fifth, you don't have to find a place to leave your vehicle, or plan a trip that circles back to pick it up.

With a coastal sampler, you can combine a trip to sheltered waters and then move on to open bays, spend a few days in a major shopping area and then sneak off to a quiet coastal village, or enjoy a few days on the mainland and a few on an inhabited island.

THE ISLANDS

The islands of Maine's coast are special places for locals and visitors alike. We are inspired by their beauty, and we relish the solitude we can find on an island. We are surprised by their variety. Some islands look like the Maine classic: an almost perfectly round island with granite shores and dense evergreen forests. Others will be long and narrow. They might have stands of birches and other hardwoods, or be covered with wild roses and raspberries. Occasionally there will be one with a beach seemingly transported from the Caribbean. (If you go for a swim you'll quickly recall your true location, however!) The latest count of Maine islands came to a remarkable 4,617.

Human inhabitants

In the past, some of the larger islands were the seasonal homes of Native Americans, and some of the earliest Europeans arriving in North America settled on Maine islands such as Damariscove. Prior to the twentieth century, 300 islands were busy with year-round residents fishing, farming, cutting timber, and quarrying granite. Island communities started to dwindle after that; there are now only 15 islands with year-round communities and another 29 with summer colonies.

When you are on an island, you may spot signs of earlier inhabitants, such as heaps of clam shells (known as "middens") discarded by Native Americans, or old building foundations. Admire these reminders of the past without disturbing them. Some sites are being monitored by archeologists who are attempting to learn more about past island inhabitants.

Wildlife

The islands are home to many kinds of wildlife. Seabirds nest on islands, away from many of the predators found on the mainland. Many seabirds return to the same islands year after year. The presence of visitors can cause birds to abandon nest sites or prevent parent birds from returning to their nests to incubate their eggs or feed their young. Predators such as gulls can swoop in when parent birds have been scared away. If you notice groups of birds leaving an island's banks while you are on the water, move away immediately to allow the birds to return.

Seabird nesting occurs during most of the boating season, from early spring to mid-August. Visitors should avoid islands known or suspected to be home to nesting birds. Nesting birds often select small, treeless islands and ledges. It is difficult to see their nests, and easy to disturb them, as many nest on the ground, so it is best to stay off shore from these islands. Even a slight disturbance can destroy an entire nest. For this reason, it is especially important not to bring pets ashore.

Bald eagles often perch and fish from islands other than the ones that hold their nests. If you spot eagles on any island, enjoy viewing them from a distance. Approaching them while they are perching and fishing makes them expend valuable energy that could be better used hunting for food for themselves or their young.

Seals frequently rest on ledges and

Low-impact island visits

As wild islands attract greater numbers of visitors, it is incumbent on all of us to do what we can to leave the islands the same, or even better, than we found them. This helps assure that they will continue to remain open for recreational use and that others can enjoy the same wilderness experience that we have.

One way to help preserve these islands is to reduce our use of them. Overnight camping is more likely to cause damage than short day visits. Damage may be caused by deliberate actions, such as building campfires, or unintentional ones, such as trampling vegetation or contributing to bank erosion while carrying gear ashore. By staying in onshore lodgings and established campgrounds, instead of camping on wild islands, we help preserve these fragile natural resources.

Using the following low-impact techniques when we do stop on islands will help us reduce the effects of our visits.

- Island soils are shallow and take years to recover once disturbed. Walk on sand beaches, rock ledges, grasses, or established trails. Avoid climbing on dirt embankments that easily erode.
- Do not build fires. They are prohibited without a fire permit, and they pose too great a risk of spreading across an isolated island. Even those built below the high tide line risk scarring rock ledges and depleting downed wood needed to replenish island soils.
- Carry out everything you bring in. If you can, take out rubbish the tide or less careful visitors brought ashore. This will protect wildlife and enhance the island experience for fellow travellers.
- Human waste and toilet paper should not be buried in the shallow soils of islands, nor left exposed to be found by animals or visitors. They should be properly disposed of in mainland sewage treatment or septic facilities. Boaters with larger boats can use their holding tank or a porta-pottie. Those with smaller boats can improvise using small containers with tight-fitting lids or closures.
- Travel in small groups. If others are already on the island, respect their privacy and select a different landing or picnic site.
- If you are planning to camp on an island, but there are no more established tenting spots when you arrive, move to another island where camping is permitted, or go back to the mainland. Do not cut, limb, or crush vegetation to make new campsites.
- Stay off known seabird nesting islands until mid-August. If you happen upon nesting birds, move

The Maine Island Trail Association

While the Maine Island Trail Association (MITA) owns no islands at all, it plays a very important role in island conservation and access. The members of the association act as stewards for a network of over 75 wild islands stretching along the coast from Portland to Machias. Through their actions and examples members hope to assure that Maine's wild islands will be conserved in a natural state, for the enjoyment of boaters today and in the future. Association members monitor the levels of use islands receive, help to educate visitors and potential visitors about careful use, and participate in island clean-ups. They help with work projects requested by island owners, such as building stairs to prevent bank erosion or cutting a perimeter trail. Those with commitments to specific islands "adopt" them.

Half of the Trail islands, those belonging to the Bureau of Parks and Lands and the U.S. Fish and Wildlife Service, are open to the general public. The other half are private islands whose owners wish to share them with careful visitors; camping is often allowed for MITA members. Members learn about low-impact use and the restrictions island owners place on access to their islands through an annual guidebook, quarterly newsletters, and association activities.

Those planning a trip along the coast should consider joining MITA. They will find the guidebook of great help, as it not only describes islands open to members but also provides valuable information on topics such as boating safety, danger areas, and low-impact techniques. Plus, membership dues are a major portion of this volunteer-based organization's budget, and would further MITA's efforts to protect Maine's wild islands and educate island visitors.

The Maine Island Trail Association's mailing address is P.O. Box C, Rockland, ME 04841. There are offices in Rockland and in Portland. The Rockland office is located at 328 Main Street; phone (207) 596-6456. In Portland, the office can be found on the waterfront at 41A Union Wharf; phone (207) 761-8225.

away so that adults can stay with their young. Likewise, if you come upon seals hauled out on ledges, keep far enough away that they don't feel pressure to jump into the water. Do not bring pets onto islands, because they can destroy nests or kill small birds.

The brochure "Fragile Lands" was used with permission as the main source for this overview of low-impact techniques. Look for it at marine establishments in Maine, or request a copy from the Maine Island Trail Association, P.O. Box C, Rockland, ME 04841; (207) 596-6456 or 761-8225.

the shores of islands. They should be observed from a distance. If your approach causes them to struggle back into the water, you are too close. This is particularly important in May and June, when the seal pups are young.

The hotline phone number to report marine mammal strandings is listed in Appendix A.

Island access

When you are out boating, how do you determine which islands you may visit? Hundreds of islands are critical to wildlife, and should be avoided. Many islands are privately held. The absence of buildings or "No Trespassing" signs should not be taken as a cue to start looking for a picnic spot. The best approach is to land only on those islands you have permission to visit. Government agencies and conservation groups have identified many islands that are appropriate for recreational access. See page 20 for suggested low-impact techniques to use when visiting these islands.

To help with your trip planning and enjoyment of the coast, many of the islands open to the public are listed in the regional "Off Shore" sections of this guide. Islands believed by their owners to provide significant nesting habitat have been excluded.

Maine's Bureau of Parks and Lands (BP&L) has identified over 30 wild islands on the coast that are suitable for low-impact recreational use. BP&L allows fires on its islands if you have obtained a fire permit. (It asks that fires be built below the high tide line and that they be on either sand or gravel, to avoid scarring ledges. Fires

should be small and contained, and made with driftwood or wood brought from the mainland.) To help you confirm that you've located the correct island, BP&L islands bear blue signs. To obtain a copy of BP&L's brochure "Your Islands on the Coast," call BP&L at (207) 287-3821, or write to 22 State House Station, Augusta, ME 04333. The brochure is updated regularly, so make sure yours is a current one. (Islands are removed from the list if eagles nest on them, for instance.)

While visitors may camp on BP&L islands, some of the more popular destinations are showing the effects of their visits. The Maine Island Trail Association (MITA), which monitors levels of use and damage to these state-owned islands, reports that campers have been cutting, limbing, or crushing vegetation to create new tent sites. It may be that boaters are arriving on summer weekends and, finding the existing tenting sites occupied, are creating new ones. MITA is concerned that the fragile ecosystems of these small offshore islands cannot withstand this level of use or abuse. MITA asks that if you arrive at an island and find the existing tenting spots taken, that you move to another island where camping is permitted, or go to mainland lodgings or campgrounds. When you are making your boating plans, select a few alternate spots to spend the night before setting out, and allow enough time to reach them should you need to. On busy weekends, you might want to exclude frequently visited islands from your list of destination options entirely. Islands observed by MITA to have had heavy summer use are identified in the text.

Two federal organizations have islands open for day use only. The U.S. Fish and Wildlife Service (207-546-2124) has a few islands in the Down East region. Fires are discouraged but can be built below the high tide line. Acadia National Park (207-288-5262) has several islands in Frenchman Bay. No fires are permitted. (Camping is available at the park's established campsites at Duck Harbor on Isle au Haut; see page 147.)

Conservation groups make islands available to small groups of careful day visitors. The Nature Conservancy protects a number of islands in Maine; some are appropriate for visits and others are set aside for nesting birds most of the boating season. To protect wildlife, no pets are permitted ashore. Fires are discouraged and must be built below the high tide line. You can get more information on the preserves by contacting the Maine Chapter's office at 14 Maine Street, Suite 401, Brunswick, ME 04011; phone (207) 729-5181. Local land trusts have islands along the coast open to day visitors as well. Any of the conservation groups would welcome your support as a member.

It is important to observe whatever restrictions (i.e., no pets ashore or no camping) these agencies and conservation groups have placed on the use of their islands. Island owners have set these restrictions to protect the resident plant and animal populations. Your adherence to their guidelines will not only contribute to the undisturbed continuation of the island ecosystems, but will also help assure that the islands remain open for future visitors to enjoy.

Some islands look like the Maine classic: an almost perfectly round island with granite shores and dense evergreen forests. Others will be long and narrow. They might have stands of birches and other hardwoods, or be covered with wild roses and raspberries. The latest count of Maine islands came to a remarkable 4,617.

HOW TO USE THIS GUIDEBOOK

The research for this guidebook

All the lodgings and campgrounds described in this book were visited by the author in 1996 or 1997, with the exception of four facilities that are noted in the text. In large towns with many lodgings, those closest to the water or of special interest to boaters were selected. A few places that might serve boaters well were not included because they were closed or the hosts unavailable at the time the research was done. None of the accommodations paid to be listed, as is sometimes the case in lodging guides.

Room rates and campsite fees are current for 1997 in most cases. (In situations where the owners could not be reached to provide 1997 rates, the 1996 figures are shown.) You may find changes when you visit.

Since some visits occurred at high tide, judgments of access to the water at low tide may be based on information from hosts or area residents. Distances given are estimates. Land distances are given in statute miles, and boating distances are given in nautical miles.

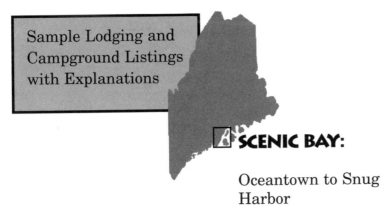

Sample Lodging and
Campground Listings
with Explanations

SCENIC BAY:

Oceantown to Snug
Harbor

Geographic regions are listed from southwest to northeast. Entries within each region are also listed in a southwesterly to northeasterly fashion, with lodgings first, followed by campgrounds.

ON SHORE

This entry provides an overview of the towns and villages in the region, along with attractions such as nautical museums and boater-oriented shops, and hiking and bicycling destinations. Inhabited islands with guest lodgings appear in this section.

OFF SHORE

Some characteristics of the boating in the region are provided under the "Off Shore" heading. Descriptions of wild islands open to visitors appear here. (Refer to pages 22-23 for the restrictions island owners place on their use.)

REGIONAL ACCESS

Launch ramps/areas with overnight parking

Launch ramp descriptions include whether the ramp is hard-surfaced and if it appeared (or was reported) that there is water at all tides. Launch areas suitable for kayaks, such as public docks and floats, are noted where there are no ramps. If floats provide access to the water for only part of the tide cycle, that is noted.

Ferries

Information appears here on car or passenger ferry service to inhabited islands that have guest accommodations. All the ferries listed will take kayaks, although some require that they be carried on a vehicle.

Public moorings, slips, dock space

Public facilities for securing sailboats are listed here. Most facilities monitor VHF Channel 9.

LODGINGS

The Oceanfront B&B

#1, Chart 13000, Lobster Cove, Oceantown

- The lodging's number appears on one of the detailed nautical chart excerpts in Appendix E.
- Chart number for the 1:40,000 scale NOAA nautical chart.
- A nearby location (harbor, point, cove, etc.) named on the nautical chart, followed by the name of the nearest village or town (if different).

Overview of lodging
Information on the lodging's distinctive features.

Breakfast/
Meals   This entry describes the meals offered, and tells which are included in the room rate. In most cases, breakfast is included. Many inns offer dinner to the public; it will be listed as "available" to guests if it is not included in the room rate. ("MAP," or Modified American Plan, means that breakfast and dinner are included in the room rate.)

Rates
- Number of rooms with private and shared baths.
- Rate range for two people in a double occupancy room ("double"), including breakfast unless otherwise noted. The Maine lodging tax of 7% is additional. Where a rate range is shown for specific months, those are the high season rates; rates at other times will be lower. Rates are subject to change without notice and should be confirmed with the innkeeper.
- Single occupancy rates are generally available, but are often not much less than the rates for doubles. Additional guests are permitted in rooms at some lodgings for an extra fee.
- Credit cards accepted, if any. Note that many B&B's do not take credit cards. ("MC" stands for MasterCard and "Amex" represents American Express.) Personal and travellers checks and cash are almost always welcome; any exceptions are noted.
- The majority of lodgings do not allow smoking indoors. If they *do* allow smoking, that is shown.
- If the lodging is reported to be wheelchair accessible in accordance with the Americans with Disabilities Act code, that is listed. Appendix D summarizes the wheelchair-accessible lodgings.
- Children are generally welcome, but there are sometimes age

restrictions as noted.

- If the owners have pets in common spaces used by guests, that is shown. If they permit guests to bring pets, that is noted.
- Most facilities permit a single night's reservation. It will be indicated if they require longer reservations in high season or on weekends.
- Months the lodging is open.

Access All distances are approximate. Entries for kayaks, trailered boats, and sailboats appear if there is access or facilities for them nearby.

Kayaks

- If there is shore access from the property, the distance boats need to be carried from guests' cars and whether there is reported to be water at all tides is indicated. Where access is restricted to some tides, an alternative launch may be suggested as well.
- If there is no access from the property, the closest launch area is listed. The distance is provided for those launch areas where you could easily move your vehicle back to your lodging after unloading your gear.

Trailered boats

- The "trailered boat" listing will appear only if the innkeepers said that they can find parking for trailers at least some of the season. Often parking is restricted to the off season, or to one trailered boat, due to space constraints. Boaters need to determine whether the innkeeper can provide parking at the time they wish to visit.
- The closest launch ramp suitable for a trailered boat is listed, with a description of its surface. Ramp conditions can change over time, and some ramps may not be appropriate for your vehicle and trailer.

Sailboats

- If there are guest moorings, that will be listed. Sailors need to contact the innkeeper to see if a mooring will be available when they wish to visit, and to determine if it is large enough, and in enough water, for their boat.
- If there are no guest moorings, nearby rental moorings, dock space, and slips are listed. Details on these can be found in the "Regional Access" notes for that area. Generally, the rental moorings, slips, or dock space will be within 1/2 mile of the lodging unless otherwise noted.

Walk to

- The availability of restaurants, grocery stores or markets, galleries, shops, laundry services/laudromats, and bicycle rentals within walking distance are indicated for those travelling by boat. These services are generally within a mile of the lodging, but can sometimes be up to a maximum of 2 miles away for more rural lodgings.

Address Street address, mailing address if different, phone number(s). The area code for Maine is "207." Toll-free phone numbers are listed when available; they start with "800" or "888."

CAMPGROUNDS

Blue Sky Campground
#C1, Chart 13000, Snug Harbor

- The campground's number appears on one of the detailed nautical chart excerpts in Appendix E. Campground numbers carry a "C" prefix.
- Chart number for the 1:40,000 scale NOAA nautical chart.
- A nearby location (harbor, point, cove, etc.) named on the nautical chart, followed by the name of the nearest village or town (if different).

Overview of campground
Information on the campground's distinctive features.

Campsites
- Total number of sites, and of the total, the number that are designed for tent use.
- Number of waterfront sites. These may be on bluffs overlooking the water.
- The percentage of campers on an average summer weekend at the campground who are tenting.
- Availability of showers, flush toilets or privies (outhouses). If they are reported to be wheelchair accessible, that is listed. Appendix D summarizes the campgrounds with wheelchair-accessible facilities.
- On-site recreation room, laundry machines, groceries, and snack bar availability.

Rates
- Fee for a tent site, generally for one family or two adults. The Maine 7% lodging tax is additional.
- Credit cards accepted, if any. ("MC" stands for MasterCard and "Amex" stands for American Express.) If personal checks are not accepted, that is noted.

- If pets are permitted, that is listed.
- Any minimum stay requirements. Some campgrounds will require longer reservations for sites directly on the water.
- Months the campground is open.

Access The information covered under this heading is generally the same as for lodgings; see above. Unlike lodgings, services such as restaurants and groceries are usually unavailable within 2 miles of campgrounds. If there are none, the "Walk to" entry does not appear.

Address Street address, mailing address if different, phone number. The area code for Maine is "207." Toll-free phone numbers are listed when available; they start with "800" or "888."

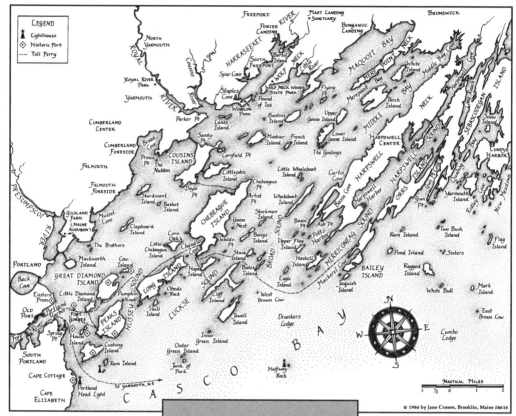

© 1986 by Jane Crosen, Brooklin, Maine 04616

THE CASCO BAY ISLANDS

were called the Calendar Islands by early visitors, since there seemed to be as many as the days in a year. Thanks to the jutting peninsulas and numerous islands, sections of the bay can be fairly sheltered. There is good gunkholing to be had here, and several uninhabited islands are open to the public.

CASCO BAY

Western Casco Bay: Portland to Freeport

ON SHORE

Portland

Allow plenty of time to explore Portland. Maine's largest city has a multitude of great restaurants, shops, museums, and cultural attractions. If you arrive by sea, you'll be right on the doorstep of the Old Port, the center of much of this activity.

Those seeking food will find everything from traditional New England seafood to an impressive array of ethnic restaurants. Within a mile of the harbor are numerous bakeries, seafood retailers, and specialty markets for those needing to stock up for the next leg of their trip.

Shoppers will discover a cluster of unique stores and galleries in the Old Port's 19th-century brick buildings, in the vicinity of Exchange, Fore, and Commercial Streets. Just uphill at 542 Congress Street is a new L.L. Bean fac-

tory store, with discounted outdoor clothing and equipment.

Nautical supplies are abundant in downtown Portland. The Chart Room at Chase Leavitt (10 Dana St., 772-3751) is a convenient place in the Old Port to purchase charts. Kayakers can stop in at Norumbega Outfitters (58 Fore St., 773-0910) to select anything from a wetsuit to a new boat. The Portland branches of Hamilton Marine (100 Fore St., 774-1772) and West Marine (127 Marginal Way, 761-7600) are two well-stocked chandleries.

The Visitors Information Center (305 Commercial St., 772-5800) is a good place to pick up walking maps and to check for current arts and entertainment information. Portland is the home to many music venues and theaters.

There are several museums in the

downtown area. Among them is the Portland Museum of Art (7 Congress Square, 773-2787). Its permanent collection includes artists with ties to Maine, such as the Wyeths and Winslow Homer, and it hosts outstanding travelling exhibits as well. The Children's Museum of Maine (142 Free St., 828-1234) is next door, with two floors of hands-on displays; it's a great place to spend a foggy day.

The Maine Island Trail Association has an office at 41A Union Wharf (761-8225), just off Commercial Street in the Old Port. Drop in on weekdays to learn more about the nonprofit organization's island stewardship activities. (See page 21 for more information on MITA.)

Peaks Island

Peaks Island lies two miles east of Portland Harbor. While many people live on Peaks just in the summer, there is a year-round community of 1000. Many residents commute back and forth by ferry to office jobs in Portland. There's a 5-mile perimeter road around Peaks; visitors can bike along and enjoy views of the mainland and surrounding islands.

Chebeague Island

Chebeague is the kind of place where residents will offer you a lift and everyone waves as a car goes by. About 350 people reside there year round, with many summer people joining them in this quiet spot not far from the busy mainland. There are many recreational opportunities on the island: bring your golf clubs for the nine-hole community course, or stow your tennis racket for a match near the harbor. Biking is a pleasure because there is so little traffic, and you can hike on the network of trails that cover the island.

Freeport and South Freeport

Downtown Freeport is best known as home to L.L. Bean, the legendary outdoor clothing and equipment store that threw away the keys years ago. (L.L. Bean is open 24 hours a day, 365 days a year on Main Street; 800-221-4221 for phone orders.) You'll find extensive sea kayaking and camping gear departments there. A variety of specialty shops, outlet stores, and restaurants flank L.L. Bean.

Even though downtown Freeport can get quite busy with shoppers, neighboring South Freeport is a relatively quiet harbor village where you can enjoy a lobster dinner by the water. Boaters lacking cars can catch an hourly on-demand shuttle bus from the South Freeport harbor to L.L. Bean in the summer.

OFF SHORE

While the coast of Maine southwest of Portland is characterized by stretches of beach and very few islands, things change dramatically once you reach Casco Bay. The region includes a series of peninsulas running parallel to one another; some of the bay's islands can be viewed as extensions of these peninsulas. The Casco Bay islands were called the Calendar Islands by early visitors, since there seemed to be as many as the days in a year. Thanks to the jutting peninsulas and numerous islands, sections of the bay can be fairly sheltered. There is good gunkholing to be had here, and several uninhabited islands are open to the public.

Portland Harbor is quite busy with boats large and small. Those in small boats should exercise caution, as cargo vessels and fast-moving ferries frequent the harbor. Ferries fan out to Peaks, Great and Little Diamond, Long, Cliff, and Chebeague Islands. Small boaters can avoid the majority of the cargo vessel traffic and the largest ferry, the one running to Nova Scotia, if they stay to the north of Fort Gorges, just outside of the harbor.

Fort Gorges makes an interesting first stop as you leave the Portland area. You can bring small boats up on the gravel beach of this city-owned property. Go inside and follow the spiral stairs to the top of this impressive granite-block Civil War fortification. You'll have a great spot for a picnic while surveying the harbor traffic.

Two Bureau of Parks and Lands (BP&L) islands of note are in western Casco Bay. Little Chebeague has lovely beaches, but skip any exploration of the interior during tick season. Jewell is a frequently visited island with rocky bluffs. There are hiking trails leading to observation towers and old gun emplacements. Jewell tends to get a lot of overnight visitors, with groups tenting on shore and many others staying aboard their boats in the anchorages. For that reason, you may find it does not provide the wilderness experience you would like. (There may also be a lot of empty six-packs on Jewell by the end of the weekend.)

The BP&L islands, as well as some others in western Casco Bay, are home to the caterpillars of browntail moths in June and July. Their tents appear on the tips of tree branches. Avoid skin contact with these caterpillars, as they can cause a severe rash.

Basket Island, southwest of Cousins Island, is cared for by the Cumberland Mainland and Islands Trust. It offers attractive pocket beaches to visitors; just watch for poison ivy. The island is for day use only; no fires are permitted.

Inhabited Long Island, between Peaks and Chebeague, has lovely public beaches.

REGIONAL ACCESS

Launch ramps with overnight parking

PORTLAND: *Portland Yacht Services* (58 Fore St., 774-1067), by the Bath Iron Works dry dock, has a concrete ramp; water at all tides.

ROYAL RIVER, YARMOUTH: There are three spots on the Royal River to leave your car if you are boating to lodgings on Chebeague or Peaks. Parking fees are lower than in Portland. *The Yarmouth Boat Yard* (846-9050), by Route 88, has a dirt ramp with water at half tide. Kayakers can launch their boats from floats at all tides. *Yankee Marina* (846-4326), next to the Lower Falls Landing complex on Route 88, has a concrete ramp with water at most tides. *The Royal River Boat Yard* (846-9577) has a concrete ramp with water at all tides. It is on the north side of the river, on Bayview Street 1/2 mile southeast of the junction with Route 88. (While you're near Lower Falls Landing, stop by Harbour Books for a great selection of marine titles, or Royal River Provisioners for tasty take-away food.)

FREEPORT: *Winslow Memorial Park* (865-4198), off the South Freeport Road, has a paved ramp; water on top 2/3 of the tide.

SOUTH FREEPORT: *Brewer's South Freeport Marine* (865-3181), at the harbor, has a spot to carry kayaks into the water at all but low tide.

Ferry service

If you're on Peaks Island and you hit bad weather, the Casco Bay Lines (774-7871) will carry kayaks as freight back to Portland. Ferries also carry cars to and from Peaks. From Chebeague Island, the Chebeague Transportation Company (846-3700) will carry kayaks as freight from the Stone Pier to Cousins Island. Casco Bay Lines will take hand-carried kayaks from the south end of Chebeague to Portland.

Public moorings, slips, dock space

PORTLAND: *DiMillo's Old Port Marina* (Long Wharf, 773-7632) has slip rentals by the Old Port. *Portland Yacht Services* (58 Fore St., 774-1067) has rental moorings by the dry dock.

PEAKS ISLAND: *Lionel Plante Associates* (766-2508) has moorings and slips by the ferry terminal. They don't monitor VHF radio.

SOUTH FREEPORT: *Brewer's South Freeport Marine* (865-3181) has moorings and dock space next to the town dock. *Strout's Point Wharf Co.* (865-3899) may have a mooring or slip available, also near the town dock.

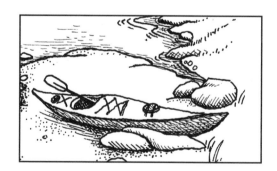

LODGINGS

Portland lodgings note

There are numerous guest accommodations within several miles of Portland Harbor. Yet because of the city's working waterfront, none of the mainland lodgings are directly on the water. Four of the lodgings close to the harbor are listed below. Contact the Visitors Information Center (305 Commercial St., 772-5800) for other Portland area suggestions.

The Danforth

#1, Chart 13290, Portland Harbor

The Danforth is a wonderful hybrid of inn and downtown hotel. The stately brick Federal mansion, built in 1821, has the appearance of an inn: there are just nine spacious guest rooms, decorated with antique and reproduction furniture. Each guest room has a working fireplace. Oriental carpets are scattered through the formal parlors, and deep paint colors on the walls highlight the ornate crown moldings. Fresh flowers are everywhere. Yet you'll find amenities and services more often found in hotels: each room has a telephone, television, hair dryer, and air conditioning. There are guest passes to a local health club, and you can have breakfast brought to your room.

There are pleasant surprises throughout the building. On the ground floor is a paneled room dedicated to playing billiards. On upper floors the sun shines through clear leaded-glass windows. As you open a door, you'll see that the doorknobs are crystal. Perched on top of the building is a cupola, providing views of the wharves and downtown Portland. Outside you'll find gardens and guest bicycles.

Innkeeper Barbara Hathaway, who has raced wooden sailboats in the past, will help ensure that your stay in this Portland historic district is enjoyable.

Meals A full breakfast is included. Barbara describes it as "always way too much, with healthy options." Favorites include stratas, pecan French toast, and baked potatoes with lobster Newburg sauce. There's always fresh fruit, espresso, cappuccino, and the morning newspapers. Box lunches can be provided.

Rates 9 rooms with private baths. $115-185 doubles late May through October. Visa, MC, Amex. Well-behaved children welcome. Well-behaved pets permitted. 2-night minimum reservation preferred for high season weekends and holidays. Open year round.

Access *Kayaks and trailered boats:* Paved public ramp at East End Beach; water at all tides. *Sailboats:* Closest facilities at DiMillo's Old Port

Marina, just under a mile away. *Walk to:* Restaurants, markets, galleries, shops, laundry.

Address   163 Danforth St., P.O. Box 10907, Portland, ME 04104.
(207) 879-8755, (800) 991-6557.

The Inn at ParkSpring
#2, Chart 13290, Portland Harbor

The Inn at ParkSpring is within a few blocks of the Portland Museum of Art and several of Portland's most creative restaurants; it is a 10-minute walk down to the Old Port. Guest rooms in the 1830's building are large and comfortably furnished with sofas and armchairs. Guests are encouraged to make themselves at home. There's a stove and refrigerator for their use, and they can help themselves to an evening brandy or chocolates in the high-ceilinged living room.

Breakfast   Guests can enjoy a large continental breakfast in the eat-in kitchen or they can have a tray brought to their room.

Rates   5 rooms with private baths, 2 with shared bath. $95-125 doubles May through October. Visa, MC, Amex. Children over 12 welcome. 2-night minimum stays preferred on summer weekends. Open year round.

Access   *Kayaks and trailered boats:* Paved public ramp at East End Beach; water at all tides. *Sailboats:* Closest facilities at DiMillo's Old Port Marina, 3/4 mile away. *Walk to:* Restaurants, markets, galleries, shops, laundry, bicycle rentals.

Address   35 Spring St., Portland, ME 04101.
(207) 774-1059.

Portland Regency Hotel
#3, Chart 13290, Portland Harbor

The Portland Regency is in the heart of the Old Port district, and is just a block from the waterfront. This fortress-like brick and granite structure served as an armory from its construction in 1895 until after World War II. Ten years ago it was ingeniously renovated, and turned into a full-service hotel. If you arrive by car, a valet will offer to park it. As you enter the lobby, a member of the staff will hold the door. Room service can bring a meal to your well-appointed room, which comes complete with mini-bar and cable television. Guests may avail themselves of the health club's sauna, steam room, and jacuzzi, or work out on the exercise equipment.

Meals   None included. Breakfast and dinner available every day, and lunch during the week. Traditional American cuisine with an emphasis on seafood is offered in the main dining room, and there's lighter fare in the attractive lounge.

Rates   95 hotel rooms. $189-229 doubles July through October. Visa, MC, Amex, Discover. Designated smoking guest rooms. One wheelchair-accessible room. Children welcome. Open year round.

Access   *Kayaks and trailered boats:* Paved public ramp at East End Beach; water at all tides. Kayakers are requested to have cable locks for kayaks if they wish to use the hotel's valet parking service. *Sailboats:* Closest facilities at DiMillo's Old Port Marina, within 500 yards. *Walk to:* Restaurants, markets, galleries, shops, laundry, bicycle rentals.

Address   20 Milk St., Portland, ME 04101.
(207) 774-4200, (800) 727-3436.

Victoria Terrace
#4, Chart 13290, Fish Point, Portland

The deck at Victoria Terrace is reason enough to stay here, although host Eva Horton has made sure that there are plenty of other good reasons. The second-floor deck commands an unobstructed 180-degree view of the islands beyond Portland's Eastern Promenade, and makes the most resolute think of whiling away the afternoon there. Back inside, guests find sunny common rooms with Scandinavian furnishings and some of Eva's sculptures. Two guest rooms are in the main house; one comes with a kitchen. The third guest room, in an adjacent building, has five skylights as well as a window looking out on Fort Gorges and Peaks Island. All three spacious guest rooms have private entrances.

There are laundry machines on site if you'd like to make your clothes more presentable, and workshops if you need to make minor equipment repairs. Between the main house and the water is a popular public park, with playgrounds and walking trails.

Breakfast   Guests can help themselves to a buffet of fresh fruit, pastries, and cereal, and sit in the cozy eat-in kitchen or on the deck.

Rates   3 rooms with private baths. $90-140 doubles. Visa, MC. Smoking permitted. Well-supervised children welcome. Cats in residence. Small well-behaved pets welcome by prior arrangement. Open year round.

Access   *Kayaks:* Closest lodgings to East End Beach; 4/10 mile along park road to beach and launch ramp with water at all tides. Eva has room to store kayaks if you arrive by water and use wheels to bring your kayaks up the hill. *Trailered boats:* Fee paved public ramp at East End Beach. *Sailboats:* Portland Yacht Services is within 1/2 mile. *Walk to:* Restaurants, markets, galleries, shops, bicycle rentals.

Address 84 Eastern Promenade, Portland, ME 04101.
(207) 774-9083.

Keller's Bed and Breakfast
#5, Chart 13290, Peaks Island

Keller's Bed and Breakfast offers four rooms downstairs from their restaurant, as well as a studio set off by itself. The studio has a private deck with glass windscreens, and the other rooms share a deck overlooking the harbor. You're so close to the harbor that you could be awakened by the first ferry of the morning blasting its horn. Each room has a refrigerator and television.

Meals A full breakfast is included, with guests choosing from the restaurant menu. Lunch and dinner are available inside the restaurant or on the waterfront deck.

Rates 4 guest rooms and 1 studio, all with private baths. $125-145 doubles. No credit cards. Smoking permitted. Children welcome. 2-night minimum stays from Memorial Day to Labor Day. Open year round.

Access *Kayaks:* Sand beach below Keller's provides access at all tides. It is an easy 75-foot carry over the lawn to rooms. *Sailboats:* Moorings and slips at Lionel Plante Associates. *Walk to:* Restaurants, grocery store, shops, laundry, bicycle rentals.

Address P.O. Box 8, Peaks Island, ME 04108.
(207) 766-2441.

Chebeague Orchard Inn
#6, Chart 13290, Great Chebeague Island

The hosts of the Chebeague Orchard Inn, Vickie and Neil Taliento, are sea kayakers who have lived on the island the past fourteen years. Neil is a Registered Maine Guide as well. They have separated their white clapboard Greek Revival home into a guest wing and a family wing. Guests have their own living room, filled with lovely watercolors. Comfortable bedrooms are furnished with antiques, colorful handmade quilts, and flowers from Vickie's garden. There are Adirondack chairs on the lawn overlooking the meadow and water beyond, and an enclosed porch for cooler days.

Breakfast You may have breakfast in the dining room, on the porch, or even in bed! The full breakfast might include homemade muffins, pancakes, or eggs Benedict.

Rates 1 room with private bath, 2 rooms with private half baths and joint shower, 2 rooms with shared bath. $75-95 doubles. For those arriving by sea kayak, there is a 15% discount. Visa, MC. Children welcome. Pets allowed on a space-available basis. 2-night minimum on July 4th weekend. Open year round.

Access *Kayaks:* Vickie and Neil can meet kayakers at the Stone Pier at the north end of the island, where there is access to a beach at all tides. They'll either load your kayaks onto a truck or give you detailed directions to the shore near their house, where there is access at most tides. You can leave your boats at the shore and walk a few hundred yards to the inn. *Sailboats:* There is a guest mooring for a small boat, up to 25 feet, at the Stone Pier, or the Talientos can help you borrow a mooring. The Stone Pier is less than 1 mile from the inn; the innkeepers can provide a lift, or you can catch the island taxi. *Walk to:* Restaurants, groceries, bicycle rentals.

Address P.O. Box 453, Chebeague Island, ME 04017.
(207) 846-9488.

Sunset House Bed and Breakfast Inn
#7, Chart 13290, Great Chebeague Island

Innkeeper Banu KomLosy has been a member of the Chebeague community for over 30 years. When her children grew up, she opened their rooms to guests. The newly renovated guest rooms are decorated with mementos of her travels: Banu has been all over Southeast Asia, and she spent several years teaching English in Laos. There is a big living room with a harbor view, and a great deck looking west over the second hole of the Great Chebeague Island Golf Course. Banu suggests sitting out on the deck in the evening to watch the night sky.

You can rent a mountain bike at the inn, and the community tennis courts are handy as well. After your workout, you can sit in the outdoor hot tub. If your clothes have seen better days, you can use the inn's washing machine. If you'd like to purchase lobsters for dinner, Banu can cook them up for you.

Breakfast Quiche, waffles, fish, or salmon souffle could be featured.

Rates 4 rooms with private baths, 1 with shared bath. $95 doubles. No credit cards. Children welcome. Open year round.

Access *Kayaks:* It is a 4-minute walk up the road to the inn from the Stone Pier and adjacent beach. Kayaks can be paddled up to the beach at all tides. The KomLosys can move your kayaks and gear to the inn on a trailer. *Sailboats:* Guest moorings. *Walk to:* Restaurants, groceries.

Address Capps Rd., P.O. Box 584, Chebeague Island, ME 04017.
(207) 846-6568.

Chebeague Island Inn
#8, Chart 13290, Great Chebeague Island

This large rustic inn just up the hill from the harbor has been welcoming guests to its spacious living and dining rooms since 1925. The 12-foot-tall stone hearth in the Great Room warms guests on cool days. They'll find comfortable chairs scattered over an oriental carpet, and an organ for those with musical talent. The wrap-around porch features plenty of rocking chairs and hanging geraniums, as well as good views of the community golf course and harbor.

The dining room, dining porch, and bar are open to the public. On Saturday nights there is musical entertainment and dancing. Bring warm clothes in the off season, as the only heat comes from the Great Room fireplace. There are bicycle rentals at the inn.

> *Meals* None included. Three meals a day are offered, with brunch on Sundays and afternoon tea some weekdays. The dinner menu features seafood and international fare, and includes vegetarian selections.
>
> *Rates* 16 rooms with private baths, 5 with shared baths. $85-125 doubles July and August. Visa, MC, Discover. Smoking permitted in some common spaces. Children welcome. Open mid-May through September.
>
> *Access* *Kayaks:* It's a 5-minute walk up the road to the inn from the Stone Pier and adjacent beach. Kayaks can be paddled up to the beach at all tides. The inn staff will move kayaks up the hill by truck. *Sailboats:* Guest moorings and dinghies. *Walk to:* Restaurants, groceries.
>
> *Address* South Rd., P.O. Box 492, Chebeague Island, ME 04017.
> (207) 846-5155.

Far Horizons Kayak Center
#9, Chart 13290, South Freeport

Ann and Chick Carroll are BCU-certified sea kayaking instructors with a beautiful home near the South Freeport harbor. In the past, the Carrolls sometimes housed a student in one of the bedrooms vacated by their grown children. It occurred to them that they could create a "kayak center," a place where paddlers would enjoy the camaraderie of staying with fellow paddlers. In Great Britain, kayak centers are popular getaways near the water for novices and experienced paddlers alike. British centers tend to feature Spartan dormitory rooms though; you'll find the opposite here.

The Far Horizons Kayak Center offers bed and breakfast accommodations to paddlers only, or paddlers and their travelling companions. While the Carrolls offer instruction and trips for small groups, there is no requirement that guests enroll in a lesson to enjoy a stay at the center. Kayaking enthusiasts may find themselves at breakfast with paddlers from a location they'd always hoped to visit, members of the center's staff, or a guest instructor from Great Britain.

The center is housed in a sunny 1830's Cape with plenty of interesting common spaces. The living room is lined with soft sofas and has a bookshelf full of seafarers' tales and other adventurers' stories. The library offers a quiet place to sit, with more books and a stereo system. Outside are the gardens: a water garden, a meditation garden, an herb garden. Ann's sculptures are integrated into her gardens. Her artistic talents are in evidence in the guest rooms too; each is designed around a different culture's folk art. The Inuit Room, for instance, has seals, caribou, wolves, and salmon stenciled on the walls, along with two outlines of East Greenland kayaks. Other rooms celebrate the folk art of Africa, America, and the northwest American coast Indians.

Breakfast A buffet of oatmeal, cereal, homemade bread, and fruit.

Rates 4 rooms with private baths, 1 with shared bath. $60-75 doubles. Visa, MC. Children welcome. Dog and cat in residence. 2-night minimum on July and August weekends. Open mid-May through September.

Access *Kayaks:* Kayakers can use the center's private low float on the Harraseeket River at all tides. It's a 3-minute walk to the center. If you arrive by water the Carrolls can provide safe kayak storage on their waterfront rack and help you move your gear. *Other:* Necky kayak rentals. Guided kayaking trips using a 47-foot support boat that sleeps 7; hot shower on board. *Walk to:* Restaurant, deli, market.

Address 13 Main St., P.O. Box 189, South Freeport, ME 04078. (207) 865-1244, (888) 375-2738.

Atlantic Seal Bed & Breakfast
#10, Chart 13290, South Freeport

Innkeeper Tom Ring grew up in this 150-year-old Cape Cod. His home reflects the maritime heritage of both South Freeport and his family. You'll find the 1860's shipping licenses of family members hung beneath his own. (Tom runs trips out to Eagle Island, home of North Pole explorer Robert Peary, and he also captains tugboats.) An old ship's compass, sextant, bell, and telescope are on display in the open common rooms. You can enjoy a view of the Harraseeket River from the back deck or from the dock. One guest room has a jacuzzi, and another has a fireplace and window seat.

Breakfast	The "hearty sailors' breakfast" might include lobster omelets if Tom found a lobster in his traps the day before. If not, guests can enjoy Featherbed Eggs or blueberry pancakes.
Rates	3 rooms with private baths. $85-135 doubles May through November. No credit cards. Children welcome. 2-night minimum on holiday weekends. Open year round.
Access	*Kayaks:* Carry boats down the back lawn and launch from the low float at 1/2 tide and higher. Kayakers can use the town dock, 500 feet away, at any tide. *Trailered boats:* Small boats may be tied to Tom's dock if they can sit on mud. The nearest paved launch is a few miles away at Winslow Memorial Park. *Sailboats:* Contact Brewer's South Freeport Marine or Strout's Point Wharf Co. *Other:* Rowboat available. *Walk to:* Restaurant, deli, market.
Address	25 Main St., P.O. Box 146, South Freeport, ME 04078. (207) 865-6112.

Porter's Landing Bed and Breakfast
#11, Chart 13290, Porter's Landing, Freeport

Owners Barbara and Peter Guffin completely renovated an old carriage house adjacent to their home to create comfortable guest quarters a mile from downtown Freeport. The large living room is furnished with inviting couches and several contemporary paintings. There are well-stocked bookshelves, including many titles by Maine authors. The cozy guest rooms have handmade quilts on the beds. Above the bedrooms is a loft with more books, a couple of armchairs, and a skylight. Guests may use the washer and dryer in the carriage house.

Barbara and Peter enjoy sea kayaking. They use a Whaler to take their three young daughters island camping.

Breakfast	Fruit, freshly baked bread, and a hot entree such as apple pancakes or an egg dish.
Rates	3 rooms with private baths. $95 doubles from Memorial Day through October. Visa, MC. Children over 12 welcome. Open year round.
Access	*Kayaks and trailered boats:* There is a dirt public ramp 1/4 mile away at Porter's Landing for use by kayakers or those with boat trailers and four wheel drive vehicles; water on the top half of the tide only. The paved ramp at Winslow Memorial Park is 3 miles away and has water for 2/3 of the tide. Kayakers can use the South

Freeport town dock at all tides. *Sailboats:* Contact Brewer's South Freeport Marine or Strout's Point Wharf Co. The Guffins can pick up sailors at the town dock, which is 1.5 miles away. *Walk to:* 1 mile to restaurants, market, L.L. Bean, shops.

Address   70 South St., Freeport, ME 04032.
(207) 865-4488.

CAMPGROUNDS

Winslow Memorial Park
#C1, Chart 13290, Stockbridge Point, Freeport

A municipal campground, with many sites overlooking Casco Bay. 1/3 wooded, fairly private sites; 2/3 open grassy sites. Sand swimming beach and trails along the Harraseeket River.

Campsites   101 sites, tenters can use any site. 23 waterfront. 50% tenters. Showers, flush toilets. Wheelchair accessible.

Rates $16-18 tent sites for non-Freeport residents, lodging tax included. No credit cards. Personal checks drawn on Maine banks only. Pets permitted. No advance reservations taken. Open Memorial Day through September.

Access   *Kayaks and trailered boats:* Paved ramp; water on top 2/3 of the tide, mud at low tide. *Other:* Overnight public parking available near the ramp.

Address   Staples Point Rd., Freeport, ME. Mail: c/o Town Office, 30 Main St. Freeport, ME 04032.
(207) 865-4198.

Recompence Shore Campsites
#C2, Chart 13290, Little River, Freeport

Very wooded, rustic campground with private sites and a few pocket beaches. There are organic gardens next to the campsites. You can purchase fresh basil for your pesto sauce, or edible flowers for your salad, from the honor-system farm stand. Down the road is Wolfe's Neck Woods State Park, with hiking trails along the water.

Campsites   104 sites, tenters can use any site. 43 waterfront. 80% tenters.

Central showers. Privies scattered through campground, a few flush toilets by office. Laundry. Basic groceries.

Rates $12-20 tent sites. Visa, MC, Discover. Pets permitted. Open Memorial Day to mid-October.

Access *Kayaks:* 1/2 tide and higher access from pocket beaches. Easiest access down 16 stair steps, between sites #92 and 94. There are also stairs by site #160 and a foot ramp by the bridge over the Recompence River. *Trailered boats:* Launch at Winslow Memorial Park paved ramp.

Address 10 Burnett Rd., Freeport, ME 04032.
(207) 865-9307.

Flying Point Campground
#C3, Chart 13290, Little Flying Point, Freeport

Mostly open sites to accommodate RV's in this small campground on Maquoit Bay. The tent sites are clustered together near the water. Very clean shower room.

Campsites 38 total sites, 7 for tenters. 21 waterfront. 20% tenters. Showers and flush toilets. Laundry.

Rates $15-17 tent sites. Visa, MC. Pets permitted. 3-night minimum on holiday weekends. Open May 1 to October 15.

Access *Kayaks:* Small gravel beach by causeway; water 1/2 tide and higher. Easy access to beach. *Trailered boats:* Winslow Memorial Park paved ramp.

Address Lower Flying Point Rd., Freeport, ME 04032.
(207) 865-4569.

Eastern Casco Bay: Harpswell to Small Point

ON SHORE

Most of the waterfront lodgings in eastern Casco Bay are in rural locations well down the peninsulas that extend into the bay. It is surprising how quiet this region is, since busy Portland and Freeport are nearby.

If you have a car, you will most likely pass through either Brunswick or Bath on your way down a peninsula to your accommodations. Both towns have fine restaurants. Brunswick is home to Bowdoin College, with the Peary-MacMillan Arctic Museum on campus. Kayakers will find displays of special interest there; see the description below. At Bath is the Maine Maritime Museum; see page 59 for information on its exhibits.

OFF SHORE

As in western Casco Bay, there are some sheltered waters and interesting places to poke around in the eastern section of the bay. You're likely to see great blue herons and osprey from your boat.

Three BP&L islands are open to low-impact visits. Strawberry Creek is a one-acre island at the mouth of the creek of the same name, in Harpswell Sound. Little Snow is in a nicely sheltered section of Quahog Bay, just east of Snow Island. Basin Island is found in The Basin, a popular hurricane hole on the New Meadows River. (Little Snow and Basin receive fairly heavy use and so should be avoided by summer weekend campers.)

Eagle Island, the summer home of Arctic explorer Admiral Robert Peary, is a state historic site open to the public. The cottage sits on a high bluff looking out over the waters of Casco Bay. It was here that Peary's wife, Josephine, received his telegram on September 6, 1909 stating that he had reached the North Pole. Visitors can wander around the large cottage, furnished much as it was when the Pearys lived there. Some of the family's personal effects are on display. Walking paths crisscross the 17-acre island, located 2 miles southwest of Harpswell Neck. The entry fee is $1.50 for those ages 12-65. Kayakers can land on the beach at any tide; there are a couple of state-maintained moorings for sailors.

REGIONAL ACCESS

Launch ramps with overnight parking

HARPSWELL: *Dolphin Marine* (833-6000) at Basin Point has a paved ramp, with water at all tides.

ORR'S ISLAND: *Lowell Prince* (833-6210) offers parking next to a gravel ramp just north of the cribstone bridge to Bailey Island. Water at all tides at the ramp. Pay parking fee at the Orr's Island Chowder House.

CUNDY'S HARBOR: *Bethel Point Boatyard and Marina* (725-8145) on Bethel Point Road provides parking 100 yards from the paved public ramp on Hen Cove. Water at all tides at the ramp.

Public moorings, slips

HARPSWELL: *Dolphin Marine* (833-6000) has moorings and a restaurant at Basin Point at the south end of Harpswell Neck.

BAILEY ISLAND: *Cook's Lobster House* (833-6641) has slips by the cribstone bridge.

SEBASCO ESTATES: *Sebasco Lodge* (389-1161) has moorings available on a first come, first served basis.

The Peary-MacMillan Arctic Museum

This museum contains artifacts, equipment, and photographs from the Arctic explorations of two Bowdoin College alumni, Robert Peary and Donald MacMillan. Among the artifacts of particular interest to paddlers is an Inuit kayak collected in North Greenland by MacMillan during an expedition spanning the years 1913-1917. The kayak was constructed of sealskin stretched over a wooden frame. The Inuit used harpoons to hunt sea mammals from their boats; the collection contains photographs and paintings of hunters with their kayaks. Also on display are several models of kayaks from different regions of Greenland, and even an Eskimo walrus-tooth kayak toy.

Of general interest are the stuffed polar bears and Arctic birds. Tools used during the exploration, such as a dog sled, are displayed in front of huge photographs of the explorers in action. This is a great little museum for children and adults alike.

The Peary-MacMillan Arctic Museum, Hubbard Hall, Bowdoin College, Brunswick, ME 04011. (207) 725-3416. Hours: Tuesday through Saturday 10-5, Sunday 2-5, closed Mondays and holidays. Free admission. Located near the Walker Art Building, on the Bowdoin campus in downtown Brunswick.

LODGINGS

The Vicarage by the Sea
#12, Chart 13290, Curtis Cove, West Harpswell

Cathedral ceilings and skylights brighten this casual, home-style B&B of recent construction. By taking a seat on the deck or in the hammock, guests can admire the gardens and woods. It is an easy amble down a wood-chip-covered path to Curtis Cove. Host Joan Peterson-Moulton loves dogs and has 3 rescued greyhounds and a terrier. Some of the dogs join guests in Joan's living room.

Breakfast   A full breakfast, with selections such as French toast and fruit.

Rates   1 room with private bath, 2 with shared bath. $65-80 doubles. No credit cards. Children or pets accepted by prior arrangement. Dogs in residence. 2-night minimum on certain weekends. Open year round.

Access   *Kayaks:* Easy carry down a gently sloping 200-foot path and then a dozen shallow stair steps to the stone beach, which is available at all tides. *Trailered boats:* Launches within a few miles include the paved public ramp at Lookout Point and the paved ramp at Dolphin Marine. *Walk to:* No nearby restaurants; boat to the restaurant at Dolphin Marine 3 miles away.

Address   Route 123, RR#1 Box 368B, South Harpswell, ME 04079. (207) 833-5480.

Harpswell Inn
#13, Chart 13290, Lookout Point, Harpswell Center

This handsome inn on Middle Bay started out as a cookhouse for the local shipyard in 1761. Additions have been built over time, and the inn now offers 11 guest rooms and 3 suites. The guest rooms range from ones furnished in a cheery summer cottage style to more formal rooms with antique beds and floral wallpaper. Guests gather round a large dining table at breakfast. Afterwards they might linger in the great room or on the porch to admire the water views.

Breakfast   Offerings such as quiche, Texas pecan waffles, or pancakes.

Rates   5 rooms and 3 suites with private baths, 6 rooms with shared baths. $59-116 guest room doubles, $135-150 for suites, mid-June through October. Visa, MC, Discover. Children over 10 welcome. Resident cat. 2-night minimum on weekends in July, August, and October. Open year round.

Access	*Kayaks:* Easy launch from the back lawn on the top half of the tide, or from the paved public ramp 500 feet away; water at all tides. *Trailered boats:* Neighboring public ramp. *Sailboats:* Innkeepers Susan and Bill Menz, sailors themselves, will pick up boaters at Dolphin Marine. *Walk to:* Restaurant and market.
Address	141 Lookout Point Rd., RR#1 Box 141, South Harpswell, ME 04079. (207) 833-5509, (800) 843-5509.

Bailey Island Motel

#14, Chart 13290, Wills Gut, Bailey Island

This small motel is adjacent to the unique cribstone bridge joining Bailey Island to Orr's Island. Guests have views of easternmost Casco Bay from their rooms or from the waterfront lawn. Comfortable rooms are newly refurbished and have framed prints of wooden boats; some rooms have antique side pieces. Cable television is included.

Owner Chip Black has lived in the area all his life, and serves on the boards of the local land trust and historical society; he's also done quite a bit of boating. Guests can ask Chip to cook up lobsters they've purchased, and then dine outside at the picnic table.

Breakfast	Homemade muffins and juice.
Rates	9 motel rooms and 1 efficiency with kitchenette, all with private baths. $85 doubles mid-June through September. Visa, MC. Children welcome. Open May through October.
Access	*Kayaks:* Launch from the motel property at half tide and higher. There is water at all tides at the gravel town landing at Garrison Cove a few hundred yards to the west; bring cars back to the motel as there is no parking provided at the landing. There's a fee gravel ramp at the north end of the cribstone bridge, with water at all tides. *Trailered boats:* Use either gravel ramp. *Sailboats:* Transient slips at Cook's Lobster House. *Walk to:* Restaurants nearby, market 1 mile away.
Address	Route 24, P.O. Box 4, Bailey Island, ME 04003. (207) 833-2886.

Orr's Island Bed & Breakfast
#15, Chart 13290, Long Cove, Orr's Island

Guests staying in this contemporary home will enjoy relaxing on the large deck overlooking sheltered Long Cove, or swinging in the hammock. They share the family living room, which has a light and open feel. At breakfast guests choose between eating in the sunny kitchen or out on the deck.

Breakfast	Full breakfast, such as bacon and eggs, blueberry muffins, and fruit.
Rates	2 rooms with private baths. $85 doubles Memorial Day through October. Visa, MC. Well-supervised children welcome. Cats in residence. Open year round.
Access	*Kayaks:* Only the energetic would want to carry their kayaks down to the water here (or back up!). From the parking spaces, there's a short slope, then 60 stair steps to the float, a 150-foot carry. Launch kayaks from the low float, where there is water on the top half of the tide. Easier kayak access and parking is available a few miles away at the north end of the cribstone bridge linking Orr's to Bailey Island; water at all tides. *Walk to:* Deli and market.
Address	Route 24, Box 561, Orr's Island, ME 04066. (207) 833-2940, (800) 550-2940.

Hazel-Bea House
#16, Chart 13290, Quahog Bay, Harpswell

Roberta and Chuck Hammond have decorated this 20-year-old gambrel-roofed house with a light Victorian touch. There are wonderful old family photographs showing shipbuilding and wood mills in down east Maine. You might opt to eat breakfast on the deck, which catches the morning sun. The deck overlooks Snow Island, with state-owned Little Snow Island hidden just beyond. You have a good chance of finding calm waters and spotting osprey in this sheltered section of Quahog Bay.

A pleasant surprise is a big indoor spa, a hot tub that is sometimes kept cool in the summer. Each guest room has a television. Chuck has extensive boating experience and he charters a 38-foot pilot house ketch.

Breakfast	Fruit, pancakes or French toast, and fruit bread.
Rates	1 room with private bath, 2 rooms with shared bath. $75 doubles. Visa, MC. Well-behaved children welcome. Resident cat. Open May through October.
Access	*Kayaks:* There's a neighborhood gravel right-of-way within 200 feet; water at all tides. *Trailered boats:* Ramps at the Great Island Boat

Yard and at Bethel Point, with fee parking. *Sailboats:* Great Island Boat Yard (729-1639) is within a mile and may have a mooring. *Walk to:* No restaurants or markets, but the Hammonds can give you a lift or call a taxi for a trip to Brunswick.

Address   Route 24, Fire Road 280; RR#2 Box 2233, Brunswick, ME 04011. (207) 725-6834.

Bethel Point Bed and Breakfast
#17, Chart 13290, Hen Cove, Cundy's Harbor

Peter and Betsy Packard are boaters who summered on a nearby island for years before purchasing this house. These warm hosts have established a B&B in a very inviting spot directly on Hen Cove. As you walk along their waterfront you may spot working boats travelling between the numerous islands, or the wreck of the Philip E. Lake, an old Grand Banks schooner. It's so quiet that you might hear the seals barking on the ledge just off shore. If there weren't so many great boating destinations nearby, it would be tempting to relax on the granite step by the pocket beach and watch the sea birds. Assuming you do get out boating, you can return to soak your weary bones in the outdoor whirlpool.

The main house was built in 1838 as a store serving the Cundy's Harbor fishing community. Today it is furnished with family antiques and hand-stenciled walls. Bedrooms have extras beds to accommodate families. A two-story addition has modern furnishings, a kitchen, living room, washer/dryer, a double bed and two singles, and padded carpeting for sleeping bags. Common rooms include the family living room and a sunny greenhouse-style dining room.

Breakfast   Choices might include omelets with home-fried potatoes, waffles with strawberries and whipped cream, or homemade coffee cake.

Rates   1 suite with private bath, 2 rooms with shared bath. $70-80 doubles, $95 for two in suite, Easter to Christmas. Visa, MC. Children welcome. Dog and cat in residence. Guest pets are negotiable. Open year round.

Access   *Kayaks:* Easy launch from the beach just steps from the house; water at all tides. *Trailered boats:* Paved public launch next door. *Sailboats:* No moorings, but sailors anchor here, with 3 or 4 feet of water at low tide. *Walk to:* Restaurants and market are two miles away in Cundy's Harbor; you can boat there for dinner and groceries.

Address   Bethel Point Rd., RR#5 Box 2387, Brunswick, ME 04011. (207) 725-1115, (888) 238-8262.

The Captain's Watch B&B
#18, Charts 13290 & 13293, Cundy's Harbor

Here's a B&B that's marked on the nautical charts: just look for the abbreviation for a "cupola" in Cundy's Harbor. The structure, built in 1862 as the Union Hotel, retains its original cupola. There is still a grand view to be had of the harbor, which is used primarily by working boats. Ask for one of the two guest rooms that provide direct access to the cupola. All the guest rooms are spacious, and furnished with the innkeepers' antiques.

Enthusiastic hosts Donna Dillman and Ken Brigham love to sail, and spend their winters aboard their 37-foot O'Day sloop in warmer climes. In the summer, Ken charters the boat for day sails and overnight trips.

Breakfast	A full breakfast, with treats such as cinnamon raisin French toast and blueberry coffee cake.
Rates	5 rooms with private baths. $95-130 doubles May to Columbus Day. Visa, MC. Children welcome on a limited basis. Maine coon cat in residence. 2-night minimum stays on weekends and holidays preferred. Open year round by reservation.
Access	*Kayaks:* Donna and Ken can meet paddlers arriving by water at a small public landing in town. As parking there is quite limited, kayakers with cars should head to the Bethel Point paved launch 2 miles away and use the fee parking area. *Trailered boats:* Bethel Point ramp. *Sailboats:* You can arrange to tie up to Ken's boat on a mooring in the harbor. *Walk to:* Restaurants, market, laundry.
Address	2476 Cundy's Harbor Rd., Cundy's Harbor, Harpswell, ME 04079. (207) 725-0979.

Sebasco Lodge
#19, Charts 13290 & 13293, Sebasco Harbor, Sebasco Estates

This waterfront resort includes a nine-hole golf course, so bring your clubs. There is a large saltwater swimming pool, two tennis courts, bicycles, hiking trails, movies, and numerous children's activities: plenty to do in addition to boating in eastern Casco Bay. Guest accommodations range from inn rooms to family-sized cottages. While the overall feel of the resort is rustic, guests tend to dress more formally for dinner.

Meals	Rates generally include both breakfast and dinner. The full breakfast might feature fresh fish. Dinner choices could be grilled yellowfin tuna, broiled scallops, ravioli, or sirloin. Box lunches can be prepared, and there is a snack bar on site.

Rates   Approximately 100 rooms between the lodges and cottages. Inn room MAP rates (which include breakfast and dinner) are $98-108 per person, double occupancy, plus gratuities. A B&B rate can be arranged. Visa, MC, Amex. Smoking permitted only in the bar. 3 wheelchair-accessible guest rooms. Children welcome. Open Memorial Day through early October.

Access   *Kayaks:* Launch at the cove by the 1st golf hole on the top 2/3 of the tide by walking over gravel and hard-packed sand from a parking spot. *Trailered boats:* Launch from the cove, using four wheel drive. *Sailboats:* Moorings are rented on a first come, first served basis adjacent to the lodge; sailors can use Sebasco's float and dock. *Walk to:* Snack bar and coin-operated laundry on site.

Address   Sebasco Estates, ME 04565.
(207) 389-1161, (800) 225-3819.

Rock Gardens Inn
#20, Charts 13290 & 13293, Sebasco Harbor, Sebasco Estates

Rock Gardens is a small resort next door to Sebasco Lodge (see above). The inn's 60 guests have access to Sebasco's golf course, saltwater swimming pool, tennis courts, and other recreational opportunities. Rock Gardens is situated on a point of land with views of the harbor and numerous Casco Bay islands. There are 3 rooms in the inn, and 10 cottages. Cottages have 2 to 4 bedrooms, and no kitchens; half the cottages are located on a bluff overlooking the water. Rooms are furnished in a Maine cottage style, with braided rugs and quilts. Art workshops in June, July, and September provide instruction in watercolor and oil landscape painting; some of the results adorn the cottages.

Meals   Rates include breakfast and dinner. The full breakfast offers fresh baked goods and eggs. At dinner there is a choice of entrees: one fresh fish, one meat or chicken, and one vegetarian, with lobster served twice a week. Lunch can be obtained at the snack bar at Sebasco Lodge.

Rates   3 rooms and 10 cottages, all with private baths. $86-112 MAP rate per person, double occupancy, plus 15% gratuity, July to Labor Day. No credit cards. No smoking in common rooms, permitted in cottages. Children welcome. Resident dog in the inn. Minimum reservation of 5 nights in July and August, shorter stays available in June and September. Open early June to third week of September.

Access   *Kayaks, trailered boats, and sailboats:* See Sebasco Lodge information. Rock Gardens is closer to the cove; you can carry a kayak from the inn down to the water. *Walk to:* At Sebasco Lodge, there is a snack bar, restaurant, laundry, and bicycle rentals.

Address Sebasco Estates, ME 04565.
(207) 389-1339.

Small Point Bed and Breakfast
#21, Charts 13290 & 13293, Small Point

While this B&B has no water access, hosts Jan and Dave Tingle will gladly pick up guests from their boats. Dave has a marine services business and can repair boats, including fiberglass kayaks. He and Jan spent several years on boats in the Caribbean, he as a captain and she as a chef. They provide attractive rooms in their 100-year-old New England farmhouse. There is a big screened porch and guest refrigerator. Jan can prepare dinner when the nearby restaurant is closed.

Breakfast Full breakfast.
Rates 1 room with private bath, 2 with shared bath. $55-80 doubles mid-June to Labor Day. Visa, MC. Children welcome by prior arrangement. Dogs in residence. Guests may bring dogs by advance arrangement. 2-night minimum some holidays and weekends. Open year round.
Access *Kayaks and trailered boats:* Closest launching area a few miles away at Head Beach (unpaved). *Sailboats:* Rental moorings adjacent to Sebasco Lodge; the Tingles will pick up boaters. *Walk to:* Restaurant.
Address Route 216, HC32 Box 250, Sebasco Estates, ME 04565.
(207) 389-1716.

CAMPGROUNDS

Orr's Island Campground
#C4, Chart 13290, Reed Cove, Orr's Island

This campground has a nice long stone beach on Harpswell Sound. Open playing fields, a volleyball set, and playground. Mix of open and wooded sites; the tent sites are mostly wooded and private. Canoe rental available.

Campsites 70 total sites, 14 designed for tents, tenters can use any site. 21 waterfront. 40% tenters. Showers, flush toilets. Laundry.
Rates $17 tent sites. Visa, MC. Pets permitted. 2-night minimum reservations, 3 nights for holiday weekends. Open Memorial Day to mid-September.

Access   *Kayaks:* Easy access from stone beach; water at least on top 2/3 of
           the tide, sometimes throughout the day depending on tide cycle.
           Trailered boats: Launch with four wheel drive from beach. *Sailboats:*
           Rental moorings. *Walk to:* 1 mile to general store.
Address Route 24, RR#1 Box 650, Orr's Island, ME 04066.
           (207) 833-5595.

Hermit Island Campground
#C5, Charts 13290 & 13293, Hermit Island, Small Point

Despite the campground's name, you can drive to it via a sandy finger of land joining the island to the Phippsburg peninsula. You also can arrive by boat, as there
are 2 large sand beaches, 5 pocket beaches, and moorings. Hermit Island caters to
tenters; it cannot accommodate RV's or travel trailers. Some campsites are situated amidst scrubby vegetation, others are open and near a beach with thickets of
beach roses. Some of the nicest sites are on bluffs overlooking Casco Bay. An extensive network of hiking trails covers the island.

Campsites 275 sites, all suitable for tents. 70 waterfront. 50% tenters, rest of
             campers are using tent trailers or pickup truck campers. A mix of
             privies and flush toilets. Central showers. Recreation center with
             video games and snack bar. Groceries and lobsters.
    Rates $23.75-33.75 tent sites, late June to Labor Day. No credit cards. Pets
             permitted. No visitors. Open May 1 to Columbus Day.
   Access *Kayaks:* Launch from boat ramp, or from one of the beaches; water
             at all tides. *Trailered boats:* Launch from gravel boat ramp.
             Sailboats: Guest moorings available. *Other:* Canoes and rowboats for
             rent.
  Address Route 216, Small Point, ME. Mail: 42 Front Street Bath, ME 04530.
             (207) 443-2101.

AS WILD ISLANDS

attract greater numbers of visitors, it is incumbent on all of us to do what we can to leave the islands the same, or even better, than we found them. This helps assure that they will continue to remain open for recreational use and that others can enjoy the same wilderness experience that we have.

See page 20 for information on low-impact techniques to use when visiting public islands.

QUIET WATERFRONT HIDEAWAYS *and some rare Maine sand beaches await discovery at the ends of these long peninsulas.*

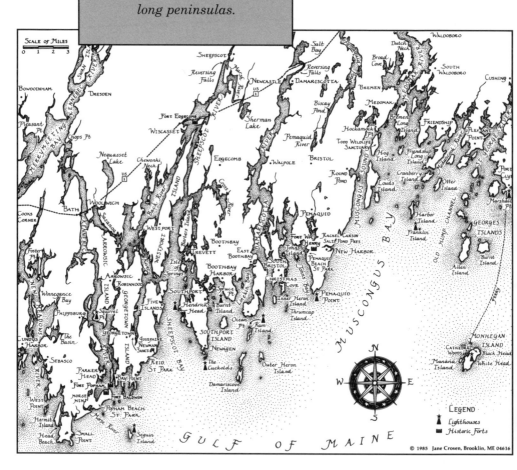

© 1985 Jane Crosen, Brooklin, ME 04616

RIVERS AND BOOTHBAY HARBOR

Kennebec and
Sheepscot Rivers

ON SHORE

Lodgings found along the Kennebec and Sheepscot Rivers are miles from busy Route 1, and have a definite hideaway feel to them. Yet if you have a car, it is easy enough to head up to Bath and enjoy a visit to the Maine Maritime Museum (see below) or go to dinner at Kristina's (442-8577) or another local restaurant.

Popham Beach
This self-contained village at the mouth of the Kennebec offers a restaurant, a market, a few places to stay, and several walking destinations. Visit the Civil War granite fort, or climb Sabino Hill to admire the view of the Seguin lighthouse from 20th-century Fort Baldwin. Walk along the miles of exposed sand beach in the state park, keeping an eye out for sand dollars.

Georgetown
At the southeastern end of Georgetown (an island linked to the mainland by a bridge) is Reid State Park. You'll find a section of shoreline good for rock-hopping and a long stretch of sand beach here. A stop at the village of Five Islands can net you a lobster dinner on the dock.

OFF SHORE

The upper reaches of the Kennebec and Sheepscot Rivers provide unlimited opportunities to explore complex saltwater estuaries. Two Bureau of Parks and Lands (BP&L) islands make interesting stops. Perkins, in the Kennebec, has a pretty lighthouse and a walking path through a hardwood forest. Goat is a little island further up the river near the village of Phippsburg. If your explorations take you onto the Sasanoa River, watch the currents of the Upper and Lower Hell Gates.

Two miles offshore from Popham Beach is Seguin Island. Visitors are welcome to go ashore to get a close-up view of the lighthouse, the second built on the coast of Maine.

SAFETY NOTE: The Kennebec dumps into the ocean the largest volume of water of any river in Maine, and the current can create dangerous conditions. This is particularly the case at the mouth of the river. The mouth of the Kennebec near Popham Beach has one of the Maine coast's most deceptive and treacherous currents, and warrants boaters' utmost caution and respect. The water can look nearly calm when viewed from shore, yet have standing waves in mid-channel where it funnels between islands. The current sweeps out toward Seguin Island.

The mouth of the Kennebec has caused problems for those in large motorboats as well as those in sailboats and kayaks; many choose to avoid it altogether, or to time their passage in light of the tide and wind. A kayaker lost her life here a few years ago after capsizing and being swept out to sea. Refer to boating guides and seek local knowledge before travelling in these waters.

REGIONAL ACCESS

Launch ramp with overnight parking

PHIPPSBURG: *Morse Cove public ramp,* at Fiddler Reach off Rt. 209, has a concrete ramp and float; overnight parking in the upper lot.

Many Maine coast B&B's were once the homes of wealthy 19th-century sea captains.

Maine Maritime Museum

The museum engages visitors in a discovery of Maine's maritime history. Boaters of all ages will find exhibits to interest them within the museum's extensive collections. You might wish to start with a guided tour through five of the original buildings of the Percy & Small Shipyard, to learn how four, five, and six-masted wooden schooners were built here 100 years ago.

In the boat shop you can view over 90 historic boats now serving as references for boatbuilders and those doing restorations. The collection includes a sailing canoe built in 1897, a lumberman's bateau for driving logs downriver to the sawmills, a beautifully restored Old Town canoe, and a North Haven racing dinghy. Visiting vessels on the riverfront may include old schooners, sloops, or fishing boats.

An extensive lobstering exhibit occupies its own building. It shows the wide variety of lobster boats used in Maine over the last 100 years. Various types of traps are on display, including the nets used to scoop lobsters up in the days when lobsters were more plentiful. There is also a large diorama of a lobster-canning factory.

The Maritime History Museum houses changing exhibits that may include beautiful half-hulls and ship models, oil paintings, artifacts from the days of steamer travel, and photographs of shipbuilders at work.

If you arrived by car, you might want to join an excursion boat for an up-close look at the Bath Iron Works shipyard, with its enormous crane towering over the city of Bath.

You can easily spend a couple of hours at the Maine Maritime Museum, and that doesn't include time spent browsing through the books in the museum store.

Maine Maritime Museum, 243 Washington St., Bath, ME 04530. (207) 443-1316. Open daily except Thanksgiving, Christmas, and New Year's, 9:30 to 5:00. Admission is $7.50 adults, $4.75 children 6-17, under 6 admitted free. $21 family admission for 2 adults and their children.

Water access: Located 1 nautical mile south of the Bath Bridge and Route 1, just south of Bath Iron Works. Kayakers are welcome to use the floats and carry their boats ashore. Moorings and possibly dock space are available for visiting sailors; there is no charge for day use. A $20 fee provides a mooring for the night and admission to the museum for two people.

LODGINGS

Popham Beach Bed & Breakfast
#22, Chart 13293, Popham Beach

Owner Peggy Johannessen has been renovating this interesting structure, built in 1883 as a U.S. Lifesaving Station and later taken over by the U.S. Coast Guard. (That this is the site of a former Coast Guard station should remind boaters that the waters at the mouth of the Kennebec are among the most dangerous on the Maine coast.) Some of the guest rooms previously accommodated rows of bunks and are quite large, with big windows opening onto great water views. The room with the wicker sofa facing the bay window is particularly nice. The cupola, where watchmen used to track ships, now lets guest scan up and down the coast. A rare Maine sand beach lies just in front of the B&B.

Breakfast	Peggy serves a two-course breakfast. The entree might be strawberry-stuffed French toast with strawberry sauce, a strata, or a frittata.
Rates	4 rooms with private baths, 1 with shared bath. $80-145 doubles mid-June to mid-September. Visa, MC. Well-behaved children over the age of 1 welcome. 2-night minimum stays from July to Labor Day, and all weekends. Open May through October.
Access	*Kayaks:* It's possible to carry kayaks on a path through the dunes to the beach, but the current can rush through here and this launch is not recommended. (See safety note above.) A better option is to launch from Atkins Bay, 1/4 mile away, with water on the top 2/3 of the tide, and to hug the western shore while exploring the Kennebec River to the north. There are quieter put-ins further north on the river, such as at the Morse Cove public ramp at Fiddler Reach. *Sailboats:* Sailors may be able to acquire a mooring in Atkins Bay from a local boater. *Walk to:* Restaurant, market.
Address	HC31 Box 430, Popham Beach, Phippsburg, ME 04562. (207) 389-2409.

Spinney's Guest House
#23, Chart 13293, Fort Popham, Popham Beach

Jack and Fay Hart operate a guest house near Fort Popham, and also rent cottages by the week. Rooms are simply furnished, and guests share the family living room. The second-floor porch looks out over the Kennebec River. It's an easy walk down to Popham Beach or the fort. Jack is a retired firefighter from neighboring Bath, and is very knowledgeable about boating in the region.

Meals	None provided; available at the lobster restaurant next door.
Rates	4 rooms sharing a bath. $55 doubles. Visa, MC. Children welcome. Open May to mid-October.
Access	*Kayaks:* Jack asks that kayakers head upriver only, to avoid the worst of the current at the mouth of the river. (See safety note above.) There is a place to carry kayaks into Atkins Bay 100 feet from the guest house, with water on the top 2/3 of the tide. *Trailered boats:* Launch at the sandy public put-in a few hundred feet further down and move vehicle and trailer back to Spinney's. Jack has a finger dock by the fort that is available to guests, with mud at low tide. *Sailboats:* Sailors may be able to obtain a mooring in Atkins Bay from a local boater. *Walk to:* Restaurant, market.
Address	HCR31 Box 395, Phippsburg, ME 04562. (207) 389-2052.

The Captain Drummond House Bed and Breakfast
#24, Chart 13293, Weasel Point, Phippsburg

This handsome Federal house was built in the late 1700's, when Maine was still part of Massachusetts, and is considered the oldest building in the Kennebec River Valley. Guests previously arrived by stagecoach or steamship, but now you can drive directly to this secluded bluff overlooking the Kennebec. The carefully restored rooms are furnished with period antiques. There is a massive fireplace in the dining room. Porches on the first and second floors offer seats to watch the river.

Breakfast	A full breakfast is served.
Rates	3 rooms with private baths. $95-130 doubles. Checks and cash preferred. Children welcome on a limited basis. Dog in residence. 2-night minimum stays on weekends and holidays preferred. Open May through October.
Access	*Kayaks:* Drive 1/4 mile to the Center Pond bridge and put in next to the fish ladder at half tide and higher; limited parking, so take cars back to the B&B. There's a gravel public put-in with water at all tides 1.5 miles north at Cranberry Point. *Trailered boats:* Launch at Cranberry Point or the Morse Cove concrete ramp upriver at Fiddler Reach. *Sailboats:* Guest mooring available with fairly difficult access. You can row in at half tide and higher, then use the ladder to reach a path to the house. *Other:* See safety note above on the Kennebec River. *Walk to:* Restaurant and market 3/4 mile away.
Address	Parker Head Rd., P.O. Box 72, Phippsburg, ME 04562. (207) 389-1394.

The Grey Havens Inn
#25, Chart 13293, Harmon Harbor, Georgetown

The Grey Havens Inn, perched high on a rocky bluff, commands an outstanding view of the open ocean. The wild shoreline might remind visitors of the bold coast of down east Maine. The rambling early 1900's Shingle architecture more often associated with classic Bar Harbor summer homes and inns is a pleasant surprise. These features combine to make you wonder if you're really still in Southern Maine, in an age of turbocharged cars and cellular phones.

The extended Hardcastle and Eberhart family has been pitching in to operate the inn for the past twenty years. They've enlarged guest rooms, added carpeting and soundproofing, but kept the features that let you feel that you've travelled back to the days of parasols and boardwalks. The dining room, for instance, is furnished with the inn's original tables and chairs, and there's a piano and tambourines. In the parlor is a huge stone fireplace and the original 12-foot picture window. Walls are made of southern pine in a tongue and groove design. (The pine was ballast on ships returning from delivering ice.) Upstairs, you'll find antique headboards, dressers, and chairs in the guest rooms, and often clawfoot tubs in the spacious baths. Most rooms have a water view; the four charming turret rooms have stunning 180-degree views. Outside, the wraparound front porch has rocking chairs serving as front row seats to the seascape just beyond the lawn.

Meals A "hearty continental" is included and served on a big buffet table. Choices include cereal, muffins, and a hot dish. The inn no longer serves dinner, but there is an open kitchen arrangement. Guests can help themselves to what they find, and it's charged to their room. The helpful innkeepers will show you how to cook lobsters if you bring some back from Five Islands.

Rates 13 rooms with private baths. $120-195 doubles, Memorial Day through October. Visa, MC. Children over 7 welcome. 2-night minimum on weekends, Memorial Day through October. Open mid-April to mid-December.

Access *Kayaks:* It's a carry over 16 stone steps, then down a path the equivalent of a couple flights of stairs to the float's ramp, which is steep at low tide. *Sailboats:* One guest mooring, plus moorings are available to rent at the Sheepscot Bay Boat Company (371-2442) at Five Islands. *Other:* Guest canoe. See safety note above on the Kennebec River. *Walk to:* Lobster dinners at Five Islands, 1.5 miles away.

Address Seguinland Rd., P.O. Box 308, Georgetown, ME 04548.
(207) 371-2616.

CAMPGROUND

Chewonki Campgrounds
#C6, Chart 13293, Montsweag Brook, Montsweag

This attractive facility has a 60' by 40' filtered saltwater swimming pool, wading pool, clay tennis court, and a day lily garden. Campsites are primarily wooded and private. Several campsites have picnic table shelters. Canoes and rowboats can be rented to take out on the quiet waters of Montsweag Brook.

Campsites 47 sites, of which 40 can accommodate tents. A handful of waterfront sites. 25% tenters. Nice shower room with flush toilets. Small recreation room with piano. Groceries.

Rates $18-28 tent sites. No credit cards. Pets permitted. 3-night minimum on holiday weekends. Open mid-May to mid-October.

Access *Kayaks:* Choice of 12-inch-high float at any tide, or launch site usable on top 2/3 of the tide. *Trailered boats:* Launch with four wheel drive from grassy ramp. *Sailboats:* Those with small boats are welcome to use the small dock on a first come, first served basis; boats may sit on mud at low tide. *Walk to:* Diner 1.5 miles away.

Address Box 261, Wiscasset, ME 04578.
(207) 882-7426.

Boothbay Harbor Area: Southport to Linekin Neck

ON SHORE

There are three distinct areas in the Boothbay Harbor region: Southport Island, the town of Boothbay Harbor, and East Boothbay on Linekin Neck.

The Boothbay Region Land Trust (633-4818) has established several preserves along the rivers open to the public; brochures with directions are distributed locally.

Southport Island

West of Southport is the Sheepscot River, east is Booth Bay. The island is connected to the town of Boothbay Harbor by a bridge over picturesque Townsend Gut. The large stands of dense evergreens covering the island help make it feel quite removed from the downtown bustle. There is a lovely little beach called Hendrick Head Beach on the western shore.

Boothbay Harbor

The town of Boothbay Harbor is a major tourist destination, with numerous shops, galleries, souvenir stores, and eateries. Most activity is centered around the harbor itself. Park your car and walk around downtown, so you don't become part of the vehicular gridlock that sometimes occurs. Tour boats can transport you to deep waters to look for whales, or take you on a day trip to Monhegan Island.

East Boothbay

East Boothbay, on Linekin Neck, has Linekin Bay to its west and the Damariscotta River to its east. Like Southport, it is only a few miles from downtown Boothbay Harbor, yet as you head down the neck the pace keeps slowing down. The drive around Ocean Point is quite scenic, and you can stop for a picnic at Grimes Cove at the southern end of the peninsula.

OFF SHORE

Damariscove Island is believed to be the site of Maine's earliest permanent European settlement. Residents made a living fishing and farming for over 300 years, before abandoning the island earlier this century. Today the Nature Conservancy cares for this nearly treeless island a few miles from the southern tips of Southport and Linekin Neck. Visitors can enjoy day visits to the southern end of the island, and use the dock and marked trails. To protect wildlife, no pets are permitted ashore. Fires are discouraged and must be built below the high tide line.

REGIONAL ACCESS

Launch area with overnight parking

BOOTHBAY HARBOR: Kayakers can launch from the *town dock* located between Piers 6 and 8. Overnight fee parking nearby includes the Cap'n Fish lot by Pier 8.

Public moorings, slips, dock space

BOOTHBAY HARBOR: *Samples Shipyard* (120 Commercial St., 633-3171) has moorings just west of the inner harbor.

Tugboat Marina (100 Commercial St., 633-4434) has moorings and dock space on the left as you enter the inner harbor. *Cap'n Fish's Marina* (65 Atlantic Ave., 633-6605) has slips and moorings on the right side of the inner harbor. *Brown's Wharf Marina* (Atlantic Ave., 633-5440) has moorings and dock space on the right side of the inner harbor.

LODGINGS

The Lawnmeer Inn
#26, Chart 13293, Townsend Gut, Southport

The Lawnmeer Inn sits near the water's edge at Townsend Gut, and draws a lot of patrons to its waterfront dining room. Guest rooms are available in the main inn and the annex. Those in the inn are individually furnished, and come with a teddy bear, while those in the annex are motel units. Adirondack chairs dot the front lawn.

Meals None included. Breakfast is served in the restaurant. When I visited, the dinner menu included a jumbo shrimp tart, lobster fradiavlo, a black bean and roasted vegetable quesadilla, and linguine with shrimp, scallops, mussels, and lobster.

Rates 13 inn rooms, 19 motel units, all with private baths. $68-128 doubles end of June to Labor Day. Visa, MC. Smoking permitted in annex rooms. Children welcome. Pets permitted in specified rooms. 2-night minimum on some holidays. Open mid-May to mid-October.

Access *Kayaks:* Carry boats across the lawn 50 yards from the parking lot to the 12-inch-high float; water at all tides. You can launch kayaks from the rocks at high tide. *Trailered boats:* Paved public ramps at Knickerkane Island Park off Barter's Island Road in Boothbay and on Murray Hill Road in East Boothbay. *Walk to:* Restaurant.

Address P.O. Box 505, West Boothbay Harbor, ME 04575. (207) 633-2544, (800) 633-7645.

Newagen Seaside Inn
#27, Chart 13293, Cape Newagen, Southport

Rachel Carson fans might want to head to the Newagen Seaside Inn: the marine biologist and author of *Silent Spring* often visited the inn's shoreline, which was a few miles from her home on Southport Island. The inn's wooded 85 acres at the tip of Southport offer a mile-long waterfront trail, a saltwater pool, freshwater pool, and tennis courts. The attractive dining room is open to the public. Bedrooms are generally fitted with reproduction furnishings; request one of the more recently redecorated rooms or a spacious room in the new wing.

Meals   A "bountiful breakfast buffet" with hot dishes is included. Dinner of international cuisine with an emphasis on seafood is available.

Rates   26 rooms with private baths. $100-175 doubles mid-July to Labor Day. Visa, MC. Wheelchair-accessible rooms. Children welcome. Open Memorial Day to mid-September.

Access   *Kayaks:* Launch from the 10-inch-high float after driving kayaks over to the dock; water at all tides. Kayakers preferring to carry boats into the water can go to Hendrick Head Beach off Beach Road. *Trailered boats:* Paved public ramps at Knickerkane Island Park off Barter's Island Road in Boothbay and on Murray Hill Road in East Boothbay. *Sailboats:* 3 rental moorings for guests. *Walk to:* No other restaurants or groceries within walking distance.

Address   Route 27, Southport Island, Cape Newagen, ME 04552. (800) 654-5242.

Albonegon Inn
#28, Chart 13293, Capitol Island

The Albonegon Inn is situated on a ledge right on the water; guests sitting in porch rockers could find themselves with salt spray in their hair. The inn's slogan is "determinedly old-fashioned" and it lives up to it. There is a delightful sense that Capitol Island's little bridge from Southport could be a sort of time tunnel, and upon crossing it you've entered a different era. The inn's casual and bright living room, with its big stone hearth and inviting sofas, the cheerful dining room, and the cozy bedrooms with their white chenille spreads all could have been decorated 50 years ago.

Three cute cottage rooms are perched on the rocks; I particularly liked little "Barnacle." One cottage has a kitchenette. (Those with a habit of snoring should request one of the cottage rooms, as the walls in the main building are reportedly thin.) There's a guest refrigerator and gas grill; you can purchase steaks, burgers, or chicken at the inn and prepare your own dinner.

All in all, when you're visiting the Albonegon Inn, it is hard to believe you're just a few miles from busy Boothbay Harbor.

Breakfast The continental breakfast includes freshly baked bread and muffins.

Rates 12 rooms in the inn, with in-room sinks, share four and a half baths. 3 cottage rooms with private baths. $73-81 doubles in the inn, $54 for singles. $83-123 for cottages. No credit cards. Children limited to certain rooms. 2-night minimum on holiday weekends. Open Memorial Day to Columbus Day.

Access *Kayaks:* Launch from the ledge next to the inn on the top half of the tide, about a 30-foot carry from your car. There's a sand and stone beach 250 yards from the inn where you can launch kayaks on the top 2/3 of the tide; return cars to the inn. *Sailboats:* Guest moorings can be arranged with notice. Advance arrangements can also be made to sublet a slip at a local marina. *Walk to:* No restaurants or groceries within easy walking distance.

Address Capitol Island, ME 04538. (207) 633-2521.

Ship Ahoy Motel

#29, Chart 13293, Townsend Gut, Southport

Here's a good choice for those watching their budgets. The Ship Ahoy provides clean motel rooms on the water near Townsend Gut, only a few miles from downtown Boothbay Harbor. The motel has been built in stages, with newer rooms closer to the water. Amenities include a swimming pool and a fishing dock.

Breakfast Not included, but the coffee shop serves muffins and cereal.

Rates 53 motel rooms. $39-59 doubles mid-June to Labor Day. Visa, MC. Personal checks on owner approval only. Smoking permitted. Wheelchair-accessible rooms. Children welcome. 2-night minimum on weekends, 3-night minimum for Labor Day. Open Memorial Day to Columbus Day.

Access *Kayaks:* Launch at all tides with a 50-yard carry from the car. You can use the 10-inch-high float or a rocky cove beyond the lawn. *Trailered boats:* Paved public ramps at Knickerkane Island Park off Barter's Island Road in Boothbay and on Murray Hill Road in East Boothbay. *Sailboats:* One guest mooring. *Walk to:* Restaurant.

Address Route 238, Southport, ME. Mail: P.O. Box 235, Boothbay Harbor, ME 04538. (207) 633-5222.

Hodgdon Island Inn
#30, Chart 13293, Hodgdon Island

This sea captain's home was built in 1810 on a small island lying between Barter's Island and the mainland. Boaters will find some sheltered waters and interesting gunkholing along the Back River, or they can head out into the Sheepscot River from here. Guest rooms have new private baths, and the common rooms are attractively furnished. Hosts Sydney and Joe Klenk have installed something the old sea captain would not have considered: a 16' by 32' swimming pool heated to a sybaritic 85 degrees. It is filtered by a copper ion system so it is refreshingly chlorine-free. Keep an eye out for Sydney's afternoon lemonade and cookies.

Breakfast	Joe says "you won't eat again until dinner" after one of Sydney's breakfasts.
Rates	6 rooms with private baths. $85-102 doubles May through October. No credit cards. Children over 12 welcome. Open most of the year.
Access	*Kayaks:* Drop off boats at a public ramp next to the Trevett Post Office and return cars 200 feet to the inn; there is easy access at all tides. *Trailered boats:* Knickerkane Island Park is 3/10 mile away and has a paved public ramp. *Sailboats:* Guests of the inn may be able to tie a small boat to the town dock; check with Joe. *Walk to:* No restaurants or groceries within walking distance.
Address	Barter's Island Rd., P.O. Box 492, Trevett, ME 04571. (207) 633-7474.

The Anchor Watch
#31, Chart 13293, Boothbay Harbor

Here's a current-day sea captain's house. Innkeeper Diane Campbell hosts the B&B, while her husband runs some of the ferries to Monhegan. Diane is a sailor who's active with the Boothbay Region Land Trust; she can steer you to several nearby preserves with hiking trails. The B&B sits on a quiet dead-end road, a 5-minute walk from downtown Boothbay Harbor. Pretty guest rooms have stenciled wall trim: look for the school of whales in one bathroom.

Breakfast	You might sit down to baked orange French toast or a French breakfast puff.
Rates	4 rooms with private baths. $99-129 mid-June to mid-October. Visa, MC. Children over 9 welcome. 2-night minimum on holidays. Open year round.
Access	*Kayaks:* Launch from the float off the Campbells' adjoining property at any tide. *Trailered boats:* Paved public ramps at Knickerkane

Island Park off Barter's Island Road in Boothbay and on Murray Hill Road in East Boothbay. *Sailboats:* Rent a mooring 1/4 mile away at Samples Shipyard and use their dinghy float, or row a couple hundred yards over to the Campbells' float. *Walk to:* Restaurants, groceries, galleries, shops, laundry, bicycle rentals.

Address   3 Eames Rd., Boothbay Harbor, ME 04538. (207) 633-7565.

Tugboat Inn
#32, Chart 13293, Boothbay Harbor

As you boat into the inner harbor, the Tugboat Inn's marina is the first one on your left. The Tugboat Inn was completely renovated in 1994 and 1995, and offers nicely appointed motel rooms right next to the marina. All the rooms have air conditioning, phones, and cable television. Children (and adults with a sense of fun) will enjoy dining in the converted tugboat. There are laundry facilities at the marina.

Meals   None included. 3 meals a day are available in the Tugboat Restaurant, which features traditional regional cuisine. There is dining on the deck and a piano bar.

Rates   64 motel rooms. $110-160 doubles late June through August. Visa, MC, Amex, Discover. Non-smoking rooms available. Wheelchair-accessible rooms. Children welcome. 2-night minimum stays on summer weekends and most holidays. Open April through November.

Access   *Kayaks:* Launch from the marina's floats. *Trailered boats:* Paved public ramps at Knickerkane Island Park off Barter's Island Road in Boothbay and on Murray Hill Road in East Boothbay. *Sailboats:* Rent moorings or dock space from the Tugboat Marina. *Walk to:* Restaurants, groceries, galleries, shops, bicycle rentals.

Address   100 Commercial St., Boothbay Harbor, ME 04538. (207) 633-4434, (800) 248-2628.

Rocktide Inn
#33, Chart 13293, Boothbay Harbor

The Rocktide Inn is located on the quieter eastern side of the harbor, 150 feet from the footbridge to the shopping district. Amenities include a large heated indoor pool and a courtesy shuttle bus into town. The attractive motel rooms have air conditioning, cable television, and phones. There are five different dining rooms, some casual, some formal, and all on the water. The dining rooms display an extensive collection of ship models, and there's an electric train that runs overhead.

> *Meals*　Full buffet breakfast included in room rate. Dinner is available and focuses on seafood.
>
> *Rates*　98 motel rooms. $105-145 doubles, late June through August. Visa, MC, Discover. Non-smoking rooms available. Wheelchair-accessible rooms. Children welcome. Open mid-June to Columbus Day.
>
> *Access*　*Kayaks:* Launch from a fairly low float at the inn. *Trailered boats:* Paved public ramps at Knickerkane Island Park off Barter's Island Road in Boothbay and on Murray Hill Road in East Boothbay. *Sailboats:* Float space is available at no charge to guests with boats under 40 feet. *Walk to:* Restaurants, groceries, galleries, shops, laundry, bicycle rentals.
>
> *Address*　45 Atlantic Ave., Boothbay Harbor, ME 04538. (207) 633-4455, (800) 762-8433.

Cap'n Fish's Motel
#34, Chart 13293, Boothbay Harbor

The owners of this motel are actually named Fish, and they run sightseeing cruises and whalewatching trips, so the motel comes by the name "Cap'n Fish's" honestly. The motel sits just behind their marina on the eastern side of the inner harbor. Guests can sit on a big patio and watch boats come into the harbor.

> *Breakfast*　Not included; buffet or menu selections available in the breakfast room.
>
> *Rates*　53 motel rooms. $67-105 doubles late June through September. Visa, MC. No personal checks. Smoking allowed in designated rooms. Wheelchair-accessible rooms. Children welcome. Open mid-May to mid-October.
>
> *Access*　*Kayaks:* Launch from the floats. *Sailboats:* Rent slip space or a mooring from Cap'n Fish's Marina. *Walk to:* Restaurants, groceries, galleries, shops, laundry, bicycle rentals.
>
> *Address*　65 Atlantic Ave., P.O. Box 660, Boothbay Harbor, ME 04538. (207) 633-6605, (800) 633-0860.

Brown's Wharf Motel
#35, Chart 13293, Boothbay Harbor

Three generations of a boating family run this motel, restaurant, and marina complex. The harbor-view restaurant's a bit of a landmark, having been in operation for over 50 years. Guests choose from attractive guest rooms or efficiencies, all with private decks.

> *Meals* None included. A full breakfast buffet is available. Guests can enjoy seafood dinners inside the restaurant or on the deck.
>
> *Rates* 70 motel rooms. $108-138 doubles. Visa, MC, Amex. Smoking permitted. Wheelchair-accessible rooms. Children welcome. 2-night minimum on weekends. Open mid-May to mid-October.
>
> *Access* *Kayaks:* Launch from the marina's dinghy float. Another option is the fee concrete ramp next door at the Carousel Marina (633-2922), best on the top 2/3 of the tide; no public parking at Carousel. *Trailered boats:* Ramp at Carousel Marina. *Sailboats:* Rent moorings or dock space at Brown's Wharf Marina. *Walk to:* Restaurants, groceries, galleries, shops, laundry, bicycle rentals.
>
> *Address* Atlantic Ave., Boothbay Harbor, ME 04538. (207) 633-5440, (800) 334-8110.

Spruce Point Inn
#36, Chart 13293, Spruce Point, Boothbay Harbor

The inn sits on 15 attractively landscaped acres at the tip of the primarily residential Spruce Point peninsula. This full-service resort, recently renovated, offers accommodations in inn rooms, cottages, and condominiums. The public dining room and other common spaces have a sense of old-time elegance.

This is the kind of place where you can keep quite busy, or simply enjoy sitting by the oceanfront saltwater swimming pool. You can opt for laps in the heated freshwater pool, or a game of tennis on one of the clay courts, and then a dip in the hot tub. You can retreat to the quiet library and browse through a great selection of boating and news magazines. Children will enjoy the recreation center's ping pong and pool tables. If you get the urge to head into town, you can hop on the shuttle bus or water shuttle to Boothbay Harbor.

There are laundry machines on site.

> *Meals* Breakfast and dinner are included in the MAP room rates. Breakfast choices range from eggs cooked to order to smoked fish plates with bagels and cream cheese. There are traditional New England dinner selections as well as creative offerings such as sashimi or blackened fish. The chef's signature dish is a cioppino with mussels, shrimp,

sea scallops, and lobster.

Rates   65 guest rooms in the inn and cottages, all with private baths. $132-198 per person, double occupancy MAP rate, mid-July to Labor Day. 15% gratuity is additional. Visa, MC, Amex. Smoking in one lounge only. Wheelchair-accessible rooms. Children welcome. Open Memorial Day to mid-October.

Access   *Kayaks:* Launch from the float at all tides, or launch from the rocky shore near the dock on the top half of the tide. (As an indication of the level of service at the inn, I was told that a paddler leery of entering a kayak from the float could ask a bellhop to come down and steady the kayak!) *Trailered boats:* Paved public launch on Murray Hill Road in East Boothbay. *Sailboats:* Guest moorings and a dinghy. *Walk to:* Shuttles can take you to town for restaurants, groceries, galleries, shops, bicycle rentals.

Address   P.O. Box 237, Boothbay Harbor, ME 04538. (207) 633-4152, (800) 553-0289.

Five Gables Inn
#37, Chart 13293, East Boothbay

This 100-year-old inn has been welcoming guests since the days they arrived by steamship from Boston. The nicely appointed rooms were renovated several years ago and are fitted with period reproduction furnishings and new baths. Five rooms have working fireplaces. Most guest rooms and the veranda offer views down the hill to Linekin Bay.

Innkeeper Mike Kennedy has worked on ships in Africa, the Far East, and the Caribbean. Recently he and his wife, De, crewed on a yacht in French Polynesia for a couple of months.

Breakfast   Mike cooks a big breakfast from which you will "walk away waddling." He prepares two hot dishes and two baked items each morning. Choices might include zucchini walnut pancakes, frittatas, or scones.

Rates   16 rooms with private baths. $90-160 doubles. Visa, MC. Children over 8 welcome. Cat in residence. Open mid-May through October.

Access   *Kayaks:* Choice of town dock 100 yards from the inn with a high float or an easier launch at the East Boothbay paved public ramp 250 yards away; water at all tides. *Trailered boats:* East Boothbay ramp. *Sailboats:* 2 guest moorings near the town dock. *Walk to*: Restaurant and market.

Address   Murray Hill Rd., P.O. Box 335, East Boothbay, ME 04544. (207) 633-4551, (800) 451-5048.

LeeWard Village Motel and Cottages
#38, Chart 13293, Linekin, East Boothbay

Here's a casual, family-oriented spot halfway down the western side of Linekin Neck. Some of the motel units and all the cottages include kitchenettes. The lawn is big enough for children to start up ball games, and they can play on the beach at most tides. Fishing poles are available for fishing from the dock. There is a washer and dryer on site.

Breakfast Not provided.
Rates 18 motel rooms, 8 cottages, all with private baths. $75-90 doubles in motel, $55-125 doubles in cottages, late June through late August. Visa, MC. Designated non-smoking rooms. Wheelchair-accessible units. Children welcome. Check with owners about bringing pets. 1-week minimum in cottages during July and August. Open May to mid-October.
Access *Kayaks:* An easy 100-foot carry across the lawn and then 16 stair steps down to the beach. Best to launch at other than high tide, as it's rocky then. *Trailered boats:* Paved public ramp on Murray Hill Road and a gravel one at Grimes Cove in Ocean Point. *Sailboats:* 6 moorings for boats up to 30 feet. Float and dock. *Walk to:* Restaurant and market 1 mile away.
Address HCR65 Box 776, East Boothbay, ME 04544. (207) 633-3681, (888) 817-9907.

Smuggler's Cove Inn
#39, Chart 13293, Linekin Neck, East Boothbay

Owner John McCarthy's father built this motel 30 years ago on the waterfront of Linekin Neck. One set of rooms is perched right at the water's edge, with decks overhanging the water at high tide. Six of the units have kitchenettes. The lawn leads down to a large heated pool and private beach.

Meals None included, but breakfast and dinner are available next door at Christopher's 1820 House. The extensive breakfast menu includes wild mushroom or smoked salmon omelets and bagels. Dinner offerings might include oven-roasted Maine scallops Mediterranean style or pistachio-battered haddock.
Rates 65 motel rooms. $60-140 doubles July and August. Visa, MC, Amex, Discover. No personal checks. Smoking permitted. Children welcome. Pets welcome. Open mid-June to mid-October.
Access *Kayaks:* Easily carried 75 yards across the lawn onto the beach;

water at all tides. *Trailered boats:* Very small trailered boats can be launched here; the closest ramp is the gravel one at Grimes Cove in Ocean Point. *Sailboats:* 5 guest moorings. *Walk to:* No groceries nearby.

Address Route 96, HC65 Box 837, East Boothbay, ME 04554.
(207) 633-2800, (800) 633-3008.

Ocean Point Inn
#40, Chart 13293, Ocean Point, East Boothbay

This complex is situated at the southern end of the peninsula, and provides a fine view of the open waters of Linekin Bay. Guests in the dining room can watch the sun set over the water; theirs is an uncommon experience in coastal Maine. The Adirondack chairs along the seawall are good sunset-watching vantage points as well. Guest rooms are found in several buildings and vary from country inn to motel-style furnishings. All rooms have cable television, a phone, and a small refrigerator. There's a large heated pool on the grounds, and guests may use the community tennis courts for a fee.

Meals A continental breakfast is included in the off-season rate. Otherwise, breakfast and dinner are available during most of the season.

Rates 61 rooms, all with private baths. $82-145 doubles July and August. Visa, MC, Amex, Discover. No personal checks. Smoking permitted except in main inn and dining room. Children welcome. 2-night minimum on weekends, 3-night minimum on holidays. Open Memorial Day to Columbus Day.

Access *Kayaks:* Launch at all tides from the gravel beach at the southern end of the property, with an easy 50-yard carry from the road. *Trailered boats:* Gravel ramp at Grimes Cove. *Walk to:* No other restaurants or groceries nearby.

Address Shore Rd., P.O. Box 409, East Boothbay, ME 04544.
(207) 633-4200, (800) 552-5554.

CAMPGROUNDS

Campers Cove Campground
#C7, Chart 13293, Back River, Boothbay

A small, quiet campground on the shores of the Back River, where you're likely to spot osprey and great blue herons. Common grassy area for horseshoe games and access to the water. Swimming float. Campsites are primarily open.

Campsites	50 sites, of which 40 are suitable for tents. 22 waterfront sites. 25% tenters. Showers and flush toilets.
Rates	$16.50 tent sites. No credit cards. Pets permitted. Open May 15 to October 15.
Access	*Kayaks:* A 30-foot carry down a dirt path to the water; access on top half of the tide. *Trailered boats:* Paved ramp at Knickerkane Island Park off Barter's Island Road.
Address	Back River Rd., Box 136, Boothbay, ME 04537. (207) 633-5013.

Little Ponderosa Campground
#C8, Chart 13293, Cross River, Boothbay

A quiet, family-oriented campground with playground and miniature golf. Gospel concerts on Saturday evenings, Sunday morning church services. Rental canoes. Tall evergreen trees provide shade but not much campsite privacy. Access to a sheltered section of the Cross River.

Campsites	100 sites, most suitable for tents. 23 waterfront. 20% tenters. Showers and flush toilets, wheelchair accessible. Recreation room with ping pong, pool, and video games. Laundry. Groceries and snack bar.
Rates	$16-22 tent sites. Visa, MC. Pets permitted. Open May 15 to October 15.
Access	*Kayaks:* A 50-foot carry over a little mud; water at mid-tide and higher. Watch the currents at Ovens Mouth. *Trailered boats:* Paved ramp at Knickerkane Island Park off Barter's Island Road.
Address	Route 27, Boothbay, ME 04537. (207) 633-2700.

Gray Homestead Oceanfront Camping
#C9, Chart 13293, Pig Cove, Southport

The Gray family has been living on Southport Island since the 1800's, and Steve Gray's parents turned part of the family's land into a campground. Steve is a lobsterman, and sells some of his catch to campers. Those lacking big cooking pots can ask Steve or his wife, Suzanne, to cook the lobsters for them. Most sites are set in the woods for privacy. There is a nice little beach that faces Squirrel Island.

Campsites	40 sites, of which 20 are designed for tents. 6 trailer sites next to the water; 6 tent sites overlooking the water. 60% tenters. Showers and flush toilets. Laundry. Live or cooked lobsters.
Rates	$15-22 tent sites. No credit cards, no personal checks. Pets permitted. Open May 1 to Columbus Day.
Access	*Kayaks:* Easy launch from sand and stone beach at all tides. *Trailered boats:* Launch from beach with four wheel drive. *Sailboats:* Moorings for rent for boats up to 30 feet, or anchor. *Walk to:* General store 2 miles away.
Address	Route 238, HC66 Box 334, Southport, ME 04576. (207) 633-4612.

Damariscotta River to Pemaquid Point

ON SHORE

Rutherford Island
Rutherford is linked to the mainland by a pint-sized swing bridge over The Gut. The classic working harbor by the South Bristol bridge stands in sharp contrast to the harbor at Christmas Cove, where you're likely to spot some very large yachts.

Pemaquid Beach
Overlooking Pemaquid Harbor is the imposing reconstruction of Fort William Henry's western tower. This stone fort, originally built in 1692, was the second of three on the point; it lasted only four years before the French destroyed it. For a small fee, you can tour both the tower and the adjacent Colonial Pemaquid Museum (677-2423). The museum houses some of the artifacts uncovered by the ongoing archeological digs at the fort and village sites. On display are pottery, pipes, coins, and some of the tools of life at this colonial outpost. A visit to one of the local sand beaches might also be in order.

OFF SHORE

Heading up the pretty tree-lined Damariscotta River you'll find sheltered coves to look around and two islands to visit. BP&L's Fort Island is a popular picnic spot; watch for strong currents around the island. Half a mile to the east is Hodgsons, a 30-acre wooded island under the care of the Damariscotta River Association (563-1393). Visitors can enjoy walking along the interior trails and seeing the mosses and ferns that grow there. Hodgsons is open to day visits only.

REGIONAL ACCESS

Launch ramp with overnight parking
CHRISTMAS COVE: *Coveside Marine* (644-8282) has a concrete ramp; water at all tides.

Public moorings, slips
CHRISTMAS COVE: *Coveside Marine* (644-8282) has moorings and slips.

LODGINGS

Coveside
#41, Chart 13293, Christmas Cove, South Bristol

Mike Mitchell has created a spot catering to boaters, offering food, lodging, and marina services to those who call at picturesque Christmas Cove. The restaurant serves three meals a day to sailors coming off yachts and others who happen by. Burgees from Tasmania, Egypt, Ireland, Melbourne, Alaska, Turkey, Germany, and Bermuda are among those tacked to the walls of the clubhouse-like bar.

Lodgings are offered in a 100-year-old inn, where there's an inviting sitting room, and in the waterfront motel rooms. The pine-paneled motel rooms have skylights, and their decks overhang the water.

Meals A continental breakfast is included in the room rate. A full breakfast, lunch, and dinner can be obtained in the comfortable dining room most of the season. Dinner entrees include grilled Atlantic tuna, basil-seared Maine salmon, and a tenderloin of beef stuffed with lobster and spinach.

Rates 5 rooms with private baths in the inn, 10 motel rooms. $65-70 for inn doubles, $85-95 for motel doubles, mid-June to Labor Day. Visa, MC. Smoking permitted in rooms. Wheelchair-accessible rooms. Children welcome. Dogs and cats in the inn. Guest pets may be permitted;

check. Motel units open mid-May to late October; restaurant and inn open for a shorter season.

Access   *Kayaks and trailered boats:* Launch from the concrete ramp right next to the motel rooms; water at all tides. *Sailboats:* Guest moorings and slips. *Walk to:* Groceries in South Bristol.

Address   HC64 Box 150, Christmas Cove, South Bristol, ME 04568. (207) 644-8282.

Ye Olde Forte Cabins
#42, Chart 13293, Pemaquid Beach

This cheerfully painted cluster of well-kept cottages is next door to the Fort William Henry restoration. Cottages provide clean, simple rooms with half baths. Showers are located in the central shower rooms. There's a well-equipped communal kitchen. Just down from the common lawn is a sand beach.

Breakfast   Not provided.

Rates   9 cottages with half baths, shared showers. $55-78 double occupancy. No credit cards. Well-behaved children welcome. Reservations for short-term stays taken after June 15. Open Memorial Day to Labor Day.

Access   *Kayaks:* Carry boats 100 feet and then down over a few rock steps and ledge to the beach. There's water at all tides. *Trailered boats:* Paved and gravel public ramp at the Colonial Pemaquid State Historic Site. *Sailboats:* Two rental moorings for cabin guests and other area visitors. *Walk to:* Restaurant, groceries.

Address   HC62 Box 85, Pemaquid Beach, ME 04554. (207) 677-2261.

Apple Tree Inn
#43, Chart 13293, Pemaquid Beach

Pat Landry's attractive Cape was built on John's Island in the 1830's and moved to the mainland in 1871. Her home has the comfortable feel of an old farmhouse. One of the guest rooms has a fireplace and sitting area. Guests share Pat's pleasant living room. It is a 2-minute walk to the lovely "Little Beach."

Breakfast   An "expanded continental" of cereal and muffins except on Sundays, when there's a hot dish.

Rates   1 room with private bath, 2 with shared bath. $60-75 doubles. No credit cards. School-age children welcome. Open year round.

Access   *Kayaks:* Launch from a sandy pocket beach 250 yards from Pat's house; water at all tides. (Those with a set of kayak wheels could easily roll their boats to and from the beach on the road.) Another option is the public paved and gravel ramp at the Colonial Pemaquid State Historic Site; water at all tides. *Trailered boats:* Launch at the historic site. *Sailboats:* May be able to rent a mooring from Ye Olde Forte Cabins (677-2261). *Walk to:* Restaurant and groceries.

Address   Snowball Hill Rd., Pemaquid Beach, ME. Mail: P.O. Box 485, New Harbor, ME 04554.
(207) 677-3491.

Pemaquid Beach House Bed & Breakfast
#44, Chart 13293, Pemaquid Beach

Laura Swift describes her place as "very casual, a B&B in the original sense of the word." Her two spare rooms and the common areas of her house show her imaginative touch as a professional interior decorator. The back deck opens onto extensive gardens that include a goldfish pond. It is a short walk to sand beaches and the Fort William Henry restoration.

Breakfast   Baked goods, fruit, and cereal.

Rates   2 rooms with shared bath. $65 doubles. Visa, MC. Children welcome. Dog and cats in residence. Guest dogs may be permitted. Open year round.

Access   *Kayaks:* Launch from sandy "Little Beach" 300 yards from the B&B; water at all tides. Another option is the public paved and gravel ramp at the Colonial Pemaquid State Historic Site; water at all tides. *Trailered boats:* Launch at the historic site. *Sailboats:* Laura and her husband, Bruce, a licensed charter boat captain, have a guest mooring at Fort William Henry; they'll pick up boaters there. *Walk to:* Restaurant and groceries.

Address   Huddle Rd., Pemaquid Beach, ME 04554.
(207) 677-3361.

MUSCONGUS BAY

New Harbor to
Friendship

ON SHORE

The quiet villages along the shores of Muscongus Bay aren't often thought of as tourist destinations, which is part of their charm. They provide evidence for the theory that the further a place is from Route 1, the more undisturbed it is. Many of their residents work in fishing and other regional occupations.

New Harbor
If you are boating from the west, New Harbor is the first sheltered spot you'll see after rounding Pemaquid Point. Nearby are the beaches and historic sites of Pemaquid Beach (see page 76) and the Pemaquid Point Lighthouse. The picturesque lighthouse is perched on tilted rock ridges that are sometimes awash in crashing surf.

Round Pond
It is fun to poke around this village just uphill from the snug harbor. Stop in at Granite Hall (529-5864), a country store with penny candy and ice cream. If you're looking for more than ice cream, head to one of the waterfront eateries and enjoy a lobster roll or shore dinner on its deck.

Friendship
Friendship's busy harbor is used almost exclusively by lobster boats. The town is "dry" and perhaps as a result has no sit-down restaurants, but you can purchase take-out food. The region is known as the home of the Friendship sloop, built originally for fishing and now adapted for recreational use.

OFF SHORE

Upper Muscongus Bay has a lot to offer those travelling in small boats. Many of the wild islands dotting the bay may remind you of those further east, with their granite shorelines and spruce trees. Attentive navigation is required as there are a lot of ledges and lobster pot buoys.

This is a delightful area often unjustly overlooked by recreational boaters. If you are driving from the south with kayaks or a trailered boat, you will appreciate how much sooner you arrive at Muscongus Bay lodgings, compared to accommodations on the shores of more eastern bays.

Boaters are welcome to stop off and explore four Bureau of Parks and Lands islands. There is a tiny stretch-your-legs island off the south end of Marsh Island called Little Marsh. Thief is a handsome high island with a pleasant meadow and walking trails. Crow, just east of Hog Island, has some sloping ledges along the shore for basking in the afternoon sun. Strawberry is a small island east of the southern tip of Oar. (The campsites on Thief and Crow may be filled on summer weekends.)

Just west of Hog Island, on eastern Hockomock Point, is the Audubon Ecology Camp (529-5148). The National Audubon Society has a nature trail through a spruce forest and a visitors center open to the public. Boaters can come ashore by the boathouse; there are four guest moorings. (Note that neighboring Hog Island is used for workshops and is not open to visitors.)

REGIONAL ACCESS

Launch ramp with overnight parking

MEDOMAK: *Broad Cove Marine* (529-5186) has a dirt ramp suitable for kayaks as well as trailered boats launched with a four wheel drive vehicle; water at all tides. From Route 32, turn east onto Medomak Road, and follow to the end.

Public moorings

MEDOMAK: *Broad Cove Marine* (529-5186) has moorings north of Oar Island.

LODGINGS

The Gosnold Arms
#45, Chart 13301, New Harbor

Guests of The Gosnold Arms can sit on the porch and watch the fishing boats entering the harbor. Another good vantage point is the inn's wharf, with its set of Adirondack chairs. The main building houses the public dining room and one group of rustic, wood-paneled guest rooms. Other rooms are located in cottages even closer to the harbor; some of these have kitchenettes.

Meals	A full breakfast of pancakes, eggs, and muffins is included. Dinner is available, with steak, prime rib, and traditional New England seafood entrees on the menu.
Rates	11 inn rooms and 15 cottage rooms, all with private baths. $79-98 inn doubles, $89-134 cottage doubles, July to Labor Day. Gratuities extra. Visa, MC. Smoking permitted in cottages. Children welcome. Dog in the inn. 2-night minimum on holiday weekends. Cottages tend to be booked by the week. Open May through October.
Access	*Kayaks:* Launch from the inn's 18-inch-high float, or from the public concrete and gravel ramp 1 mile away at the head of the harbor; water at most tides. *Trailered boats:* Use the New Harbor ramp. *Sailboats:* 3 guest moorings, dinghy. *Walk to:* Restaurant, grocery store.
Address	HC61 Box 161, New Harbor, ME 04554. (207) 677-3727.

The Briar Rose Bed and Breakfast
#46, Chart 13301, Round Pond

Anita Palsgrove's charming B&B is situated in the midst of the interesting village of Round Pond. The B&B is done in an early 1900's country style, with folk art and stenciled walls. The comfortable parlor has a wealth of books and magazines waiting to be perused. A number of the books reflect Anita's interest in gardening.

Breakfast	Anita uses herbs from her garden to prepare a full breakfast, and is happy to cater to dietary restrictions. A typical breakfast might be multi-grain pancakes or French toast made of locally baked bread.
Rates	2 rooms with private baths, 1 two-room suite sharing a bath. $65-80 doubles. No credit cards. School-age children welcome. Open year round.

> *Access*   *Kayaks and trailered boats:* 350 yards to a fee paved ramp, with water at all tides. *Sailboats:* Check with the Padebco boatyard (529-5106) for unoccupied moorings in Round Pond, or call Broad Cove Marine in Medomak. *Walk to:* Restaurants, groceries, country store.
>
> *Address*   Route 32, P.O. Box 27, Round Pond, ME 04564.
> (207) 529-5478.

Cap'n Am's Oceanside Bed N' Breakfast
#47, Chart 13301, Ames or Flood's Cove, Friendship

The innkeepers' grandfather was a Latin scholar who selected a line from Horace to describe this tranquil spot on Muscongus Bay: *Ille terrarum mihi praeter omnes angulus ridet.* ("This corner of the earth seems most beautiful of all.") John Flood and his sister Mary Flood Thompson welcome guests to the property their grandfather purchased in 1900 from Captain Ambrose Simmons. Visitors can walk along the one and a half miles of shore frontage, and hike out to Ames Island at low tide.

The B&B sits close enough to the cove that you can hear the water lapping at the shore. Built in the early 1800's, it is full of rocking chairs and fireplaces, and has a rustic charm. The large sitting room centers on a stone hearth, and as you look around you will discover intriguing mementos of bygone days. The guest rooms have stenciled walls and are outfitted with family antiques. Large groups can request the enclosed sleeping porch with three double beds. From the sleeping porch, you can look out over the cove without lifting your head from the pillow.

There are several cottages on the grounds, which are generally rented by the week. Guests can use the Keowee kayaks and tennis courts. There are laundry machines on site.

> *Breakfast*   Might be pancakes, eggs, or blueberry crepes.
>
> *Rates*   3 rooms with shared baths. $55-65 doubles. No credit cards. Children over 1 year old welcome. Dogs and cats in residence. Open mid-June to mid-September.
>
> *Access*   *Kayaks:* An easy 75-foot carry to the gravel beach; water at all tides. *Trailered boats:* There are a few launch ramps in Friendship; the one with the most parking is a gravel one across from Garrison Island. *Sailboats:* 2 guest moorings. *Walk to:* No restaurants or groceries nearby; can boat to Friendship.
>
> *Address*   Flood's Cove, Box 639, Friendship, ME 04547.
> (207) 832-5144.

Harbor Hill Bed and Breakfast
#48, Chart 13301, Friendship Harbor

Innkeeper Liga Jahnke was studying for the Power Squadron exam when I visited, and had recently purchased a 14-foot Cape Cod cat boat built in Pemaquid. Her 100-year-old saltwater farmhouse is just uphill from Friendship's working harbor. There are water views from the terrace and the guest rooms, and through a frame of tall flowers outside the big kitchen window. Two of the guest rooms are in the house and are furnished with elegant Empire pieces. A third, more casual, room is in a cottage behind the house.

Breakfast	The Scandinavian breakfast includes fruit, baked goods, and a hot dish such as a shrimp omelet or Danish pancakes. Special diets can be accommodated.
Rates	3 rooms with private baths. $85-90 doubles. No credit cards. Children welcome. Dog and cats in residence. Pets allowed by prior arrangement. 2-night minimum on weekends. Open Memorial Day to Labor Day, and autumn weekends by reservation.
Access	*Kayaks:* Can be launched from the public float 500 feet down the hill. If you arrive by sea, you can use kayak wheels to roll your boat uphill, or the innkeepers can help you move your boat. Another launch option is the gravel public ramp across from Garrison Island; water at all tides. *Trailered boats:* Launch at ramp opposite Garrison Island. *Sailboats:* Sailors may be able to obtain permission to pick up a private mooring in the harbor. *Walk to:* Take-out food and groceries. Guests are welcome to bring take-out food back to the B&B for dinner.
Address	Town Landing Rd., P.O. Box 35, Friendship, ME 04547. (207) 832-6646.

Friendship By-the-Sea
#49, Chart 13301, Friendship

While this B&B is a half mile from the harbor, it provides a comfortable home base for day trips in the Friendship area. Barbara and Jay Thompson call this 1805-built Cape Cod home, and welcome guests to share their living room. Guest rooms are pleasantly cozy. Three acres of woods, fields, and blueberry patches surround the old farmhouse. Next to the house is the "buoy tree" festively hung with lobster pot buoys, reminiscent of a Jamie Wyeth painting.

Breakfast	Could include baked eggs, French toast, or muffins made with very fresh blueberries.

Rates   3 rooms with shared bath. $50-55 doubles. No credit cards. Check in advance about bringing children or pets. Cat in residence. 2-night minimum on weekends and holidays. Open June to mid-September.

Access   *Kayaks and trailered boats:* Public launch with the most parking is a gravel one opposite Garrison Island; water at all tides. *Sailboats:* Sailors may be able to obtain permission to pick up a private mooring in the harbor. *Walk to:* Take-out food and groceries.

Address   Shipyard Lane, P.O. Box 24, Friendship, ME 04547. (207) 832-4386.

CAMPGROUND

Saltwater Farm Campground
#C10, Chart 13301, Between McCarthy Point and Thomaston

Nine miles up the St. George River from Port Clyde, Saltwater Farm Campground provides pleasant river-view sites. The RV and trailer sites are open; the tent sites are wooded, fairly private, and nearest the water. Swimming pool and playground. Fresh flowers in the shower house.

Campsites   38 sites total, 8 for tents. 1 waterfront tent site. 20% tenters. Showers and flush toilets. Recreation center with ping pong, TV, lending library, video games. Laundry. Basic groceries.

Rates $17 tent sites. MC, Visa. Pets "encouraged." 3-night minimum for Maine Lobster Festival weekend. Open mid-May to mid-October.

Access   *Kayaks:* A 50-foot carry from last tent site to the water; water on top 2/3 of the tide. *Trailered boats:* Launch at concrete ramp in Thomaston. *Walk to:* Nearby snack bar open on weekends, 1 mile to market.

Address   Wadsworth St., P.O. Box 165, Thomaston, ME 04861. (207) 354-6735.

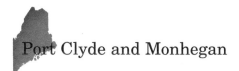

Port Clyde and Monhegan

ON SHORE

Port Clyde

Port Clyde is known as a jumping-off point for ferry passengers bound for Monhegan, but it is worth a visit in its own right. A number of artists live in the region, and you'll find some interesting little galleries and shops in this village at the end of a peninsula. It is also home to a large fleet of working boats.

Monhegan Island

Monhegan is a place of few vehicles, few year-round residents, and lots of tame deer. It can feel a bit crowded at midday, when the day-trippers are ashore, but otherwise it is a pleasantly remote spot. Large sections of the island are preserved in a wild state; visitors can hike on 17 miles of trails along the cliffs and through the woods. Several high headlands on the eastern side drop off precipitously into the ocean. A picturesque shipwreck lies past Lobster Cove at the southern end. A trail map can be obtained on the island; be aware that it is not drawn to scale.

In the village are the studios of a good number of resident artists. Monhegan has been the home and inspiration of a number of notable artists, including Rockwell Kent and Jamie Wyeth. Above the village, at the high point of the island, stands the lighthouse. Next to it is the Monhegan Museum (596-7003), which houses artifacts such as fishing gear and household furnishings from earlier times on the island.

OFF SHORE

Monhegan lies 10 miles south of Port Clyde. Small boaters should carefully evaluate their skills, equipment, and the weather before setting out, as much of the journey is through open seas. The ferry from Port Clyde will carry kayaks. Sailors may find the harbor more open than they'd like.

REGIONAL ACCESS

Launch ramp with overnight parking

PORT CLYDE: *Concrete public ramp, with water at all tides.* Parking available from the *Monhegan-Thomaston Boat Line* (372-8848) and the *Ocean House* (372-6691).

Ferry service

The *Laura B* passenger ferry travels between Port Clyde and Monhegan at least once a day from spring through fall. The ferry will transport kayaks as freight. Contact the Monhegan-Thomaston Boat Line (372-8848).

Public moorings

PORT CLYDE: *Port Clyde General Store* (372-6543) has moorings in the harbor.

LODGINGS

Ocean House
#50, Chart 13301, Port Clyde

The Ocean House sits just uphill from the Port Clyde harbor. Built in the 1820's as a sail loft, it now offers pleasant, simply furnished rooms. If your boat's on a mooring, you can keep an eye on it from your room or the second-floor porch. The common room has a VCR with tapes for rainy days.

The Seaside Inn across the road is under the same ownership and charges the same rates. Rooms in the Seaside, while clean, are in need of a facelift, so make a room in the Ocean House your first choice.

> *Meals*   Not included in the room rate. A hearty breakfast with home fries and pancakes is available. Dinner is offered by reservation Monday through Friday, with a single entree per evening followed by homemade pie or strawberry shortcake.
>
> *Rates*   Ocean House: 7 rooms with private baths, 2 with shared bath. Seaside Inn: 1 room with private bath, 2 with half baths, 6 with shared baths. $56-75 doubles, with $5 surcharge for single-night stays. No credit cards. Smoking discouraged. Children welcome. Pets discouraged. Open May to mid-October.
>
> *Access*   *Kayaks and trailered boats:* Launch from the concrete public ramp a few hundred feet away, with water at all tides. *Sailboats:* Rent moorings from the Port Clyde General Store. *Walk to:* Restaurants, groceries, galleries, shops.
>
> *Address*   P.O. Box 66, Port Clyde, ME 04855.
> (207) 372-6691, (800) 269-6691.

The Trailing Yew
#51, Chart 13301, Monhegan Harbor

The Trailing Yew is a friendly place that might bring your experience at summer camp to mind. While accommodations anywhere on Monhegan tend toward the informal, the lodgings here are quite rustic. Of the four main buildings, three are lit with kerosene lamps. There is an average of one bathroom for every five bedrooms. Guests are encouraged to bring sleeping bags in spring and fall as buildings are unheated. Everyone gathers promptly for the big dinner served family-style at long tables in the dining hall. Afterward, they might adjourn to the pleasant common rooms, one of which has a working pump organ.

Meals   Breakfast and dinner are included. Breakfast consists of homemade doughnuts, eggs, bacon, and cereal. At dinner there are two entrees (one meat and one fish), as well as soup, bread, and dessert.

Rates   34 rooms with shared baths. $56 per night for adults, $15-32 for children. No credit cards. Smoking permitted in guest rooms. Children welcome. Pets permitted. Open mid-May to Columbus Day.

Access   *Kayaks:* Come in at either Fish Beach or Swim Beach in the harbor at any tide; secure kayaks above the high tide line. The Trailing Yew is just a few minutes' walk away. *Sailboats:* A rental mooring may be available from Shining Sails Guesthouse (596-0041). *Walk to:* Restaurants, market, galleries, shops, laundry.

Address   Monhegan Island, ME 04852.
(207) 596-0440.

Monhegan House
#52, Chart 13301, Monhegan Harbor

Monhegan House has been welcoming visitors every summer since 1870 to its central location in the village. The general store, post office, and church are all a stone's throw from the front porch, which is lined with a row of white rockers that catch the afternoon sun. There's a big stone hearth in the sitting room in front of the public dining room. The inn offers four floors of guest rooms with oak country antique dressers and beds covered with white chenille spreads. The bathroom facilities are located on the second floor. The higher floors provide the best vistas of the harbor and barren Manana Island.

Meals   None included. A full breakfast is available. The dinner menu has seafood, steak, pasta, and vegetarian entrees.

Rates   32 rooms with shared baths. $80 doubles, $48 singles. Visa, MC, Amex, Discover. Children welcome. Open Memorial Day to mid-October.

Access   *Kayaks:* Come in at either Fish Beach or Swim Beach in the harbor at any tide; secure kayaks above the high tide line. The walk to the inn takes just a couple of minutes. *Sailboats:* A rental mooring may be available from Shining Sails Guesthouse (596-0041). *Walk to:* Restaurants, market, galleries, shops, laundry.

Address   Monhegan Island, ME 04852.
(207) 594-7983, (800) 599-7983.

The Island Inn

#53, Chart 13301, Monhegan Harbor

With its flags flying high above the cupola, The Island Inn will catch your eye long before you enter the harbor. Once you've secured your boat, it is an easy stroll up the hillside to the inn. It's a toss-up whether the inn or the lighthouse in the middle of the island provides the best spot on Monhegan to watch the sun set over the water. If you choose the inn for your sunset-viewing, you then have to decide between the dining room and the wide front porch.

New owners Howard Weilbacker and Philip Truelove are remodeling the inn in stages during the winters. The parlor has been stylishly redecorated with Oriental carpets and inviting chairs, and some of the guest rooms have been completed. Some guest rooms are in the nearby Pierce Cottage. The inn can arrange laundry service.

Meals	A "filling" breakfast with pancakes and eggs is included. Lunch, afternoon tea, and dinner are available in the dining room. Dinners feature roast meats and fresh fish.
Rates	7 rooms with private baths, 29 with shared baths. $110-175 doubles July through late August. Visa, MC. Children welcome. Pets permitted. Open Memorial Day to Columbus Day.
Access	*Kayaks:* Come in at nearby Swim Beach at any tide, and leave kayaks on the lawn. *Sailboats:* One mooring for a small boat, or call Shining Sails Guesthouse (596-0041) for a possible rental mooring. *Walk to:* Restaurants, market, galleries, shops.
Address	P.O. Box 128, Monhegan Island, ME 04852. (207) 596-0371.

Shining Sails Guesthouse

#54, Chart 13301, Monhegan

Hosts John and Winnie Murdock are among the hardy residents who stay on Monhegan all year round. They've lived on the island for 20 years, and are raising three children there. John works as a lobsterman during Monhegan's restricted season, which runs from January through June.

Their guest house has apartments as well as guest rooms. The apartments include kitchens, and some units have private decks. Visitors can sink into the sofa in the big common room and gaze out into the harbor. On the lawn are a picnic table and barbecue fireplace for outdoor suppers.

Breakfast	Bagels, muffins, cereal, and fruit.
Rates	3 guest rooms, 4 apartments, all with private baths. $70-155 doubles

May to Columbus Day. $5 surcharge for single-night stays. Visa, MC, Amex, Discover. Well-supervised children welcome. Open year round.

Access   *Kayaks*: Come in on the little beach near the guest house, north of Smutty Nose Island, or use Swim or Fish Beach in the main harbor; access at any tide. *Sailboats:* A rental mooring at the north end of the harbor, beyond the dock. *Walk to:* Restaurants, market, galleries, shops, laundry.

Address   P.O. Box 346, Monhegan Island, ME 04852.
(207) 596-0041.

Tribler Cottage
#55, Chart 13301, Monhegan

This cottage was first used as guest lodgings in the 1930's, by owner Richard Farrell's grandmother. Today Richard and his wife, Martha Yandle, provide four apartments with full kitchens, and a guest room with refrigerator and toaster oven. The little sitting room has a good selection of books, and many of Richard's appealing landscape photographs hang on the walls.

Breakfast   Not provided.

Rates   4 apartments and one guest room, all with private baths. $65-100 doubles July and August. $5 surcharge for single-night stays. No credit cards. Children welcome. Dog in residence occasionally. Open year round.

Access   *Kayaks:* Come in at either Fish Beach or Swim Beach in the harbor at any tide; secure kayaks above the high tide line. The walk to the cottage takes just a few minutes. *Sailboats:* A rental mooring may be available from Shining Sails Guesthouse (596-0041). *Walk to:* Restaurants, market, galleries, shops, laundry.

Address   Monhegan Island, ME 04852-0307.
(207) 594-2445.

Hitchcock House
#56, Chart 13301, Monhegan

The Hitchcock House sits at the top of a steep hill a five-minute hike from the harbor. Guests are rewarded with great views of the waters both east and west of the island. The large common deck is built around old trees and provides a good lookout point, particularly from the hammock. Two efficiencies in the house and one in a cottage have their own decks. The guest rooms are equipped with refrigerators, and an outdoor grill is available.

Breakfast	Not provided.
Rates	3 efficiencies with private baths, 2 rooms with shared bath. $50-75 doubles. No credit cards. Smoking discouraged. Inquire about bringing pets. Open year round.
Access	*Kayaks:* Come in at either Fish Beach or Swim Beach in the harbor at any tide; secure kayaks above the high tide line. *Sailboats:* A rental mooring may be available from Shining Sails Guesthouse (596-0041). *Walk to:* Restaurants, market, galleries, shops, laundry.
Address	Monhegan Island, ME 04852. (207) 594-8137.

ON THE MAINE COAST,

B&B's have been created from a former lighthouse keeper's home, a coast guard station, a tavern, lodgings for granite quarry workers, carriage houses, and a number of grand old summer cottages. When you stay in these well-restored structures, you can start to peel back layers of the area's history. It becomes easier to imagine the days of steamships and waterfront boardwalks.

OFFSHORE ISLANDS

in Penobscot Bay with guest lodgings include Vinalhaven, Islesboro, and Isle au Haut. Campgrounds are found on Warren Island and Isle au Haut.

© 1995 by Jane Crosen, Penobscot, ME 04476

WESTERN PENOBSCOT BAY

Tenants Harbor to South Thomaston

ON SHORE

St. George Peninsula

The accommodations on the St. George peninsula facing Penobscot Bay are found at Tenants Harbor, Clark Island, and Waterman Beach. These are pleasantly quiet locations, yet it's easy to drive to Rockland, Rockport or Camden if you're looking for things to do on a rainy day.

South Thomaston

Buildings in this pretty little village are clustered next to the reversing falls. The Old Post Office Chandlery (594-9396), an interesting gallery filled with nautical paintings and ship models, is right across from the public boat launching ramp. Birch Point State Park, a few miles away, has a lovely sand beach by the Muscle Ridge Channel.

Matinicus Island

Matinicus Island is the most remote island in Maine with a year-round community. Many of the families living there are descendants of the island's earliest settlers. Twenty miles south of Rockland, Matinicus is a difficult place to reach, but it will reward you for your efforts. It offers visitors two white sand beaches and a network of walking trails covering its 750 acres. Matinicus is noted for the visits of migratory birds. You can join a guided trip to Matinicus Rock to view the protected puffin colony.

It should go without saying that this trip is for expert boaters in good weather only. Because of the distance from shore and dearth of landing spots en route, this destination is not recommended for kayakers or others in small boats.

OFF SHORE

From Tenants Harbor and Clark Island it is a short paddle or sail to several pretty islands, and Waterman Beach and South Thomaston put you close to the lovely granite-ringed islands along the Muscle Ridge Channel. Enjoy these islands from your boat unless you have permission to visit them, as they are all privately owned.

REGIONAL ACCESS

Launch ramps with overnight parking

TENANTS HARBOR: *Concrete public ramp*, with water at all tides. Three parking options: *Town Hall lot,* 1/4 mile south on Route 131 (use spots furthest from building); *Odd Fellows Hall lot,* 1/4 mile away, with better trailer parking, uphill from launch, take right and then left off Route 131; *Cod End Marina* (372-6782), next to ramp.

CLARK ISLAND: *Wheeler's Bay Marine* (596-0091) off Clark Island Road has a new concrete ramp with water at all tides.

Ferry service and flights

The Maine State Ferry Service provides car ferry service between Matinicus and Rockland a few times a month during the summer. The ferry will not take hand-carried kayaks. Call the Maine State Ferry Service at 624-7777 for general schedule information, or 596-2202 for the Rockland terminal. Boaters running into difficulties on the island can arrange for transport with local fishermen or Penobscot Air Service (596-6211).

Public moorings

TENANTS HARBOR: *Cod End Marina* (372-6782) has moorings.

CLARK ISLAND: *Wheeler's Bay Marine* (596-0091) has moorings. They don't monitor VHF radio.

MATINICUS: *The harbormaster* (366-3610) can direct sailors to rental moorings.

LODGINGS

Harbor View Guest House
#57, Chart 13301, Tenants Harbor

The Nilands' guest house provides inexpensive accommodations just up the hill from the public launch area. The guest living room is done in a nautical theme. Ruffles decorate the guest rooms, two of which face the harbor. The Nilands moved to Tenants Harbor for the sailing, and Bob has a 40-foot wooden sloop.

Breakfast   Muffins.

Rates   3 rooms with shared bath. $35-55 doubles. No credit cards. Children welcome. 2-night minimum on festival weekends. Open mid-June to mid-October.

Access   *Kayaks and trailered boats:* 500 feet to the concrete public ramp, with water at all tides. Four-hour parking limit, so bring car back to house. Boat trailers can be parked at the Odd Fellows Hall, near the guest house. *Sailboats:* Moorings at Cod End Marina. *Walk to:* Restaurants, groceries.

Address   Route 131, P.O. Box 268, Tenants Harbor, ME 04860. (207) 372-8162.

The East Wind Inn
#58, Chart 13301, Tenants Harbor

The East Wind Inn houses an outstanding collection of fine antiques. Owner Tim Watts, a native of Tenants Harbor, has furnished guest rooms and common spaces with his collection of early 1800's pine and mahogany pieces. This is a country inn with an elegant side to it. There are guest rooms in the inn itself, as well as in the adjacent Meeting House. Three very attractive apartments with cooking facilities and decks have been added recently in a third building. All the guest accommodations have harbor views.

Meals   A full breakfast with a choice of entrees such as pancakes or Belgian waffles is included. The public dining room offers dinner selections such as baked Maine salmon, saute of Maine crab cakes, Mediterranean lamb, and grilled eggplant torta.

Rates   15 guest rooms, 3 suites, and 4 apartments, all with private baths; 7 rooms with shared baths. $82 for shared bath doubles, $120 for private bath doubles, $150-260 for suites and apartments, mid-June to Labor Day. Visa, MC, Amex, Discover. Smoking permitted in guest rooms. Well-behaved children welcome. Black Labrador at the inn. Guest pets by prior arrangement. Open April through November.

Access   *Kayaks:* Can launch from the inn's float, or use the concrete public ramp within 200 yards; water at all tides. Four-hour parking limit by the ramp, so bring vehicles back to inn. *Trailered boats:* Use neighboring public ramp. *Sailboats:* Moorings at Cod End Marina. *Walk to:* Restaurants, groceries.

Address   P.O. Box 149, Tenants Harbor, ME 04860.
(207) 372-6366, (800) 241-VIEW.

The Craignair Inn at Clark Island
#59, Chart 13301, Clark Island

Just beyond the Craignair Inn is the causeway to Clark Island, a wonderful 200-acre island with hiking trails leading to a swimming quarry, fog forests, fields of old apple trees, tidepools, and sand beaches. The inn was built in 1928 to house people working in the nearby granite quarries. The sitting room is furnished with antiques from owner Terry Smith's trips to Asia and India, and Asian and Indian artwork hangs on the guest room walls.

Meals   A full breakfast is included. The dining room is open Monday through Saturday; the house specialty is a bouillabaisse of shrimp, clams, mussels, fish, and lobster.

Rates   8 rooms with private baths, 14 with shared baths. $79-102 doubles, July to Labor Day. Visa, MC, Amex. Smoking permitted in some guest rooms. Children welcome. Small to medium-sized dogs permitted. 2-night minimum on holiday weekends. Open mid-May to mid-October.

Access   *Kayaks:* Can be driven to the causeway and dropped off; from there it's a 30-foot carry, best on top 2/3 of the tide. Another option is a concrete launch a few miles away at Wheeler's Bay Marine; water at all tides. *Trailered boats:* Launch at Wheeler's Bay Marine. *Sailboats:* Moorings at Wheeler's Bay Marine. Someone from the Craignair can meet sailors there. *Walk to:* No other restaurants or groceries nearby.

Address   Spruce Head, ME 04859.
(207) 594-7644, (800) 320-9997.

The Blue Lupin Bed and Breakfast
#60, Charts 13303 & 13305, Waterman Point, Waterman Beach

Here's a bed and breakfast ideally located right next to a beach and a popular lobster shack. Helen Mitchell's house is 35 feet from the water's edge, with a grand view of the Muscle Ridge islands. After living here 20 years, she decided to add a new wing and open a B&B. Each attractive room has a television and VCR; two have private decks. The VCR movie library numbers more than 200. Guests can enjoy fields of blue lupins in the spring, and a walk along Waterman Beach anytime. On their return from a walk, they might want to stop in at Waterman Beach Lobsters for a piece of homemade pie.

Breakfast	Full breakfast.
Rates	2 rooms and 1 two-room suite with private baths, 1 room with shared bath. $65-85 doubles, $120 for two in suite. Visa, MC. Well-behaved children welcome. Cat in residence. Open June to mid-October.
Access	*Kayaks:* Easy 75-yard carry across the lawn and then down 4 granite steps to the stone beach; access at all tides. *Trailered boats:* Paved public ramp in South Thomaston. *Walk to:* Restaurant.
Address	Waterman Beach Rd., HC33 Box 647, South Thomaston, ME 04858. (207) 594-2673.

Weskeag at the Water Bed & Breakfast Inn
#61, Charts 13303 & 13305, Weskeag River, South Thomaston

This inn is located in the village of South Thomaston, right next to the reversing falls. Within a few steps are a general store, post office, and a nautical gallery. The inn is eclectically furnished in a ruffled Victorian style. Look for the old family tintypes in the halls. There are two common rooms, one with a large screen television and VCR. Guests can bring take-out food back from the general store and eat on the deck overlooking the river.

Breakfast	Full breakfast buffet.
Rates	4 rooms with private baths, 4 with shared baths. $65-95 doubles. Visa, MC. Children welcome. Dog in residence. Open year round.
Access	*Kayaks:* Kayakers can explore the estuary and marshes above the falls by putting in from the property. It's a carry over the lawn and down 18 steps to some rocky slabs; access at most tides. Timing is critical for those wishing to paddle safely under the bridge and through the reversing falls. 100 yards from the inn, and below the falls, is the paved public launch on the Weskeag River, with water at all but dead low tide. Another put-in for kayakers is the sand beach

at Birch Point State Park, a few miles from town and closer to the Muscle Ridge Channel. *Trailered boats:* Neighboring public ramp. *Walk to:* Take-out food, groceries, gallery.

Address   Route 73, P.O. Box 213, South Thomaston, ME 04858.
(207) 596-6676, (800) 596-5576.

Tuckanuck Lodge
#62, Chart 13303, Old Cove, Matinicus Island

Matinicus is so far off shore, and there are so few residents, that the Maine State Ferry Service makes only infrequent trips. If you do make the trip, Bill Hoadley will welcome you to his house 1/4 mile from the harbor. Bill describes his home as quiet and rustic. (I was unable to visit.) Look for a house with natural cedar shakes. He rents bikes to visitors and offers dinner to guests on nights when the island's restaurant is closed.

Breakfast   Cereal, fruit, homemade English muffins.
Rates   5 rooms with shared baths. $60-70 doubles, or $80 for Saturday-night-only stays, mid-June to mid-September. No credit cards. Bill prefers checks to cash because there is no bank on the island. Well-behaved children welcome. Dog in residence, guest pets welcome. Open year round.
Access   *Kayaks:* While I don't recommend kayaking to Matinicus, should you choose to, come in at the harbor and wheel boats up to the house or check with Bill about shoreline storage. *Sailboats:* Contact the harbormaster to rent a mooring. *Walk to:* Restaurant, market.
Address   Shag Hollow Rd., P.O. Box 217, Matinicus, ME 04851.
(207) 366-3830.

CAMPGROUND

Lobster Buoy Campsite
#C11, Charts 13303 & 13305, Waterman Beach

This small oceanfront campground provides convenient access to the Muscle Ridge island chain or the Weskeag River. There is a real sense of being at the water's edge in the open, closely clustered sites bordering 400 yards of attractive stone beach. The owners are boaters who ask those going out on the water to leave a float plan with them. A social hour at 7 p.m. features homemade desserts such as fudge brownies and whipped cream.

Campsites	40 sites total, 20 for tents. A group camping area is available also. 10 waterfront sites. 25-50% tenters. Showers, flush toilets and a few privies. Day room with tables, books, and a camper-written anthology. Basic groceries.
Rates	$13.50 tent sites. No credit cards; personal checks at owner discretion. 1 pet per site permitted. Open mid-May to mid-October.
Access	*Kayaks:* Launch at any tide from the designated launch area or from the beach in front of some campsites. *Trailered boats:* Small boats can be launched from the beach using four wheel drive vehicles, or use the South Thomaston paved ramp. *Sailboats:* Rental moorings or anchorage. *Other:* The small island closest to the Lobster Buoy is privately owned. The island owners request that you do not land on it.
Address	Waterman Beach Rd., HCR33 Box 625, South Thomaston, ME 04858. (207) 594-7546.

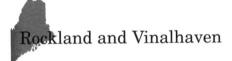

Rockland and Vinalhaven

ON SHORE

Rockland

Rockland seems like a town with a mission. It used to be that people passed Rockland by, complaining of the stench from the fish rendering plant. The plant closed years ago, and now the town is presenting visitors with plenty of reasons to stop. The harbor is filling with recreational as well as working boats. There are new shops, galleries, and eateries along Main Street. Waterfront festivals include Schooner Days in early July and the Maine Lobster Festival on the first weekend in August.

The Farnsworth Museum (19 Elm St., 596-6457) is one of the finest art museums in the Northeast. It has a broad range of American paintings, from primitives through modern works, and many focus on Maine subjects. To house its growing collection of works by N.C., Andrew, and Jamie Wyeth, it will be opening the "Farnsworth Center for the Wyeth Family in Maine" in the summer of 1998.

Downtown Rockland is home to one of the Maine Island Trail Association's offices. Stop by 328 Main Street or call 596-6456 to learn about the network of islands the Association's members care for. (See page 21 for more information on MITA.)

Vinalhaven

Vinalhaven is a large island in the middle of Penobscot Bay. It is a crossing of 13 nautical miles from Rockland to Carver's Harbor, where the town of Vinalhaven is located. During the 19th and early 20th centuries, the island was a center for the granite quarrying industry; as you walk on the island you will see reminders of those times. The highly irregular shoreline makes for great gunkholing, whether by boat, on foot, or by bicycle. As you travel on shore, it seems that everywhere you look there is a new perspective on the water. Biking is a pleasure since there are few cars on the paved roads.

Vinalhaven is not a common tourist destination. Services are geared toward those who make their living there year round, in industries such as fishing. As I was told, "people don't come here to shop." Visitors come for the natural beauty of the island and the surrounding waters. Pick up an island map showing all the public open spaces, and make sure to visit one of the quarries. You can walk from town to the Nature Conservancy's Lane's Island Preserve. There you'll find 40 acres of bayberry bushes, cobble beaches, and spectacular granite shoreline.

OFF SHORE

Near Rockland Harbor are two lighthouses. The one at Owls Head is particularly photogenic, and there is another at the end of the Rockland Breakwater.

The waters around Vinalhaven are full of green islands and intriguing coves. You can stop and visit four small Bureau of Parks and Lands (BP&L) islands in the vicinity. Tiny Ram Island is actually two islets, east of the midpoint of Leadbetter Island and a few miles from Carver's Harbor. In Seal Bay you'll find Little Hen and Hay Islands. Up by North Haven is pretty Little Thorofare Island, just north of Calderwood Island.

Participants in Hurricane Island Outward Bound School activities may be camped on BP&L or other islands near Vinalhaven. A white flag flying on an island means that a student is "soloing," or camping alone. Try to avoid them, and don't tempt them with food from your cache of goodies.

The trip out to Vinalhaven is a long one, whether you depart from the Rockland area or from Deer Isle. Kayakers and others with small boats should carefully assess their skills, equipment, and the weather before deciding to make the crossing. You can take the ferry instead, and save your boating for the interesting waters surrounding the island.

REGIONAL ACCESS

Launch areas with overnight parking

ROCKLAND: Kayakers can launch from the cove next to *Knight Marine Service* (594-4068 or 594-9700, 525 Main St.) on the top 2/3 of the tide, and park at the marina.

VINALHAVEN: Those with kayaks and trailered boats can use the concrete *public ramp* in Carver's Harbor; water at all tides. Parking in town lot.

Ferry service

There is frequent car ferry service to Vinalhaven from Rockland. The ferry will not take hand-carried kayaks. Call the Maine State Ferry Service on 624-7777 for general schedule information, or 596-2202 for the Rockland terminal. It is advisable to make reservations for vehicles; this is done in person or in writing no more than 30 days in advance.

Public moorings, dock space

ROCKLAND: *The harbormaster* (584-0312 or 594-0314) has transient moorings and dock space near the town landing. *Knight Marine Service* (594-4068 or 594-9700) has moorings and dock space at the north end of town, by the ferry terminal.

VINALHAVEN: Contact *Hopkins Boatyard* (863-2551) for moorings in Carver's Harbor.

LODGINGS

Lathrop House
#63, Chart 13305, Rockland Harbor

This yellow Queen Anne guest house is a block up from Rockland's public landing. Proprietor Liz Godley has seen boaters in need of a hot shower before. When I stopped by she'd just received a note from two New Hampshire sailors thanking her for the "...pampering you gave to two wet, busy mariners."

Liz has decorated the guest rooms around different themes. I particularly liked the Presidential Room, with its pictures of Franklin D. Roosevelt and Winston Churchill hung by the four-poster bed. (She used to have a life-sized cardboard President Bush in the room, but guests kept asking that he be moved.) Some rooms can easily accommodate children.

Breakfast Fruit, muffins, cereal, and a boiled egg.
Rates 1 room with private bath, 6 with shared baths. $55-65 doubles. Smoking permitted on the enclosed porch. No credit cards. Children welcome. Well-mannered pets welcome. Open May through October.
Access *Kayaks:* Launch from a hand-carry ramp just north of the public

landing or from the Snow Marine Park paved ramp by the Hurricane Island Outward Bound School; water at all tides at either location. *Trailered boats:* Use the Snow Marine Park ramp. *Sailboats:* Contact the harbormaster. *Walk to:* Restaurants, groceries, galleries, shops, laundry.

Address   16 Pleasant St., Rockland, ME 04841.
(207) 594-5771.

Trade Winds Motor Inn
#64, Chart 13305, Rockland Harbor

The Trade Winds is located right next to Harbor Park and the public landing. Many of the motel rooms have good views of Rockland's busy harbor. Accommodations range from standard rooms to spacious suites. Amenities include an indoor pool, jacuzzi, steam room, and sun deck. If you've been sitting in your boat too long, you can use the stair climbers or ski exercisers in the fitness room for a fee. There are laundry facilities on site.

Meals   Not included. Breakfast and dinner are available in the adjoining steak and seafood restaurant.
Rates   140 motel rooms and suites. $70-99 rooms, $99-125 suites late June to early September. Visa, MC, Amex, Discover. Local checks only. Designated non-smoking rooms. Wheelchair-accessible rooms. Children welcome. Pets permitted. Open year round.
Access   *Kayaks:* Carry 150 yards to the hand-carry ramp just north of the public landing; water at all tides. *Trailered boats:* Launch at the Snow Marine Park. *Sailboats:* Public landing 300 yards away; call the harbormaster. *Walk to:* Restaurants, groceries, galleries, shops.
Address   2 Park View Dr., Rockland, ME 04841.
(207) 596-6661.

Capt. Lindsey House Inn
#65, Chart 13305, Lermond Cove, Rockland

While this inn is located in downtown Rockland, sitting inside it you might be tempted to believe you're in Great Britain. Cues include the dark wood paneling, deep paint colors, and handsome fabrics. There's also the afternoon tea and scones, and sometimes, cucumber sandwiches. The library comes complete with reading chairs and a chess set. Guest rooms have televisions and phones.

Meals   A cold continental breakfast buffet is included. Dinner is available

	next door at The Waterworks, with pub food and Maine microbrews.
Rates	9 rooms with private baths. $95-160 doubles, Memorial Day to mid-October. Visa, MC. One wheelchair-accessible room. Children over 10 welcome. Open year round.
Access	*Kayaks:* Launch from the hand-carry ramp just north of the public landing or from the Snow Marine Park paved ramp by the Hurricane Island Outward Bound School; water at all tides at either location. *Trailered boats:* Use Snow Marine Park ramp. *Sailboats:* Contact Knight Marine Service. *Walk to:* Restaurants, groceries, galleries, shops, laundry.
Address	5 Lindsey St., Rockland, ME 04841. (207) 596-7950, (800) 523-2145.

The Old Granite Inn
#66, Chart 13305, Lermond Cove, Rockland

Innkeeper Stephanie Clapp has an infectious enthusiasm for the city of Rockland. She is delighted to see the renaissance it is undergoing, and points to the quality of the collections at the Farnsworth Art Museum and the rapid growth of the harbor as examples of the good things happening there. She and her husband, John, have numerous boating interests: together they restored and lived aboard a 100-year-old Baltic Trader; she serves on the local harbor commission; he builds cabinets for ships.

The inn is constructed of gray granite blocks and faces the terminal for the North Haven and Vinalhaven ferries (and Concord Trailways buses). Rooms are decorated with some wonderful family heirloom furniture, and come in a variety of sizes and decor. One has mementos of Maine's noted senator, Margaret Chase Smith. Another has a bathroom completely papered with old nautical charts, courtesy of a Vinalhaven ferry captain. Downstairs is a welcoming sitting room.

The innkeepers can help arrange for bicycle rentals.

Breakfast	Stephanie's experience as a bakery owner and pastry chef shows in the breakfast menu. The buffet utilizes organic fruit and might include blackberry poppy seed pound cake or blueberry tarts, along with eggs any style and strong coffee.
Rates	8 rooms with private baths. 2 single rooms share a bath. $79-109 doubles, $59 singles, mid-June to late September. Visa, MC, Amex, Discover. 3 wheelchair-accessible rooms. Well-behaved children welcome by reservation. Open year round.
Access	*Kayaks:* Kayakers arriving by water can come in at the cove by Knight Marine Service on the top 2/3 of the tide; it's 250 yards to the inn. Kayakers with cars can drive to a hand-carry ramp just north of

the public landing or to the Snow Marine Park paved ramp by the Hurricane Island Outward Bound School; water at all tides at either location. *Trailered boats:* Use the Snow Marine Park ramp. *Sailboats:* Contact Knight Marine Service. *Walk to:* Restaurants, groceries, galleries, shops, laundry.

Address 546 Main St., Rockland, ME 04841.
(207) 594-9036, (800) 386-9036.

Old Harbor Inn Bed & Breakfast
#67, Chart 13305, Old Harbor, Vinalhaven

Robert Phillips welcomes guests to share his quiet waterfront summer cottage a mile and a half from the town of Vinalhaven. The living room and deck command a grand view to the west that takes in Greens Island. Robert's interesting hand-made furniture and carvings are scattered through the house. Ask for the newly constructed guest room upstairs with its own deck. Guests may use the kitchen to cook supper.

Breakfast Muffins.
Rates 2 rooms with shared bath. $60-80 doubles. No credit cards. Smoking permitted. Children welcome. Dog in residence; guests may bring dogs. Open Memorial Day through September.
Access *Kayaks:* Kayakers can paddle to the cove 75 yards in front of the house; best on top 2/3 of the tide. *Trailered boats:* Concrete public ramp in Carver's Harbor. *Sailboats:* Robert can arrange for a nearby mooring or dock space for sailors. *Walk to:* Restaurants, groceries, shops, bicycle rentals 1.5 miles away.
Address Old Harbor Rd., Vinalhaven, ME 04863.
(207) 863-0946.

Tidewater Motel
#68, Chart 13305, Carver's Harbor, Vinalhaven

The Tidewater Motel was built partly on a granite bridge that allows water to flow between Carver's Harbor and a saltwater pond. Consequently, some rooms are not just waterfront, they have water beneath them as well! Many of these pleasant rooms have decks for watching the busy working waterfront. Some rooms include kitchen facilities. From the Tidewater's location in the middle of town, it is a short stroll to restaurants, groceries, shops, and the post office. There are bike rentals on site, and laundry service is available.

Breakfast   Not provided.
    Rates   12 motel rooms. $85-95 doubles July and August. No credit cards.
              Children welcome. Open year round.
   Access   *Kayaks and trailered boats:* Concrete public ramp adjacent to the motel;
              water at all tides. Owner Phil Crossman can help you obtain a car ferry
              reservation if you'd prefer to skip the open water crossing to Vinalhaven,
              and you call him more than a month in advance. *Sailboats:* Hopkins
              Boatyard has moorings. *Walk to:* Restaurants, groceries, shops.
  Address   Main St., P.O. Box 546, Vinalhaven, ME 04863.
              (207) 863-4618.

The Fox Island Inn
#69, Chart 13305, Vinalhaven

This inviting inn is uphill from town, just past the blue galamander formerly used
to haul granite from the quarries to the harbor. Innkeeper Gail Reinertsen, a
marathon runner, provides particularly comfortable sitting rooms. Bookshelves
are full of good recent novels and books on Maine. You can settle in with a book on
the architecture of North Haven summer cottages, a guide to Maine coast ghosts,
or a collection of Maine humor. Bedrooms range from snug to spacious, and have
handmade quilts on the beds. Guests can prepare meals in a separate kitchen, and
borrow one of Gail's single-speed bikes.

Breakfast   Homemade bread, fruit, and cereal.
    Rates   6 rooms with shared baths. $50-65 doubles. No credit cards. Children
              over 8 welcome. 2-night minimum on July and August weekends.
              Open June through September.
   Access   *Kayaks and trailered boats:* 1/4 mile to concrete public boat launch,
              with water at all tides. *Sailboats:* Hopkins Boatyard has moorings.
              Walk to: Restaurants, groceries, shops.
  Address   Carver St., P.O. Box 451, Vinalhaven, ME 04863.
              (207) 863-2122.

Payne Homestead at the Moses Webster House
#70, Chart 13305, Vinalhaven

Moses Webster, a partner in Vinalhaven's granite industry, had this mansard-
roofed house built in 1873. The Paynes have turned it into a child-friendly B&B:
there's a playroom with games, VCR, and children's videos. There's space to play
on the deck or in the backyard. The Victorian decor includes antique beds and a
tin ceiling in the first-floor bedroom.

Breakfast The family-style breakfast might feature eggs or pancakes.
Rates 5 rooms with shared baths. $75-90 doubles, with $5 surcharge for single-night stays. No credit cards. Children welcome. 2-night minimum reservation in July and August. Open April through November.
Access *Kayaks:* Less than 1/4 mile to concrete public boat launch, with water at all tides. *Sailboats:* Hopkins Boatyard has moorings. *Walk to:* Restaurants, groceries, shops, bicycle rentals.
Address Atlantic Ave., P.O. Box 216, Vinalhaven, ME 04863. (207) 863-9963.

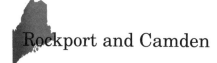

Rockport and Camden

ON SHORE

Rockport

If you come into Rockport Harbor, there are two interesting sights in the harbor park. One is the remnants of a lime kiln and the other, a statue of local celebrity Andre the Seal. In the pretty town up the hill you'll find some shops and galleries, including Anne Kilham's (236-0962), and the Maine Photographic Workshop (236-8581). Beauchamp Point is worth a visit, with its hiking paths and Children's Chapel overlooking the bay. Cow aficionados should get directions to the "Oreo cows," Belted Galloway cattle with distinctive white midsections.

Out on Route 1 is Maine Sport Outfitters (236-7120), which you'll find is well stocked with sea kayaking equipment, camping gear, and outdoor apparel.

Camden

Camden is popular with vacationers on their way to Bar Harbor, who stop to admire the windjammers in the harbor and shop in the wide range of gift shops near the waterfront. Route 1 runs right through the center of town, creating some interesting traffic patterns in July and August.

There are plenty of places to get a tasty bite to eat; just follow your nose. If you're in need of groceries, a good place to restock is French & Brawn (1 Elm St., 236-3361), a couple hundred yards from the town landing. They have gourmet food, fresh bakery bread, and a deli, and will deliver to boats in the harbor. The free Camden Shuttle will take you to the IGA on the outskirts of town.

A great book shop, The Owl and Turtle (8 Bayview St., 236-4769), has strong selections of nautical titles and charts. You'll find books on boat building and maintenance, navigation, maritime history, and pictorials. You can even pick up a few hair-raising boating adventure stories for the next leg of your trip.

Right near the public landing is an office of the Rockport-Camden-Lincolnville Chamber of Commerce (236-4404). They can provide you with maps and information on current events. If you arrive in town without a lodging reservation, they can help you find a place to spend the night. Camden Accommodations and Reservations (77 Elm St., 800-236-1920) is a private agency that can help you locate a room in the region.

North of town is Camden Hills State Park, with hiking trails leading to Mt. Battie and Mt. Megunticook. (Those with cars can opt to drive to the top of Mt. Battie.) There is something quite striking about the view of Camden Harbor and Penobscot Bay from these high lookout points.

OFF SHORE

Those in small boats may enjoy touring around the Rockport and Camden Harbors; just be alert to larger boats. Head out to Curtis Island at the Camden Harbor entrance and enjoy the town park there. Once outside of the harbors, the coast is fairly straight and open to the winds sweeping along Penobscot Bay.

REGIONAL ACCESS

Public moorings, floats, dock space

ROCKPORT: *The harbormaster* (236-0676) has some transient dock space on a first come, first served basis. *Rockport Marine* (236-9651) has moorings.

CAMDEN: *The Camden Yacht Club* (236-3014, channel 68) is open to the public and has moorings, inner harbor floats, and a launch shuttle service. *P.G. Willey* (236-3256) has dock space, outer harbor moorings, and inner harbor floats; they don't monitor VHF. You can reserve dock space from the *harbormaster* (236-7969). The yacht club, P.G. Willey, and the town landing are on the west side of the inner harbor. On the east side, *Wayfarer Marine* (236-4378, channel 71) has harbor floats, outer harbor moorings, dock space, and a launch shuttle service.

LODGINGS

Samoset Resort

#71, Chart 13305, Jameson Point, Between Rockland and Rockport

This full-service resort is easy to spot from the water since the granite Rockland Breakwater extends from its golf course. If you've been cooped up on your boat too long, here's a great place to get some exercise. You can start by walking to the lighthouse at the end of the nearly mile-long breakwater. Then you can golf on the championship 18-hole course, play tennis or racquetball, swim laps in an indoor or outdoor pool, or pedal a rental bicycle. The fitness center has aerobics classes, Nautilus equipment, treadmills, and stair climbers. Once you're nicely tuckered out, you can sit in one of three jacuzzis or go for massage therapy.

You can get three meals a day at "Marcel's," or have them brought to your room. The hotel rooms tend to be capacious, with decks overlooking the golf course and water. There are coin-operated laundry facilities on site.

Meals	None included; breakfast, lunch, Sunday brunch, and dinner available. There are dinner choices such as filet mignon, grilled free-range chicken, and country rabbit pie, as well as seafood and vegetarian entrees.
Rates	150 hotel rooms, 72 time-share condominiums. $230-305 hotel room doubles July and August. Visa, MC, Amex, Discover. Non-smoking guest rooms. Wheelchair-accessible rooms. Children welcome. Open year round.
Access	*Kayaks:* Access to the water from the property is possible but awkward because the golf course separates the parking lot from the waterfront. Kayakers can come in on the float off the breakwater. There is easier kayak access from the Snow Marine Park paved ramp in Rockland; water at all tides. *Trailered boats:* Use Snow Marine Park ramp. *Sailboats:* 2 moorings next to the breakwater in front of the resort are available on a first come, first served basis. *Walk to:* No groceries within walking distance.
Address	Rockport, ME 04856. (207) 594-2511.

Oakland Seashore Motel and Cabins

#72, Chart 13305, Pine Hill, Rockport

A real surprise awaits those who turn off busy Route 1, with its fast food restaurants and superstores, and head down the dirt road leading to this wooded enclave.

They'll find 11 classic tourist cabins dating from the late 1940's right on the open waters of Penobscot Bay. There's nothing fancy about these cabins, with their wooden interior walls and metal shower stalls, but they're clean, and some have kitchenettes. Most perch on ledge just above the water. There's also a simply furnished motel set back off the water.

Breakfast	Not provided.
Rates	11 cabins, 10 motel rooms. $50-88 cabins, $47-77 motel rooms, July to Labor Day. No credit cards. Children welcome. Pets permitted. Open Memorial Day to mid-October.
Access	*Kayaks:* Rather easy carry down a 50-foot slope to a cove with a nice stone beach; water at all tides. *Trailered boats:* Launch at the fee paved ramp at Rockport Harbor Park. *Walk to:* Restaurant, market.
Address	Route 1, Rockport, ME. Mail: RFD #1 Box 1449, Rockland, ME 04841. (207) 594-8104.

Sign of the Unicorn Guest House
#73, Chart 13305, Rockport

Winnie Easton-Jones has been hosting guests for over 20 years and has yet to tire of it. She delights in helping her guests fulfill their travel plans, whether it involves picking them up at Rockland Harbor or pointing them in the direction of scenic spots on Beauchamp Point. Besides running the guest house, she also teaches French and runs art workshops. Her house is cheerfully decorated and guests have free run of the kitchen. One of the guest rooms has its own grand piano and extensive book collection. Winnie can help with laundry.

Breakfast	"A combination of down home and French country breakfast." Guests might sit down to eggs with cheese and portabella mushrooms or bananas Foster French toast.
Rates	1 room with private bath, 3 rooms with shared bath. $85-140 doubles late May through October. Visa, MC. Well-mannered children over 6 welcome. Guest dogs sometimes permitted. Open year round.
Access	*Kayaks and trailered boats:* Launch at fee paved Rockport Harbor Park ramp; water at all tides. *Sailboats:* Guest mooring for a boat up to 21 feet, or contact the harbormaster or Rockport Marine. Winnie can pick up sailors at the harbor. *Walk to:* Restaurants, market, shops.
Address	191 Beauchamp Ave., P.O. Box 99, Rockport, ME 04856. (207) 236-8789, (800) 789-8789.

Camden Harbour Inn
#74, Chart 13305, Camden Harbor

These are the closest lodgings to the Camden Yacht Club. Some of the large bedrooms in this elegant Victorian inn have harbor-view balconies or fireplaces. Guests receptive to ghosts might wish to avoid rooms #26 and #28, as there have been unexplained accounts of slammed drawers, yanked sheets, and lights going on and off in those rooms.

Meals   A full country breakfast is included most of the year and is served on the porch in good weather. Dinner is available; appetizers could be crab cakes or mango-spiced shrimp, with entrees of grilled salmon filet or crispy striped bass.

Rates   22 rooms with private baths. $175-225 doubles mid-June to mid-October. Visa, MC, Amex, Discover. Smoking permitted in guest rooms. Wheelchair-accessible rooms. Children over 12 welcome. Open year round.

Access   *Kayaks and trailered boats:* Sea Street paved public ramp; water at all tides. *Sailboats:* The Camden Yacht Club is 500 feet from the inn. *Walk to:* Restaurants, groceries, galleries, shops, laundry, bicycle rentals.

Address   83 Bayview St., Camden, ME 04843.
(207) 236-4200.

Hartstone Inn
#75, Chart 13305, Camden Harbor

Innkeepers Peter and Sunny Simmons' enthusiasm for sailing is evident in their inn's library. Guests are invited to make selections from the huge stack of *WoodenBoat* magazines or the collection of "coffee table" sailing books and take them up to their rooms. Peter serves on Camden's harbor commission.

The guest rooms in the inn are furnished primarily with early 1900's country oak dressers and headboards. Particularly nice are the two rooms on the third floor with high ceilings and four-poster beds. Downstairs is a sitting room with comfortable sofas, and a separate television and game room. In the carriage house are two suites with kitchen facilities. All the guest rooms have phones.

Breakfast   Sunny recommends that guests plan to skip lunch, as she serves a big breakfast. Visitors have a choice of entrees; one favorite is French toast made with Grand Marnier.

Rates   8 rooms, 2 suites, all with private baths. $75-135 doubles mid-June through October. Visa, MC, Amex, Discover. Limited rooms for children. Pets permitted in one suite. Open year round.

Access   *Kayaks:* Kayakers can drop off their boats by the floats at the public landing 1/4 mile away and bring their cars back to the inn's lot. Another option is the paved ramp at Sea Street; water at any tide. *Trailered boats:* Sea Street ramp. *Sailboats:* Contact Wayfarer Marine, the harbormaster, or P.G. Willey. *Walk to:* Restaurants, groceries, galleries, shops, laundry, bicycle rentals.

Address   41 Elm St., Camden, ME 04843.
(207) 236-4259.

The Owl and the Turtle Harbor View Guest Rooms
#76, Chart 13305, Camden Harbor

These guest rooms are 100 yards across a parking lot from the public landing and are in the midst of downtown activities. From the third-floor deck you can watch the windjammers come in or gaze at Mt. Battie. Rooms are simply furnished, with paneled walls, air conditioning, televisions, and phones. There's no sitting room, but you can walk downstairs to the wonderful Owl and Turtle Bookshop and browse through the extensive nautical section to your heart's content.

Breakfast   Continental breakfast with homemade bread or muffins is brought to your room.

Rates   3 rooms with private baths. $70-80 doubles mid-June to mid-October. MC, Visa, Discover. Children welcome. 2-night stays preferred in July and August. Open year round.

Access   *Kayaks:* Kayakers coming by sea can carry boats from the public floats to the guest house, where there is locked storage. There are reserved car parking spots adjacent to the busy public parking area. (You might wish to lock your kayaks to your car with a cable.) *Trailered boats:* Sea Street paved ramp. *Sailboats:* Contact Wayfarer Marine, the harbormaster, or P.G. Willey. *Walk to:* Restaurants, groceries, galleries, shops, laundry, bicycle rentals.

Address   8 Bayview St., P.O. Box 1265, Camden, ME 04843.
(207) 236-9014.

Lord Camden Inn
#77, Chart 13305, Camden Harbor

The Lord Camden is a 100-year-old brick building on busy Main Street, a block from the harbor. Rooms are furnished with elegant reproduction four-poster or brass beds, televisions, and phones. Most have balconies for viewing the harbor or hills. Some rooms have kitchenettes.

Breakfast Continental.
Rates 31 rooms with private baths. $128-178 doubles late June to mid-October. Visa, MC. Smoking permitted. Children welcome. Open year round.
Access *Kayaks:* Launch from the paved Sea Street ramp. Other options are the town landing floats and a small beach at the head of the harbor, both 300 yards away. All have water at all tides. The inn can provide indoor kayak storage if you arrive by sea. *Trailered boats:* Launch at Sea Street ramp. *Sailboats:* Contact Wayfarer Marine, the harbormaster, or P.G. Willey. *Walk to:* Restaurants, groceries, galleries, shops, laundry, bicycle rentals.
Address 24 Main St., Camden, ME 04843.
(207) 236-4325, (800) 336-4325.

Highland Mill Inn
#78, Chart 13305, Camden Harbor

This converted woolen mill offers newly built rooms in town, but away from the traffic of Main Street. Some rooms have decks directly over the Megunticook River and guests can enjoy the sound of water flowing over the mill wheel. Rooms are attractively furnished with a combination of antiques and reproductions; half have canopy beds. All the rooms have air conditioning, televisions, and phones.

Breakfast Continental breakfast of muffins and bagels can be brought to your room.
Rates 24 rooms with private baths. $79-169 doubles mid-June through October. Visa, MC, Amex. Wheelchair accessible. Well-behaved children welcome. Open April through October.
Access *Kayaks:* Launch from the paved Sea Street ramp. Other options are the town landing floats and a small beach at the head of the harbor, both 250 yards away. All have water at all tides. *Trailered boats:* Launch at Sea Street ramp. *Sailboats:* Contact Wayfarer Marine, the harbormaster, or P.G. Willey. *Walk to:* Restaurants, groceries, galleries, shops, laundry, bicycle rentals.
Address Corner of Mechanic and Washington Streets, P.O. Box 961, Camden, ME 04843.
(207) 236-1057, (800) 841-5590.

The Camden Riverhouse Hotel
#79, Chart 13305, Camden Harbor

This newly renovated building is just across the Megunticook River footbridge from the downtown shopping district. Don't plan on paddling up to the doorstep though, as there's a waterfall before the harbor. Large hotel rooms have air conditioning, televisions, and phones. Amenities include an exercise room, indoor pool, and spa.

Breakfast Muffins, croissants, and cereal.

Rates 35 hotel rooms. $149-179 doubles mid-July to late August. Visa, MC, Amex, Discover. Wheelchair accessible. Children welcome. Open year round.

Access *Kayaks:* Launch from the paved Sea Street ramp. Other options are the town landing floats and a small beach at the head of the harbor 300 yards away. All have water at all tides. The hotel may be able to provide indoor kayak storage if you arrive by sea. *Trailered boats:* Launch at Sea Street ramp. *Sailboats:* Contact Wayfarer Marine, the harbormaster, or P.G. Willey. *Walk to:* Restaurants, groceries, galleries, shops, laundry, bicycle rentals.

Address 11 Tannery Lane, Camden, ME 04843.
(207) 236-0500, (800) 755-RIVER.

Windward House

#80, Chart 13305, Camden Harbor

Innkeepers Sandy and Tim LaPlante like to provide the extra touches that make a stay special. They serve breakfast by candlelight and garnish plates with fresh edible flowers. They offer afternoon lemonade and cookies to guests on the deck overlooking their gardens. The LaPlantes have stocked the library with lots of books and complimentary port and sherry. Chess, checkers, and backgammon are available in the game room. Their 1854 Greek Revival house is located near the harbor, at the beginning of the historic district on High Street. The lovely guest rooms are all furnished with queen-sized beds.

Breakfast Full gourmet breakfast with "decadent" coffee cake, a fruit dish, and entrees such as a specialty French toast, frittata, or omelet.

Rates 8 rooms with private baths. $100-170 doubles mid-June to mid-October. Visa, MC, Amex. Children over 12 welcome. Open year round.

Access *Kayaks and trailered boats:* Launch 1/2 mile away at the paved Sea Street ramp; water at all tides. *Sailboats:* Contact Wayfarer Marine, the harbormaster, or P.G. Willey. *Walk to:* Restaurants, groceries, galleries, shops, laundry, bicycle rentals.

Address 6 High St., Camden, ME 04843.
(207) 236-9656.

Abigail's Bed & Breakfast
#81, Chart 13305, Camden Harbor

As you walk into this B&B you'll find welcoming parlors on either side. Both have fireplaces and country touches such as counted cross-stitch pictures and cheerful folk art. The original wood floors have been nicely restored in this 1847 Federal house in the historic district.

Two guest rooms are in the main building and two are in the carriage house. All have sitting areas and four-poster beds. The carriage house rooms have kitchenettes, and one has a large jacuzzi. Outside, past the flower gardens, you can pick up the Megunticook Trail to Mt. Battie.

Breakfast You can enjoy breakfast in the dining room or have it brought to your room on a tray. House specialties include walnut banana bread, scones, and waffles with blueberries and whipped cream.

Rates 4 rooms with private baths. $118-155 doubles July through October. Visa, MC, Amex. Children welcome. Open April through December.

Access *Kayaks and trailered boats:* Launch 1/2 mile away at paved Sea Street ramp; water at any tide. Kayaks can be stored in the barn. *Sailboats:* Contact Wayfarer Marine, the harbormaster, or P.G. Willey. The Misners can meet sailors at the harbor. *Walk to:* Restaurants, groceries, galleries, shops, laundry, bicycle rentals.

Address 8 High St., Camden, ME 04843.
(207) 236-2501, (800) 292-2501.

Hawthorn Inn
#82, Chart 13305, Camden Harbor

This stately Victorian sits just uphill from the head of the harbor. The parlors and dining room catch the sea breeze, and guests sitting on the porch can keep an eye on the waterfront and Wayfarer Marine. Interesting architectural elements include a formal curved staircase in the entry hall, turrets, and stained-glass panels. Innkeepers Patty and Nick Wharton have fitted the house with period antiques and reproductions. There are guest rooms in the main house and the adjacent carriage house. Rooms in the latter have harbor views from their patios, gas fireplaces or jacuzzis, VCRs, and phones.

Breakfast The Whartons specialize in "exotic" egg dishes. They put out a fresh fruit bowl and have baked goods such as lemon black walnut bread.

Rates 10 rooms with private baths. $90-185 doubles May through October. Visa, MC, Amex. Children over 12 welcome. Dog in residence. Open March through December.

Access   *Kayaks:* Kayakers can carry or wheel boats the 200 yards between the inn and the beach at the head of the harbor in Harbor Park, passing through the inn's backyard and the Camden library's parking lot. Another choice is the paved ramp at Sea Street. Water at all tides at both locations. *Trailered boats:* Launch at Sea Street. *Sailboats:* Contact Wayfarer Marine, the harbormaster, or P.G. Willey. *Walk to:* Restaurants, groceries, galleries, shops, laundry, bicycle rentals.

Address   9 High St., Camden, ME 04843.
(207) 236-8842.

Maine Stay
#83, Chart 13305, Camden Harbor

The Maine Stay is graciously hosted by a three-person team: Peter Smith, his wife, Donny Smith, and her identical twin sister Diana Robson. If there were an award for the profession of innkeeping, these folks would be in line for it. They work hard to help you get the most from your visit to the region. They'll provide detailed information on area attractions and how to reach them. Camden Hills State Park abuts their property; they'll gladly drop you off at a trail head in the park and direct you on the way to return. If you're struck by a particularly tasty breakfast, they'll print off the recipe from the computer.

The Maine Stay is a handsome white Greek Revival house with dark green shutters, built in 1802. It stands on a wooded property in the midst of the High Street district of 66 homes on the National Register of Historic Places. The inn combines elegant and homey features in a happy melding. Family antiques and oriental rugs furnish the spacious rooms. Two parlors with fireplaces are open to guests. If it's available, stay in the Carriage House Room, private quarters with a long window seat, shelves of books, a Vermont Castings wood stove, and a French door that opens onto a stone patio and the gardens.

Breakfast   Peter announces breakfast on a bosun's pipe. Egg casseroles and souffles are among the house favorites.

Rates   6 rooms with private baths, 2 with shared bath. $75-125 doubles June through October. Visa, MC, Amex. No smoking anywhere on the property. Children over 8 welcome. Open year round.

Access   *Kayaks and trailered boats:* Launch 1/2 mile away at the Sea Street paved ramp; water at any tide. *Sailboats:* Wayfarer Marine is a 10-minute walk away. The innkeepers can pick up sailors at docks in Camden or Rockland. *Walk to:* Restaurants, groceries, galleries, shops, laundry, bicycle rentals.

Address   22 High St., Camden, ME 04843.
(207) 236-9636.

The High Tide Inn
#84, Chart 13305, Between Camden and Lincolnville

Accommodations are scattered over this waterfront property, located a few miles north of Camden. There's the main inn, with its enclosed porch giving guests at breakfast a sweeping view of boats and islands in Penobscot Bay. Inn bedrooms are attractively furnished and the beds covered with quilts. There's a group of modern motel units right by the water; some of them have an extra bedroom for families or friends travelling together. There are some older motel rooms and several rustic cabins on the grounds as well. From the lawn, you can walk down a set of stairs to the cobblestone beach.

Breakfast	Home-baked continental breakfast might include popovers or banana bread.
Rates	5 inn rooms, 17 motel rooms, 6 cabins, all with private baths. $95-135 inn rooms, $65-145 motel rooms, $60-140 cottages, double occupancy, late June to mid-October. Visa, MC, Discover. Smoking permitted except in the inn. Children welcome except in the inn guest rooms. Cats in the inn. 2-night minimum on holidays and July and August weekends. Open mid-May to mid-October.
Access	*Kayaks:* Kayakers can drive down near the water, then carry their boats down 18 wooden stair steps to the cobble beach that allows launching at all tides. *Trailered boats:* Launch at Lincolnville Beach paved ramp. *Walk to:* Restaurant.
Address	Route 1, HR60 Box 3183, Camden, ME 04843. (207) 236-3724.

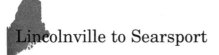

Lincolnville to Searsport

ON SHORE

Lincolnville
Except for the presence of Route 1, Lincolnville seems far removed from the bustle of Camden just south of it. From the sand beach you can look out over the waters of Penobscot Bay to Islesboro. Near the beach are lobster restaurants, a grocery store, and the shops of several craftspeople.

Islesboro Island
Islesboro is a lovely 10-mile-long island three miles east of Lincolnville. It is in the midst of many smaller islands, so interesting boating opportunities abound. Biking on the level terrain is pleasant, with new vistas opening up to both the eastern and western parts of Penobscot Bay as you ride along. You can admire the grand summer "cottages" (actually, mansions) as you travel on land or sea. At the south end of the

island is a town beach with a picnic area. There is frequent car ferry service supporting Isleboro's 600 year-round residents and numerous summer visitors.

Belfast

Travelling by car, you may have missed Belfast because Route 1 bypasses it. If so, next trip put on your turn signal and take a look around. Like Rockland, it is cleaning up its waterfront and welcoming boaters. The harbormaster's office has orientation packets, and there is an information center down on the waterfront. Pick up a copy of the walking tour brochure. The tour takes you past some lovely Victorian, Greek Revival, and Federal buildings in the downtown historic district. A quarter mile from the harbor is the excellent Belfast Co-op (123 High St., 338-2532), with whole foods grocery, bakery, deli, and cafe.

Searsport

The old sea captains' homes lining Route 1 bear testimony to Searsport's ties to the 19th-century shipping industry. You can learn more about this history at the Penobscot Marine Museum (see below). Antique hunters will want to allocate some time to pursuing their interest in the many shops in and near Searsport. Those in need of boating supplies can stop in at Hamilton Marine (548-6302) on Route 1.

OFF SHORE

Along the mainland from Camden to Searsport, the coastline is fairly straight with few coves and no islands nearby. Keep in mind that there is a shipping channel not far off shore. The gunkholing opportunities are much better circling Islesboro.

Just to the south of the Islesboro ferry landing at Grindel Point is Warren Island. The entire island is a state park; there are designated camp sites, picnic tables, a hand pump for drinking water, and privies. A network of trails helps you explore the island's 129 acres. The state maintains a dock and moorings on the eastern side.

REGIONAL ACCESS

Launch ramp with overnight parking

LINCOLNVILLE: *Paved public ramp* and sand beach next to the ferry landing; water at all tides. Pay parking fee at the ferry terminal.

Ferry service

There is frequent car ferry service between Lincolnville and Islesboro. Call the Maine State Ferry Service at 624-7777 for general schedule information, or call the Lincolnville office at 789-5611. Kayaks must be transported on top of vehicles; they will not be taken as freight.

Public moorings

BELFAST: *The harbormaster* (338-1142) and *Belfast Boatyard* (338-5098) have moorings. SEARSPORT: One mooring belonging to the Penobscot Marine Museum and one belonging to the town are available at the town landing. Contact the *harbormaster* at 548-2985.

LODGINGS

The Spouter Inn
#85, Chart 13309, Lincolnville

There is a "Spouter Inn" at the beginning of *Moby Dick*, in case the name of the Lippman's home seems familiar. The Lippmans have done a wonderful job restoring this 1832 Colonial and seamlessly adding a carriage house for additional accommodations. Wood-burning fireplaces abound: there's one in most bedrooms, the library, and the parlor. Guest rooms are tastefully furnished with four-poster beds or carved country oak furniture and quilts. Two have their own sun decks and three have jacuzzis.

The inn is located in the village of Lincolnville, just across the road from sandy Lincolnville Beach. Bike rentals can be arranged.

Breakfast   Baked goods, a fruit dish, and a hot dish such as puffed pancakes or spinach quiche.

Rates   7 rooms with private baths. $75-165 Memorial Day to Columbus Day. Visa, MC, Amex, Discover. Children over 7 welcome. 2-night minimum in high season. Open year round.

Access   *Kayaks:* Launch at any tide from the sand beach 100 feet from the house. *Trailered boats:* Paved public ramp a few hundred feet away, by the ferry landing. *Walk to:* Restaurants, groceries, shops.

Address   Route 1, P.O. Box 270, Lincolnville Beach, ME 04849. (207) 789-5171.

The Dark Harbor House
#86, Charts 13305 & 13309, Ames Cove, Dark Harbor

This Georgian Revival was built 100 years ago as a summer mansion for a Philadelphia banker. As guests enter the front door, they walk into a grand entry hall with a double staircase flanking it. The library is filled with magazines, and the inviting salmon-colored parlor has comfortable sofas. There are some massive headboards and four-poster beds in guest rooms, half of which have wood-burning fireplaces. Overall, there is a feeling of relaxed elegance about the inn.

Paths through the woods lead down to Ames Cove. Guests can borrow the inn's three-speed bicycles.

Meals   A full breakfast is included. Dinner is available; the chef cooks everything from French to Thai cuisine, offering red meat, poultry, fish, shellfish, and vegetarian choices.

Penobscot Marine Museum

The Penobscot Marine Museum celebrates the shipbuilders, sea captains, and crews of Penobscot Bay. During the years 1770 to 1920, over 3000 vessels of all types were built by workers in the region. The towns with the most activity were Belfast, Searsport, and Camden/Rockport. Searsport, in particular, was known for the sea captains originating there. Between 1870 and 1900, over 200 men from Searsport were captains of deep water merchant vessels.

The museum is housed in eight historic buildings in downtown Searsport. One building holds a collection of regional recreational and working boats. Recreational boats present include a 1910 Adirondack guide boat, a birch bark canoe from the 1930's, and a 1903 North Haven dinghy. Working boats of note are a 30-foot-long smelt scow built in nearby Winterport, several pea pods, and a 1913 salmon wherry.

Another building at the museum provides a re-creation of a 19th-century sea captain's home, complete with personal mementos. (It may remind you of the B&B where you're staying!) Other exhibits feature ship models, oil paintings, four well-preserved figureheads from the 1850's, and old photographs of sailors and their families at sea.

If the weather has been calm on your trip, attend a showing of the 1929 film "Rounding Cape Horn," and see the crew getting tossed about on the sea.

Penobscot Marine Museum, Church Street at Route 1, P.O. Box 498, Searsport, ME 04974. (207) 548-2529. Open daily from Memorial Day to Columbus Day. Hours are 9:30 to 5:00, Monday through Saturday; noon to 5:00 on Sundays. Admission is $5.00 for adults, $1.50 for children 7-15, and free for children 6 and under.

Water access: A museum guest mooring in Searsport Harbor is available for visitors. Contact the harbormaster on 548-2985. It is a half mile from the harbor to the museum at the northern end of town.

Rates   10 rooms with private baths. $105-245 doubles. Visa, MC. Children over 12 generally welcome. Pets generally not permitted. 2-night minimum on holiday weekends. Open mid-May to mid-October.

Access   *Kayaks:* Most kayakers will prefer to take their cars and kayaks over to Islesboro on the ferry, and use the paved public ramp near the Islesboro ferry terminal, where there is water at all tides. It's possible to approach the inn from the water, but it is difficult to spot the inn because of the woods near the shore. Also, the path to the inn is 250 yards long and overgrown. If you choose to paddle from the mainland, keep in mind that the open crossing can be quite windy, and that it intersects a shipping channel. *Trailered boats:* Launch at the public ramp. *Sailboats:* Guest mooring in Ames Cove. *Walk to:* Restaurant.

Address   Main Rd., P.O. Box 185, Dark Harbor, Islesboro, ME 04848. (207) 734-6669.

Belfast Bay Meadows Inn
#87, Chart 13309, South of Belfast

The common rooms and bedrooms in this century-old summer home are furnished with comfortable antiques and lots of oil paintings and oriental rugs. The newly remodeled annex offers modern furnishings. Guests eating breakfast on the deck can look down the meadow to Penobscot Bay. This is a child-friendly spot, with a big set of play equipment in the yard, plenty of room to run around, and even a children's dinner menu.

Meals   Breakfast is included; there is a choice of three entrees, one of which is a lobster and sweet pepper omelet. Dinner is available in summer every day except Tuesday, with seafood and beef on the menu.

Rates   7 rooms in the inn, 12 in the annex, all with private baths. $85-145 doubles July and August. Visa, MC, Amex, Discover. Wheelchair accessible. Children welcome. The owners' dogs are in the inn; guest pets permitted. Open year round.

Access   *Kayaks:* Drive 1000 feet down a mowed meadow path to within 30 feet of the shore. Any car with average or better clearance should be able to travel this path, except if the field is quite wet. It's an easy carry down a 30-foot wooden ramp to the stone beach, with access at all tides. *Trailered boats:* Paved fee ramp at Belfast town landing. *Sailboats:* Call inn for mooring arrangements. *Walk to:* 1 mile to restaurants, groceries, shops, laundry.

Address   90 Northport Ave., Belfast, ME 04915. (207) 338-5715, (800) 335-2370.

The Jeweled Turret Inn
#88, Chart 13309, Belfast

An eye-catching turret with stained-glass windows gives this Queen Anne Victorian its name. Innkeepers Cathy and Carl Heffentrager, who moved here from Anchorage, have done an admirable job restoring this intriguing building. Interesting features include tin ceilings, detailed woodwork, and a fireplace built from the original owner's collection of semi-precious stones and rocks. The four parlors and the guest rooms are tastefully furnished with period antiques and lacy window treatments. The decor is romantic without being stylized.

Breakfast The gourmet breakfast could include a fruit dish, scones, and a hot dish such as sourdough waffles.

Rates 7 rooms with private baths. $70-95 doubles mid-June to mid-October. Visa, MC. Children over 12 welcome. 2-night minimum on holidays. Open year round.

Access *Kayaks:* Launch from a stone beach on Commercial Street 1/4 mile from the inn, or use the beach next to the town landing 1/2 mile away; both have water at all tides. *Trailered boats:* Launch at fee paved ramp by town landing. *Sailboats:* Contact the harbormaster or Belfast Boatyard. *Walk to:* Restaurants, grocery store, food co-op, shops, galleries, laundry.

Address 40 Pearl St., Belfast, ME 04915. (207) 338-2304, (800) 696-2304.

The Thomas Pitcher House
#89, Chart 13309, Belfast

At the time this house was built, in 1873, it was considered state of the art, with its central heat and hot and cold running water. When Ron and Fran Kresge undertook a substantial renovation, they were able to keep many of its charming features while providing modern day conveniences. The 11-foot ceilings downstairs show off the large bay windows, crown moldings, and ceiling medallions. Comfortable furnishings include Victorian accents. One of the two guest parlors has big stacks of regional, travel, and home-renovation magazines next to the VCR and games.

Breakfast The main dish might be a baked raisin bread French toast puff or *apfelpfannkuchen*, a German apple pancake.

Rates 4 rooms with private baths. $65-85 mid-May to mid-October. Visa, MC. Children over 12 welcome. Open year round.

Access *Kayaks:* Launch from the beach next to the town landing 3/10 mile away; water at all tides. *Trailered boats:* Launch at fee paved ramp by town landing. *Sailboats:* Contact the harbormaster or Belfast Boatyard. The innkeepers will pick up sailors at the town dock. *Walk to:* Restaurants, grocery store, food co-op, shops, galleries, laundry.

Address 19 Franklin St., Belfast, ME 04915. (207) 338-6454, (888) 338-6454.

Thurston House
#90, Chart 13309, Searsport

This attractive 1831 Colonial home is on a quiet side street in town, near the fascinating Penobscot Marine Museum. Two guest rooms are in the main house, and two more are in the carriage house. The carriage house rooms work nicely as a suite to accommodate families or groups of friends travelling together.

Breakfast The "Forget about Lunch" breakfast of three courses might include a freshly prepared local fruit dish, a hot bread such as apple streusel muffins, and an entree such as ham and eggs of free-range chickens.

Rates 2 rooms with private baths, 2 rooms with shared bath. $45-65 doubles, or $105 for the carriage house suite, June through October. (Rates include lodging tax.) Visa, MC, Amex. Children welcome. Open year round.

Access *Kayaks and trailered boats:* 1/2 mile to the public boat landing with paved ramp. *Sailboats:* Contact the harbormaster. The innkeeper can meet boaters at the landing. *Walk to:* Restaurants, groceries, shops.

Address 8 Elm St., P.O. Box 686, Searsport, ME 04974. (207) 548-2213, (800) 240-2213.

Homeport Inn
#91, Chart 13309, Searsport

This sea captain's mansion is filled with curios the captain might have brought back from his 19th-century travels. Numerous oriental carpets furnish the comfortably old-fashioned rooms. Guests can walk along the extensive grounds to the waterfront, or rent bikes from the innkeepers and pedal into town.

Breakfast Might feature blueberry pancakes or an egg dish.

Rates 7 rooms with private baths, 3 rooms with shared baths. $55-85 doubles May through October. Visa, MC, Amex, Discover. Children over 3 welcome. Dog and cat in residence. Open year round.

Access *Kayaks:* The inn is 350 yards from the water; kayakers can drive with their boats to within 75 yards and carry boats over the rocks to the water; better at mid-tide and higher due to seaweed. *Trailered boats:* Launch at paved town ramp. *Sailboats:* Contact the harbormaster for a mooring in the harbor, 1 mile away. *Walk to:* Restaurants, groceries, shops.

Address 121 East Main St. (Route 1), P.O. Box 647, Searsport, ME 04974. (207) 548-2259, (800) 742-5814.

Captain A. V. Nickels Inn
#92, Chart 13309, Searsport

Two comfortable parlors await guests at the Captain A.V. Nickels Inn. One has a piano that guests are invited to play. The other has big windows, soft sofas, and a lovely old-time tin ceiling. Guest rooms are decorated with a Victorian flavor. Visitors can borrow the house dog, Boots, and walk down the lawn to the water's edge, where there is a 100-yard shoreline.

Breakfast   Could be pancakes or Belgium waffles.

Rates   5 rooms with private baths, 4 with shared baths. $55-95 doubles. Visa, MC, Amex. Children welcome. Dog in residence. Pets allowed, $5 surcharge. Open year round.

Access   *Kayaks:* Kayakers can drive their cars 300 yards over the mowed lawn to the water's edge, then carry their boats over rocks; better at mid-tide and higher due to seaweed. *Trailered boats:* Launch at paved town ramp. *Sailboats:* Contact the harbormaster for a mooring in the harbor, 1 mile away. *Walk to:* Restaurants, groceries, shops.

Address   Route 1, Box 38, Searsport, ME 04974.
(207) 548-6691, (800) 343-5001.

Hichborn Inn
#93, Chart 13309, Stockton Springs

Nancy and Bruce Suppes offer accommodations in their elegantly restored 1849 Italianate Victorian in the quiet village of Stockton Springs. They've furnished the house with oriental carpets and period antiques, including beautiful sleigh beds and brass beds. Common rooms include a stately "gent's parlor" where raspberry cordials, sherry, and brandy are served. Guests are encouraged to play the baby grand piano in the music room.

Nancy and Bruce are both sailors. Bruce also spends time in a smaller boat (an Alden ocean shell) and on larger ones (he serves as the chief engineer on oil tankers).

Breakfast   A hearty breakfast emphasizing local products. It might start with a cold fruit soup, followed by a house favorite such as crepes made with raspberries picked on the property.

Rates   2 rooms with private baths, 3 rooms sharing 2 baths. $60-85 doubles. No credit cards. 2 Maine coon cats in residence. Open year round; by reservation only in winter.

Access   *Kayaks and trailered boats:* A few miles from the inn is a gravel ramp at Fort Point on Cape Jellison, with water at all tides. Four wheel drive vehicles are best for launching trailered boats. *Sailboats:* The

Suppes will pick up sailors at Searsport or Belfast. For moorings, call the Searsport harbormaster, Belfast harbormaster, or Belfast Boatyard. *Walk to:* No restaurants or groceries nearby, but the Suppes will give you a lift to a restaurant or the market.

Address Church St., P.O. Box 115, Stockton Springs, ME 04981. (207) 567-4183, (800) 346-1522.

CAMPGROUNDS

Warren Island State Park
#C12, Chart 13309, Warren Island

Warren Island is the state's only "improved" island campground. There are well-spaced designated camp sites. Picnic tables and a hand pump for drinking water are provided. Hiking trails run along the shore and through the interior of this large wooded island. Signs of 19th-century habitation include old building foundations and a tombstone.

Access is by private boat only. Those with kayaks and small trailered boats should consider using the ferry service from Lincolnville to Islesboro to eliminate the open Penobscot Bay crossing. (The crossing can be quite rough when windy, and it bisects a major shipping channel.) There is a public ramp next to the Islesboro ferry landing; from there it is 1/2 mile to the dock on Warren Island's eastern side.

Campsites 9 sites include 2 with Adirondack shelters. 3 waterfront. Privies, wheelchair accessible.

Rates $12 per site for Maine residents, $16 for non-residents, including lodging tax. Park manager collects fees on site; cash or checks only. Pets permitted. Reservations taken for groups of over 6 people; write to the address below and enclose a check with a nonrefundable $10 deposit payable to "Treasurer, State of Maine." On arrival, group pays $3 per person per night. Open Memorial Day to Labor Day.

Access *Kayaks:* Paddle from Lincolnville or from the public ramp next to the Islesboro ferry landing, and land on the rocky beach of Warren at any tide. *Sailboats:* Small boats can be tied to the dock; a few moorings are maintained. *Boat to:* A convenient snack bar next to the Islesboro ferry landing.

Address Warren Island. Mail: P.O. Box 105, Lincolnville, ME 04849. (207) 236-3109 (Camden Hills State Park).

The Moorings
#C13, Chart 13309, East of Patterson Point, Belfast

This campground was opened a few years ago and is arranged to accommodate primarily trailers and RV's. The open sites provide views of Penobscot Bay. Three tent sites are located away from the water, near the road. Large stone beach. Playground, volleyball set. There is a daily group grocery store run.

Campsites	47 sites, 3 for tents. 10 waterfront. 15% tenters. New showers and flush toilets, wheelchair accessible. Small recreation room with pool table. Laundry.
Rates	$21-25 per site, June 15 to September 15. Visa, MC. Pets permitted. Open May 1 to November 1.
Access	*Kayaks:* Easy 50-foot carry across gravel to water; access at any tide. *Trailered boats:* Launch at paved ramp at Belfast town landing.
Address	Route 1, RR#1 Box 69, Belfast, ME 04915. (207) 338-6860.

Searsport Shores Camping Resort
#C14, Chart 13309, South of Searsport

Attractively situated on a northern stretch of Penobscot Bay, Searsport Shores has 1200 feet of ocean frontage. Hammocks and chairs are set out along the waterfront. Tenters have an area of their own with wooded, private sites. These sites are set away from parking, with wheeled carts provided for moving gear. Group sites available. Special activities for children and a playground with a nautical theme. Lobster bakes. A few new rental cabins.

Campsites	120 sites, with 40 designated for tents. 20 waterfront. 33% tenters. Showers and flush toilets, wheelchair accessible. Large recreation room with pool table, ping pong, VCR, and library. Laundry. Camp store with microwave.
Rates	$15-20 tent sites. Visa, MC, Discover. Personal checks drawn on Maine banks only. Dogs permitted. Open May 15 to October 15.
Access	*Kayaks:* Easy launch from gravel beach at any tide, with 250-foot carry on graded path to water. *Trailered boats:* Launch at paved ramp at Searsport town landing.
Address	216 West Main St. (Route 1), Searsport, ME 04974. (207) 548-6059.

SEA KAYAKERS

and those with trailered boats can easily launch from the scenic shores of many mainland campgrounds.

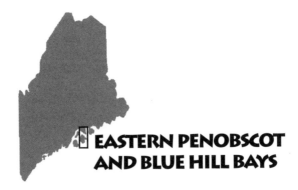

EASTERN PENOBSCOT AND BLUE HILL BAYS

Castine to
Little Deer Isle

ON SHORE

Castine

Castine is filled with 18th and 19th-cen-
tury white clapboard Georgian and
Federal houses sheltered by stately elm
trees. Visitors can enjoy a self-guided
walking tour of this genteel town, using
a detailed brochure available from local
merchants. History buffs can dig into
accounts of the town's successive occupations by French and British forces.

Castine is home to the Maine Maritime Academy (326-4311). Its training
ship, *State of Maine,* is often in the harbor and available for public tours. L.L.
Bean's Atlantic Coast Sea Kayaking
Symposium (800-341-4341, ext. 6666)
has been held on the Maine Maritime
Academy campus every summer for
many years, and serves as a great
introduction to boating skills, equipment, and the town.

The Brooksvilles

The small communities of West
Brooksville, South Brooksville, and
Brooksville are found on the western
side of the Blue Hill peninsula. The
inland landscape is characterized by
rolling hills and long stretches of rock-
strewn blueberry barrens. Lodgings in
this region are pleasantly remote from
most things except the sea. In Buck's
Harbor there are a few restaurants and
a general store. It's an easy drive to
Blue Hill for dining and entertainment
(see page 149).

Little Deer Isle

This island lies to the south of
Eggemoggin Reach and is joined to the
Blue Hill peninsula by a dramatic suspension bridge built in 1939. Driving
on this bridge in the fog can be an act of
faith. Little Deer Isle, in turn, connects

to Deer Isle via a scenic causeway, with boulders serving as guardrails.

OFF SHORE

Between Castine and Cape Rosier are several islands and sheltered Smith Cove. Holbrook Island Sanctuary is a state park on Cape Rosier. There is water access from either side of the neck separating Smith Cove from the cove formed by Nautilus and Holbrook Islands. (Note that the park is not on Holbrook Island, which is private.) Hiking trails lead through upland, salt marsh, and beaver dam habitats. Birders could find themselves busy here.

Eggemoggin Reach is a popular sailing shortcut between Penobscot and Blue Hill Bays. Boaters might want to take a look at Buck's Harbor or swing by pretty Pumpkin Light, and then head down to the spidery suspension bridge.

REGIONAL ACCESS

Launch area with overnight parking

BUCK'S HARBOR: *Buck's Harbor Marine* (326-8829) will allow kayakers who use their parking lot to launch from floats or off their rocky shore; water at all tides at floats.

Public moorings, dock space

CASTINE: *Eaton's Boatyard* (326-8579) has moorings and dock space. *The harbormaster* (326-4471) has dock space. BUCK'S HARBOR: *Buck's Harbor Marine* (326-8829) has moorings.

LODGINGS

The Holiday House
#94, Chart 13309, Castine Harbor

The Holiday House is aptly named. It's a very relaxed spot whose owners enjoy seeing guests sink into the living room couch and nod off. Sara and Paul Brouillard have created a B&B that is boater, pet, and child-friendly. When I visited, they had just placed a ping pong table over the large oriental rug in their second living room; intergenerational matches were proving popular. There are even crayons in the television room! On the grounds are a slide, a swing, and a tree house.

This 1893 "summer cottage" was built so close to the water that it is protected by a seawall. Many of the spacious, simply furnished guest rooms have great water views. Porch choices include spaces open to the sun, screened, or enclosed, for a total of 250 linear feet.

Breakfast   Choices such as croissants, yogurt, cereal, English muffins, and melons.

Rates   7 rooms with private baths, 2 with shared baths. $75-115 July into September. Visa, MC. Smoking permitted. Children welcome. 3 cats, 2 dogs, and a hamster in residence. Well-behaved leashed pets accepted; they cannot be left unattended in rooms. Open June through October.

Access   *Kayaks:* Easy 50-foot carry across the lawn from your car to the water. The cobble beach provides access at all tides. *Trailered boats:* Paved and concrete ramp by the town landing. Parking limited to 3 hours at the landing. *Sailboats:* Three guest moorings by the house, or the innkeepers can pick up guests at the harbor. *Walk to:* Restaurants, market, shops, laundry.

Address   Perkins St., P.O. Box 215, Castine, ME 04421. (207) 326-4861.

The Pentagoet Inn
#95, Chart 13309, Castine

The Pentagoet Inn has been welcoming guests since the days they arrived by steamship. It is located in the heart of the historic district, just up the hill from the harbor. The inn is comfortable, yet there is a sense of Victorian-era elegance as well. Innkeepers Virginia and Lindsey Miller host chamber music evenings in the late summer and fall; Lindsey sometimes plays the piano in the parlor. Guest rooms feature tall windows and a few have turrets.

There are afternoon refreshments such as iced tea and cookies or mulled cider and scones. Wine and cheese are served in the evening.

Breakfast   Starts with early coffee set out by guest rooms, followed by a cold buffet of whole-grain cereal, bread, fruit, and yogurt. It's capped off with a cooked entree such as eggs to order or sourdough pancakes.

Rates   16 rooms with private baths. $95-125 doubles. Visa, MC. Older children welcome. Dog and cat in parlor. Generally no minimum stay requirements. Open Memorial Day to mid-October.

Access   *Kayaks and trailered boats:* The inn is 1 steep block, 500 feet, uphill from the harbor. There is a paved and concrete ramp at the town landing; water at all tides. Parking limited to 3 hours at the landing, so move your vehicle to on-street parking. The inn has no off-street parking. *Sailboats:* Call Eaton's Boatyard or the harbormaster. *Walk to:* Restaurants, market, shops, laundry.

Address   Main St., P.O. Box 4, Castine, ME 04421. (207) 326-8616.

The Castine Inn

#96, Chart 13309, Castine

Across the street from the Pentagoet Inn, the Castine Inn also has been hosting visitors for nearly 100 years. Tom and Amy Gutow are avid sailors and the newest owners of the inn. He is the chef, and she is running the inn and looking after the extensive formal gardens. The large deck and some of the traditionally furnished guest rooms overlook the gardens and the harbor. The Gutows display the work of different local artists on a rotating basis.

Meals   A full breakfast is part of the room rate and might feature French toast or waffles made with whatever fruit is in season. Dinner is available to inn guests and the public. Tom uses fresh regional ingredients to prepare traditional and creative international recipes.

Rates   20 rooms with private baths. $85-135 doubles, mid-June to Columbus Day. Visa, MC. No smoking on the property. Children over 5 welcome. 2-night minimum July, August, and holidays. Open May into December.

Access   *Kayaks and trailered boats:* The inn is 1 steep block, 500 feet, uphill from the harbor. There is a paved and concrete ramp at the town landing; water at all tides. Parking limited to 3 hours at the landing, so move your car back to the inn. Vehicles with trailers park on the street. *Sailboats:* Call Eaton's Boatyard or the harbormaster. *Walk to:* Restaurants, market, shops, laundry.

Address Main St., P.O. Box 41, Castine, ME 04421.
(207) 326-4365.

By-the-Sea B&B
#97, Chart 13309, Smith Cove, West Brooksville

Pat and Fred Perkins retired to this small saltwater farm on family land after years of full-time farming. When they built the house they included a modest two-bedroom unit with living room, microwave and refrigerator, and separate entrance. You can book one or both of the country-style bedrooms. From the living room you can see Smith Cove and Cape Rosier, as well as the Perkins' sheep, chickens, and geese.

Breakfast Hearty, with choices such as biscuits, pancakes, and bacon and eggs.
Rates 2 rooms with shared bath. $65 doubles. No credit cards. Well-behaved children welcome (the Perkins raised ten). Pets may be permitted, call ahead. Open year round.
Access *Kayaks and trailered boats:* 1/2 mile to the scenic Brooksville town landing and picnic area; water on top half of the tide. Four wheel drive vehicles should be used with trailers. *Walk to:* No restaurants or groceries within walking distance; can boat to Castine two miles away.
Address Town Landing Rd., RR#1 Box 252, West Brooksville, ME 04617.
(207) 326-9122.

Buck's Harbor Inn
#98, Chart 13309, Buck's Harbor, South Brooksville

Buck's Harbor has long been known as a "hurricane hole" for sailors, providing protection from the winds that sweep along Eggemoggin Reach. The inn is adjacent to the Buck's Harbor Yacht Club. Rooms are simply furnished with country oak beds and dressers. There is a wood stove and TV in the living room, and breakfast is served in a pleasant sun room. Owner Peter Eberling thinks of the inn as a little hotel; he says he will even carry your bags!

Peter and his wife used to sail a 24-foot boat that they trailered all over the west coast and Mexico.

Breakfast Full breakfast cooked to order. Specialties include homemade bread and Swedish pancakes.
Rates 6 rooms with shared baths. $65 doubles. Visa, MC. Children welcome. Open year round.

> *Access*   *Kayaks:* Kayakers may launch from the floats or rocky shore of Buck's Harbor Marine and pay for car parking in their lot; water at all tides at floats. Other choices are the dirt town ramp at West Brooksville and the concrete public ramp at Sedgwick. *Trailered boats:* Ramps at West Brooksville and Sedgwick. *Sailboats:* Rent a mooring from Buck's Harbor Marine or obtain a guest mooring at the Buck's Harbor Yacht Club. *Walk to:* Restaurant, market.
>
> *Address*   P.O. Box 268, South Brooksville, ME 04617.
> (207) 326-8660.

Eggemoggin Reach Bed & Breakfast
#99, Chart 13309, Deadman Cove, Brooksville

Susie and Michael Canon built their attractive post-and-beam home and adjacent lodge and cottages based on traditional New England designs. The buildings are nestled into the evergreens near the water. The spacious guest rooms have separate sitting areas, and most include efficiency kitchens. Two of the cottages and all of the lodge rooms provide private screened porches or decks.

People tend to linger on the main porch after breakfast, to enjoy the spectacular views of the Reach and Pumpkin Light. Cape Rosier and Camden's Mt. Battie are visible in the distance. This is a quiet spot on a quiet peninsula.

> *Meals*   There is a breakfast buffet first, followed by a hot entree. House specialties include baked French toast and Eggs Eggemoggin. The Canons can arrange a shoreside lobster dinner for parties of eight or more.
>
> *Rates*   1 room in the main house, 6 rooms in the lodge, and 3 cottages, all with private baths. $140-165 doubles from mid-June to mid-October. Visa, MC. Children over 12 welcome. 2-night minimum on high season weekends. Open mid-May to mid-October.
>
> *Access*   *Kayaks:* Carry boats 10 steps down from the house, then 18 steps down to the waterfront, with access at all tides to a small gravel pocket beach. Kayaks can be left at the shore. *Trailered boats:* Launch at concrete public ramp at Sedgwick. The long dirt road to the house is steep and narrow in spots. *Sailboats:* 2 guest moorings and dock. Moorings are open to southwest winds; sailors may wish to go to Buck's Harbor in heavy weather. *Other:* Dinghy and canoe available. *Walk to:* No restaurants or groceries within walking distance; can boat to Buck's Harbor.
>
> *Address*   Herrick Rd., RR#1 Box 33A, Brooksville, ME 04617.
> (207) 359-5073.

Oakland House – Shore Oaks Seaside Inn
#100, Chart 13309, Herricks, Brooksville

This rustic resort was started by Jim Littlefield's great-grandparents in 1889, when steamboats brought guests to their landing. Today Jim and Sally, his wife, offer a waterfront inn, cottages, and a public dining room. The extensive wooded grounds include hiking trails and a lake. There is a half mile of shore frontage along Eggemoggin Reach with several wonderful pocket beaches, tide pools, and rock outcroppings. It feels a bit like summer camp for grown-ups.

Shore Oaks Seaside Inn was built as a Craftsman-style summer "cottage" in 1907; Jim and Sally have recently completed a tasteful restoration. Guest rooms are furnished with country oak and painted metal beds the Littlefields found stored on the property. The wraparound porch has some very inviting rockers. Jutting out over the waters of Eggemoggin Reach is a lovely gazebo. Views are to the west: Pumpkin Light, Cape Rosier, and the Camden Hills.

Simple log cabins built by Jim's father are scattered over the property and generally are available only by the week.

Meals   In high season (mid-June through August) a full breakfast and dinner are included in the room rate and served in the old hotel up the hill from the inn. Breakfast is made to order. Dinner entrees might include grilled swordfish, seared sea scallops, chargrilled boneless chicken breast, a New York strip sirloin, and a vegetarian option. There is a lobster picnic on the beach Thursday nights. Box lunches are available at an extra fee. In the off season, when the dining room is closed, a continental breakfast is served.

Rates   Shore Oaks Seaside Inn has 7 rooms with private baths, 3 with shared baths. The rate per person from June 15 through August, including breakfast and dinner, is $56-86 (MAP). Spring B&B rates for the inn are $51-74 for double occupancy rooms; fall B&B rates are $68-115. 15% gratuity extra. No credit cards. Children over 14 welcome. 2-night minimum on weekends in the inn. Open early May through October.

Access   *Kayaks:* Drive to one of a few different stone beaches on the property, some of which provide water access at all tides. There is also beach access to a lake. *Trailered boats:* Four wheel drive vehicles can launch small trailered boats at a dirt ramp on the property. Another option is the Sedgwick concrete public ramp. *Sailboats:* Several guest moorings. The Littlefields can have a rowboat meet you at a mooring if you call ahead. *Walk to:* No groceries within walking distance; can boat to Buck's Harbor.

Address   Herrick Rd., RR#1 Box 400, Brooksville, ME 04617.
(207) 359-8521, (800) 359-RELAX.

Eggemoggin Inn
#101, Chart 13309, Eggemoggin, Little Deer Isle

This former summer "cottage" was once part of a colony inhabited by wealthy Philadelphia families 100 years ago. It features a big wraparound porch full of rockers that afford occupants views of the Reach and the steep Deer Isle suspension bridge. I found the interior rather quirky and in need of some refurbishing, but the porch and proximity to the water nearly make up for it.

Breakfast   A continental or eggs-and-bacon breakfast available in the dining room at an extra charge.

Rates   1 room with private bath, 8 rooms with shared baths. $65-90 doubles from mid-June to late September. 15% gratuity extra. No credit cards. Children welcome. Guests may bring pets if kept in their car. 2-night minimum in July and August. Open Memorial Day to mid-October.

Access   *Kayaks:* Easy access to the water at any tide. It's a 30-foot carry from the car to the beach, with just five steps down. *Trailered boats:* Use nearby community launch or launch in Sedgwick or Brooklin. *Sailboats:* 2 moorings available. *Walk to:* No restaurants or groceries within easy walking distance.

Address   RFD Box 324, Little Deer Isle, ME 04650.
(207) 348-2540.

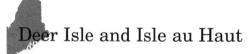

Deer Isle and Isle au Haut

ON SHORE

Deer Isle remained isolated until the completion of the suspension bridge in 1939. It still feels refreshingly detached from the mainland. The pace of life seems to get slower as the roads get narrower. The island is nearly an hour's drive from Route 1, so it is skipped by tourists hurrying to Bar Harbor. Some of the lodgings are concentrated in the towns of Deer Isle and Stonington; others are scattered in rural communities with such wonderfully evocative names as Oceanville and Sunset.

On the western part of Deer Isle, the Nature Conservancy has two lovely holdings that can be reached on foot. Barred Island overlooks Penobscot Bay. It can be accessed at lower tides by crossing a sand bar; trails to it begin at the entrance to Goose Cove Lodge in Sunset. Crockett Cove Woods, in Burnt Cove, has trails through dense ferns and erratic boulders in a coastal fog forest.

Town of Deer Isle

The town of Deer Isle lies at the midpoint of the island at Northwest Harbor. Several galleries display the work of area artists and craftspeople.

Stonington

Until a few years ago, Stonington was accurately described as an "unspoiled fishing village." It still possesses an active working waterfront in the tradition of down east Maine. There are many boats in the harbor, and most belong to fishermen. But times are changing, and shops and galleries have moved into vacant storefronts in response to the rising number of visitors arriving by car and windjammer. It remains a delightful place to visit nevertheless. The islands of Merchant Row still cluster just off shore, and the fog still settles in to remind you of the fickleness of Maine weather.

Isle au Haut

The mountains of Isle au Haut rise high above the neighboring Merchant Row islands, making it easy to pick out from a distance. Over half of the island's wooded land is held by Acadia National Park. Miles of marked hiking trails follow the rumbling popplestone beaches and forested ridge lines of this magnificent retreat.

Isle au Haut is 5 miles from the mainland, and home to 70 year-round residents. In summer, the mailboat from Stonington can drop day visitors off at the village or at Duck Harbor, where there is better access to the park. Since park day visitors are limited to 50, when you find the perfect scenic overlook, you'll have the company of just those you brought with you.

OFF SHORE

The Deer Isle archipelago has been sparking the imagination of small boaters for years. Many islands are round, ringed with granite, and covered with evergreen forests or wildflower meadows: the classic Maine island for some. Others bear the scars of quarrying, with discarded granite chunks heaped along their shores. Boaters sometimes smell the banks of island roses before they see them. The islands of this region are numerous, and many are available for careful visits.

Kayakers in particular are drawn to this area, with its nearly infinite choices of paddling routes and the partial shelter from prevailing winds provided by the archipelago. Because of island density and the likelihood of fog, competence with a chart and compass is essential for all boaters visiting the area.

There are more Bureau of Parks and Lands (BP&L) islands in this region than in any other region on the coast of Maine. Heading from west to east near Stonington, boaters will encounter Weir (just off shore and 1/2 mile northwest of Moose), Steves (west of Wreck), Harbor, Wheat, Hell's Half Acre (northwest of Devil), and Little Sheep. Potato lies east of Stinson Neck, and Apple is located in Fish Creek a mile northwest of Campbell Island. With the exception of Harbor, which is several acres in size, these BP&L islands are small beauties. Harbor Island has room for wildflower meadows as well as woods. Some BP&L islands have started showing the signs of increased visitation, so walk gently to leave no trace of your visit. Campers should steer away from Steves, Harbor, Wheat, and Hell's Half Acre, as they receive a high number of overnight visitors.

The Nature Conservancy has three wonderful islands in Merchant Row available for day visits. Wreck Island has a lovely beach and meadows, and nearby Round is wooded. Millet is covered with spruce and fir trees, and ringed with granite. To protect wildlife, no pets are permitted ashore. Fires are discouraged and must be built below the high tide line.

While you're out boating you might want to pass near Crotch Island to view the renewed quarrying operations. There is still call for the fine granite that was used extensively in the construction of major public buildings, bridges, and monuments one hundred years ago.

Boaters can come ashore on the cobble beach at Acadia National Park's Duck Harbor on Isle au Haut. Hiking trails radiate out from the harbor. You can approach nearby Western Ear by boat, or walk to it at low tide from Western Head. No fires are permitted on Western Ear.

REGIONAL ACCESS

Launch area with overnight parking

STONINGTON: Kayakers can use the *town recreational dock* to launch boats off the fairly high float; water at all tides. The town recreational dock is toward the eastern side of the harbor, near Bartlett's Market. Do not use the large dock for working boats further to the west. Closest overnight parking will be on Seabreeze Avenue at the *Isle au Haut Co.* (367-5193 or 367-6516) when it opens its new parking facility (planned for June, 1997); some of the parking will be inside an old cannery building. Away from the water, there is a *town lot* on a diagonal from Connie's Restaurant on Route 15A, beyond the ball field and on the left as you head toward Burnt Cove. To reach *Steve's Parking* (367-5548), take a left 1/4 mile past Connie's Restaurant onto Weedfield Road. Steve's can shuttle you back to the dock.

NOTE: The Stonington recreational dock can get very congested. Leave room for others, particularly when you're packing and unpacking gear.

Ferry service

The Isle au Haut Co. (367-5193 or 367-6516) can carry kayaks to or from Stonington on its mailboat in a pinch.

Public moorings

STONINGTON: *Billings Marine* (367-2328) on Moose Island, just west of town, has rental moorings that can be reserved in advance. They also have dock space.

LODGINGS

Pilgrim's Inn
#102, Chart 13305, Northwest Harbor, Deer Isle

This Greek Revival structure was built in sections in Newburyport, Massachusetts and shipped to Deer Isle in 1793. Owners Jean and Dud Hendrick have furnished the spacious rooms with simple, comfortable antiques and spread rugs over the wide pumpkin pine floorboards, giving their inn a colonial feeling. Carefully chosen regional art, along with prints by Winslow Homer and the Wyeths, complement the furnishings. Baths feature locally quarried granite. Common spaces include a game room, a library, and two rooms with eight-foot-wide hearths.

Outside are gardens where the Hendricks grow their herbs and vegetables. There's a small house next to the inn with two housekeeping units; the deck overlooks the mill pond and Northwest Harbor. Mountain bikes are available to guests.

Meals   Both breakfast and dinner are included in the room rate. Meals are served in a rustic converted barn that is attached to the inn. The full breakfast utilizes local products and offers a choice of two creative entrees. Dinner is open to the public by reservation. Hors d'oeuvres might include a tortilla with black beans or a lamb, feta cheese, and eggplant pizza. The single entree dinner could be a seafood ragout, Deer Isle farm-raised chicken, or North Atlantic salmon. (They are happy to accommodate vegetarians and those with dietary restrictions.)

Rates   10 guest rooms with private baths, 2 with shared bath. $160-185 for 2 people, MAP rate, in July and August, plus 15% gratuity. The MAP rate for two in the housekeeping units is $215. Visa and MC. Children over 10 welcome. Dog in residence. Open mid-May to mid-October.

Access   *Kayaks:* Launch next to the road a few hundred feet west of the inn and bring cars back to the inn; mudflats are likely at low tides. Kayakers paddling to the inn can approach the inn property directly at mid-tide and higher. Dud has kayaking experience and can offer insights about area paddling. *Trailered boats:* Launch from the nearby dirt ramp with four wheel drive, and return vehicle to the inn. *Sailboats:* The Hendricks will pick up sailors from Billings Marine in Stonington. *Walk to:* Market, galleries.

Address   Deer Isle, ME 04627.
(207) 348-6615.

Deer Isle Village Inn
#103, Chart 13305, Northwest Harbor, Deer Isle

Hosts Bobbie and Paul Zierk have run this homey B&B at the head of the harbor for the past several years. Bobbie describes it as the kind of place "where you can put your feet up." The screened front porch provides a fine place to watch the sun set over the water. Ask for the room with the unique hand-crafted twig bed and desk.

Breakfast	Fruit cup, a hot dish, and homemade coffee cake.
Rates	4 rooms with shared baths. $60 doubles. No credit cards. Children over 12 welcome. Open year round.
Access	*Kayaks:* Can be carried a couple hundred yards down the lawn and across Route 15 to the water, at half tide and higher. A quarter mile to the west is a dirt ramp, with water the majority of the tide. Bring your car back to the inn as there is no parking at the ramp. *Trailered boats:* Use the local ramp; a four wheel drive vehicle is preferable. *Walk to:* Restaurants, market, galleries.
Address	P.O. Box 456, Deer Isle, ME 04627. (207) 348-2564.

Goose Cove Lodge
#104, Charts 13305 & 13313, Stinson Point, Sunset

Goose Cove Lodge provides a rustic get-away with plenty of amenities, including comfortable lodgings and fine dining. The seascape here is very much part of your stay. The view from the dining room and many of the cottages and rooms is of the open ocean. The property slopes down to a 400-foot shoreline with a cobblestone beach and a fragrant bank of rugosa roses. There are nature trails on the property leading to the Nature Conservancy's lovely Barred Island, which you can walk to at low tide. The innkeepers, Joanne and Dom Parisi, are active volunteers with the Island Heritage Trust, which helps manage the preserve. The resort welcomes guests of all ages, and offers children's programs.

Lodging choices include cottages tucked into the evergreens or rooms in and near the main lodge. The recently remodeled cottages feature living rooms, kitchenettes, fireplaces, and decks. Most rooms near the lodge have shared decks and either a fireplace or a wood stove. The main building has a large library. There is a celestial telescope for viewing planets on clear nights.

Meals	Breakfast and dinner are included during the high season. Dinner is optional off-season, but from what I heard you shouldn't miss it. At breakfast there is a hearty buffet, with a couple of hot entrees such

as frittatas or brioche with cheese, as well as bread, scones, ham, and so forth. There are two seatings for dinner, with children eating earlier. The four-course dinners emphasize seafood, and include a primary appetizer and entree. Vegetarian options are available.

Rates 13 cottages, 12 rooms and suites, all with private baths. $85-130 MAP rate (includes breakfast and dinner) per adult late June to early September. $94-170 off-season B&B rate for double occupancy rooms. Visa, MC, Amex. No smoking in main lodge or on nature trails; smoking permitted in guest rooms. Children welcome. Owners' cats in lodge. 1-week minimum reservations for most rooms in July and August, unless space is available; 2-night minimum other times. Open mid-May to mid-October.

Access *Kayaks:* Drive boats down to the beach, where it is an easy launch at any tide. *Trailered boats:* Small boats can be launched from the beach using four wheel drive vehicles. *Sailboats:* Guest moorings. *Other:* Guests may borrow single and double Keowee kayaks and canoes, and a sailboat can be rented. *Walk to:* No groceries within walking distance.

Address P.O. Box 40, Sunset, ME 04680.
(207) 348-2508.

Burnt Cove Bed & Breakfast
#105, Charts 13305 & 13313, Burnt Cove, West Stonington

Host Diane Berlew has decorated her airy contemporary home with several paintings of the nearby Brooksville hills and primitive statues from her stint in the Peace Corps. The living room's cathedral ceiling and tall picture windows, a second-floor interior balcony, and an inviting deck all let you keep an eye on the working harbor. You might spot the lobster boat belonging to Diane's husband, Bob Williams. His family has lived in Burnt Cove for several generations. Diane has worked the stern of his boat, so either of them can fill you in on lobstering.

The Nature Conservancy's Crockett Cove Woods Preserve is a short walk from the B&B.

Breakfast Homemade continental of fruit, muffins, bread, and granola.
Rates 1 room with private bath, 2 with shared bath. $60-85 doubles. Rooms can accommodate 3-4 people. Visa, MC. Children over 12 welcome. Cat in residence. Open May through October.
Access *Kayaks:* Put in at Bob's launch area just across the road, within 200 yards of the house; water at most tides. There is an alternate put-in 100 yards further along for use at low tide. *Trailered boats:* Small trailered boats can be launched at Bob's unpaved launch area.

Sailboats: Two moorings. *Walk to:* Full grocery store 1/4 mile away. Hosts can give you a lift to town for dinner.

Address Whitman Rd., RFD#1 Box 2905, Burnt Cove, Stonington, ME 04681. (207) 367-2392.

Island House

#106, Charts 13305 & 13313, Stonington

While the Island House does not provide access to the water, its hilltop location provides some exceptional vistas of the islands surrounding Deer Isle. Walking about in this 1988 redwood contemporary, you almost feel that you're in an immaculate tree house. Your view is of treetops, water, and islands; there are no other dwellings sharing the summit. All but one of the bedrooms are quite spacious, and the exception provides the most outstanding view. "The Lookout," a delightful guest room at the top of a spiral staircase, offers a captain's watch/bedroom with a platform bed situated so that you can view the entire horizon. Since there are windows running around the perimeter of the room, you have unobstructed views of Penobscot Bay, Blue Hill, Mount Desert Island, and the Camden Hills. And from the 14' by 75' deck there's a grand view of Isle au Haut on a clear day.

A stay at the Island House would be a luxurious way to begin or end a camping or sailing trip. The light and airy rooms are casually elegant, with modern furnishings. The huge baths would be especially appreciated by salt-encrusted boaters. The common room has several distinct seating areas, so you can mingle or not with other guests over evening refreshments.

Innkeeper Rebecca Cennamo is interested in creating a "quiet ambiance" for people who love the natural world. Ask her to show you the medicine circle carved into the rocky summit. The grounds include an outdoor hot tub and a pond that attracts blue herons. A trail leads to a local sand beach.

The hosts will do guest laundry, water supply permitting.

Breakfast There's a continental breakfast for early risers, followed by a full healthful breakfast.

Rates 5 rooms with private baths. $110-150 doubles July and August. Also a two-bedroom guest house with partially stocked kitchen, $150-300 depending on the number of guests. Visa, MC, Amex. Guest house is wheelchair accessible. Children welcome. Guest pets may be accepted. Open June through September.

Access *Kayaks:* Launch at town recreational dock, with high float. *Trailered boats:* Closest ramps with parking are in Sedgwick (concrete) and Brooklin (unpaved). *Sailboats:* Rebecca will pick up sailors at Billings Marine. *Walk to:* 1 mile to restaurant, 1.5 miles to grocery store.

Address   Weedfield Rd., RFD#1 Box 3227, Stonington, ME 04681.
(207) 367-5900.

Pres du Port
#107, Charts 13305 & 13313, Stonington

"Pres du Port" is French for "Near the Harbor," and Charlotte Casgrain's home is, with views of the working waterfront from the large sun room and second-story deck. Charlotte, a retired French teacher, converted her summer home into a B&B twelve years ago. Rooms are cheerfully decorated, with bold colors and murals on the walls.

Breakfast   Buffet, with cereal, yogurt, bread or muffins, and fresh fruit.
Rates   1 efficiency with private bath, 2 rooms with shared baths. $75 doubles July and August. No credit cards. Smoking allowed in sun room, not in guest rooms. Children generally welcome. Cat in residence. 2-night minimum on weekends. Open mid-June to mid-October.
Access   *Kayaks:* Two nearby launching choices, in addition to the town recreational dock. Guests have permission to access the shore 200 feet away, over adjacent property and down 10 steps to ledge; good at some tides. Another option is a public right-of-way 500 feet west of the B&B, with access at all tides; unload boats and then move cars back to the B&B, as there is no parking at the right-of-way. *Sailboats:* Billings Marine is less than a mile away. *Walk to:* Restaurants, markets, shops.
Address   West Main St. and Highland Ave., P.O. Box 319, Stonington, ME 04681.
(207) 367-5007.

Boyce's Motel
#108, Charts 13305 & 13313, Stonington

This well-kept motel in the middle of town offers pleasant rooms at reasonable rates. Some units include kitchen facilities and living rooms; one has a washer and dryer. The window boxes are full of flowers. A small deck for motel guests is situated across the street on the harbor.

Breakfast   Not provided.
Rates   11 motel rooms. $40-85 mid-June to late September. Visa, MC, Amex, Discover. Some non-smoking rooms. Children welcome. Pets welcome. Open year round.

Access *Kayaks:* The town recreational dock, with an 18-inch-high float, is 500 feet away. *Trailered boats:* Closest ramps with parking are in Sedgwick (concrete) and Brooklin (unpaved). *Sailboats:* Billings Marine is 1 mile away. *Walk to:* Restaurants, markets, shops.

Address Main St., P.O. Box 94, Stonington, ME 04681.
(207) 367-2421, (800) 224-2421.

Inn on the Harbor
#109, Charts 13305 & 13313, Stonington

Past visitors to Stonington might remember the Captain's Quarters on Main Street. Under the energetic new ownership of Christina Shipps, it has been extensively remodeled and become the Inn on the Harbor. The guest rooms that face the ocean come complete with binoculars. There's a large deck right on the water that entices guests to sit and watch the return of Stonington's large fleet of fishing boats. Deck loungers can sip a cafe latte from the inn's afternoon espresso bar.

A caution to light sleepers: most rooms are situated directly on the town's busiest street.

Breakfast Cereal, muffins, and homemade bread.
Rates 13 rooms with private baths. $100-125 doubles. Visa, MC, Amex. One wheelchair-accessible unit. Children over 12 welcome. Open April through December.
Access *Kayaks:* The town recreational dock, with an 18-inch-high float, is 500 feet away. There is no on-site parking at the inn; guests park cars on the street or in a nearby town lot. Inn-to-inn paddlers should call in advance to arrange kayak storage, as there is limited space to leave boats on the property. *Sailboats:* A guest mooring is available; additional moorings can be obtained at Billings Marine, 1 mile away. *Walk to:* Restaurants, markets, shops.
Address Main St., P.O. Box 69, Stonington, ME 04681.
(207) 367-2420, (800) 942-2420.

Ocean View House
#110, Charts 13305 & 13313, Staple Point, Stonington

The delightful cupola on the Ocean View House is original to the inn, and affords an outstanding view of the town, the harbor, and the islands beyond. Other architectural elements of note in this 110-year-old building are flooring of alternating dark and light woods, as you'd find on a ship, and tin ceilings. Previous occupants have included quarry workers and a schooner captain. Today's guest rooms feature furniture restored by the innkeepers and attractive quilts. The friendly hosts, Christine and Jack Custer, report that they have a number of kayakers and sailors stay with them. Guests should allow time to look over the old local maps and photographs in the comfortable living room.

Breakfast	Christine specializes in baked goods such as quiche, tarts, French oven pancakes, and coffee cake.
Rates	8 rooms sharing 2 full baths. $60 doubles. No credit cards. Smoking limited to common rooms. Children welcome. Open last week of June through August.
Access	*Kayaks:* The town recreational dock, with an 18-inch-high float, is 200 yards away. The Custers have had guests arrive by kayak and carry their boats up to the inn. *Trailered boats:* Closest ramps with parking are in Sedgwick (concrete) and Brooklin (unpaved). *Sailboats:* The innkeepers will pick up sailors at Billings Marine, 1 mile away. *Walk to:* Restaurants, markets, shops.
Address	Corner of Main St. and Sea Breeze Ave., P.O. Box 261, Stonington, ME 04681. (207) 367-5114.

The Keeper's House
#111, Charts 13305 & 13313, Robinson Point, Isle au Haut

This B&B is particularly easy to spot from the water, since Robinson Light, an active lighthouse, is on the grounds. The keeper's quarters were unoccupied for many years before Jeff and Judi Burke converted them into a B&B in 1986. The Burkes offer guests a special get-away on this remote six-mile-long island. Rustic accommodations are provided in bright and airy rooms, many of which have grand views looking west toward the Camden Hills. Kerosene lamps and candles are the evening light sources, and the Burkes cook using gas and a generator.

A path from the property links into the extensive Acadia National Park trail system. Guests can borrow single-speed bikes to ride on the island's dirt roads.

Meals	Three meals a day are included in the room rate. Breakfast might feature homemade granola, fruit, and lemon pancakes. A box lunch is provided. Dinner is a set entree; the Burkes are happy to cater to dietary restrictions. The entree is often a seafood dish, with chicken once or twice a week, and lobster on Sundays.
Rates	Four rooms in the main house, plus 2 in outbuildings. All rooms share baths. $250-285 for two, including 3 meals a day. No credit cards. Children welcome. A dog in residence. 2-night minimum stays. Open May through October.

Access	*Kayaks:* This trip is not recommended for inexperienced kayakers, as the paddle from Stonington is at least six miles and the waters can become quite rough. Kayakers can paddle up to the Burkes' float, which is in the water most of the season. The Isle au Haut Co. will carry kayaks as freight if necessary. *Sailboats:* Contact Payson Barter at 335-2151 to request a mooring in the harbor 1 mile away. Jeff can pick up sailors there. *Walk to:* Limited groceries near the town landing.
Address	P.O. Box 26, Isle au Haut, ME 04645.
	(207) 367-2261 (off-island number).

Oceanville Seaside Bed & Breakfast
#112, Charts 13313 & 13316, Oceanville

Two seasoned sea kayakers, Kathy and Tim Emerson, are the hosts at this cozy B&B just off the Deer Isle Thoroughfare. Their 1850's saltwater farmhouse still has its original tin ceilings and wide floorboards. From the living room and screened porch you can look out on the water and beyond, to the mountains of Mount Desert Island. There's a second-floor suite that's ideal for a family or group of friends.

Kathy and Tim are quite familiar with the wonderful wild islands in the area; in fact, Tim's family owns one a short paddle from the house. His parents were the first to place a privately owned island on the Maine Island Trail.

Meals	A full breakfast is included and might feature an eggs Florentine souffle. Kathy may be able to serve dinner to hungry boaters by prior arrangement, or the Emersons can provide transportation to a restaurant.
Rates	1 suite with private bath, 1 room with shared bath. $65 double with shared bath, $80 for 2 in suite, mid-June to mid-October. No credit cards. Children over 5 welcome. Dog in residence. Guests may bring dogs that will stay outdoors; there is a dog pen. Open year round by reservation.
Access	*Kayaks:* Carry 50 feet down a nicely sloped ledge at any tide; there is also access from a beach at high tide. *Trailered boats:* Launch from the ledge using a four wheel drive vehicle. *Sailboats:* Deepwater mooring and dock. *Walk to:* No restaurants or groceries nearby.
Address	Fire Lane 32, Oceanville, ME. Mail: RR#1, Box 890, Stonington, ME 04681.
	(207) 367-2226.

The Inn at Ferry Landing
#113, Charts 13309 & 13316, North Deer Isle

This 1840's farmhouse sits right on Eggemoggin Reach, and the living room and new deck provide panoramic views of sunrises as well as sunsets on the Reach. Spacious living and guest rooms are filled with antiques and oriental carpets, for elegant yet comfortable surroundings. Host Jean Wheeler is a sailor who enjoys welcoming boaters and cyclists to the inn; her husband, Gerald, is a professional musician in nearby Blue Hill.

Breakfast Homemade coffee cake, blueberry pancakes, and omelets are among the staples.

Rates 4 rooms with private baths. $95-125 from Memorial Day to mid-October. A two-bedroom annex may be available for stays of 3 nights or more. Visa. Children over 10 in main house, children of any age welcome in annex. Dog in residence. Open year round.

Access *Kayaks:* Very convenient access to a stone beach 50 feet from the house; water at any tide. *Trailered boats:* Use four wheel drive to launch from the adjacent gravel right-of-way and return vehicle to inn grounds. *Sailboats:* Can anchor nearby until the Wheelers get a guest mooring. *Walk to:* Nearest restaurant is 2 miles away; can boat to it.

Address Old Ferry Rd., RR#1 Box 163, Deer Isle, ME 04627. (207) 348-7760.

CAMPGROUNDS

Duck Harbor Campground, Acadia National Park
#C15, Charts 13303, 13305 & 13313, Duck Harbor, Isle au Haut

Duck Harbor is located near the southern end of Isle au Haut, in a dramatic off-shore section of Acadia National Park. (Isle au Haut can be reached only by the mailboat from Stonington or by private boat.) There are 5 three-sided shelters in the trees near the harbor; each shelter will hold up to six people. Tents can be used only inside the shelters. The shelters don't provide a water view, but there are nice sunning rocks by the water just 50 yards away. There's a cobble beach and an extensive network of hiking trails.

It is essential to have a reservation before heading out, as sites often fill up in summer. Check in with the ranger when you arrive.

Campsites   5 sites with shelters. Chemical toilets. Water pump 300 yards from the campsites. Visitors are required to pack out their trash.

Rates   From June 15 to September 15, it is $25 per shelter for up to three nights. The rest of the season it is $25 for up to five nights. To obtain reservations, request a Special Use Permit in person at park headquarters or by mail. Mail requests to: Isle au Haut Reservations, Acadia National Park, P.O. Box 177, Bar Harbor, ME 04609. Requests must be postmarked April 1st or later. Enclose a nonrefundable check with mail reservation requests. No telephone reservations. No pets. Campground open May 15 to October 12.

Access   *Kayaks:* This trip is not recommended for inexperienced paddlers, as the paddle from Stonington is 10 miles and the waters can be quite rough in exposed sections. Land kayaks on cobble beach past the dock. The mailboat can carry kayaks if the weather turns bad. *Sailboats:* Can anchor in cove and bring dinghy over to dock.

Address: Isle au Haut, ME. Mail: Acadia National Park, P.O. Box 177, Bar Harbor, ME 04609.
(207) 288-3338.

Sunshine Campground
#C16, Charts 13313 & 13316, Conary Cove, Sunshine

This pleasant little campground on Deer Isle is near the village of Sunshine. All the sites are wooded; some have tent platforms tucked further back from the campground loop for more privacy. There is no water access from the sites, but the helpful owners can direct kayakers to a nearby put-in. Playground.

Campsites   22 sites, with 7 designated for tents. No waterfront sites. 50% tenters. Showers and flush toilets. Small recreation room with ping pong and magazines. Laundry. Camp store.

Rates $12 tent sites. Visa, MC. No personal checks. Pets permitted. Open Memorial Day to October 15.

Access   *Kayaks:* The owners, the Rices, can point out a launch spot into Conary Cove within 300 yards of the campground; drop off boats and bring car back to campground. Access is an hour or so either side of high tide, otherwise it is mud. Water access at all tides at the Stonington town dock. *Trailered boats:* Closest launches with parking are in Sedgwick (concrete) and Brooklin (unpaved).

Address   RR#1 Box 521D, Deer Isle, ME 04627.
(207) 348-6681.

Western Blue Hill Bay: Brooklin to Surry

ON SHORE

Brooklin

Toward the eastern end of Eggemoggin Reach is the campus of the WoodenBoat School (Naskeag Rd., 359-4651). Boaters will spot it northeast of Babson Island; they can borrow a mooring or bring kayaks ashore. It's fun to walk by workshops and see students engaged in traditional and modern boatbuilding classes. There is a great library with more sailing periodicals than you can imagine, published in a number of different languages. Reference books are available to the public during business hours.

Blue Hill

Blue Hill has been a magnet for musicians, artists, and craftspeople for years. Visitors can attend classical music concerts at Kneisel Hall (374-2811) or hear nationally known folk artists at the Left Bank Cafe (374-2201). Artisans display their work in galleries in and around Blue Hill. There's an abundance of fine restaurants and markets, including the Blue Hill Food Co-op (374-2165) on the eastern side of town. Hikers will enjoy the trail to the fire tower on the town's namesake, located two miles to the north.

OFF SHORE

Two little BP&L islands are a short hop from the Naskeag Point launch ramp. Little Hog, just east of Hog Island, and Sellars Island are open to visitors. Weekend campers may find the few camping spots occupied on these small islands, so they should have alternate destinations in mind when planning trips to Little Hog or Sellars.

REGIONAL ACCESS

Launch ramp with overnight parking

BROOKLIN: *WoodenBoat School* (Naskeag Rd., 359-4651) has a dirt ramp suitable for kayaks or trailered boats launched with a four wheel drive vehicle; water at all tides. Check with a member of the staff before launching, to determine where you should leave your car.

Public moorings

BROOKLIN: *WoodenBoat School* (Naskeag Rd., 359-4651) has moorings for rent on a first come, first served basis.

LODGINGS

The Lookout
#114, Chart 13316, Flye Point, North Brooklin

The Lookout sits right at the tip of Flye Point in Blue Hill Bay. It was built in the late 18th century by innkeeper Butch Smith's ancestors; members of his family have welcomed guests for the past 100 years. The inn sits on a rise with vegetable gardens and meadows sweeping down to the water's edge. There is a pleasant beach, and at low tide you can walk out the bar toward Flye Island. The attractive dining room serves meals to the public. Guest rooms are located upstairs. Several rustic cabins are rented by the week in high season; they may be available off peak for shorter stays.

Meals	A full breakfast is included in the inn room rates. Specialties include buttermilk blueberry pancakes or raisin bread French toast. Butch says the dinners utilize "fine ingredients, served simply," such as local seafood and red meats. There is an extensive wine list.
Rates	11 rooms with shared baths in the inn. $70-95 doubles in July and August. Visa, MC, Amex, Discover. Children welcome. Cats in common areas. Open April through October; dinner available Memorial Day to Columbus Day.
Access	*Kayaks:* Launch from a nice beach at any tide. You can drive down to it and drop off boats, as it is 300 yards from the inn. The beach is located north of the bar to Flye Island. *Trailered boats:* Launch off the ledge by the beach or from the hard-packed dirt ramps at the WoodenBoat School or Naskeag Point. *Sailboats:* Guests have anchored on the Blue Hill Bay side of the point. *Walk to:* No groceries nearby.
Address	HCR64 Box 4025, Flye Point, North Brooklin, ME 04616. (207) 359-2188.

The Blue Hill Inn
#115, Chart 13316, Blue Hill

A stay at the Blue Hill Inn puts you in the midst of the fine galleries, music venues, and restaurants for which the town is noted. Housed in a classic white clapboard building, the inn has been in operation since 1840. Very attractive period antiques fill the rooms and contribute to the elegant yet inviting atmosphere. Guest rooms feature large antique headboards; several have sitting areas or fireplaces. Original wide wood floorboards are in evidence throughout the inn.

Meals Both breakfast and dinner are generally included in the room rate. At breakfast, selections might include omelets with your choice of cheese and filling, or waffles with strawberries or sauteed apples. Dinner is served Wednesday through Sunday nights. It starts with hors d'oeuvres in the parlor by the fireplace. Five courses of French cuisine, with 2 entree choices, are served by candlelight in the dining room. Local produce, fish, and baked goods are featured, and dietary restrictions can be accommodated. There are 140 entries on the wine list.

Rates 11 rooms with private baths. $160-220 for two people with breakfast and dinner (MAP rate) from July through October. Rates are reduced by $20 per person on nights when dinner is not served or if guests choose to dine elsewhere. 15% gratuity extra. Visa, MC. Two rooms can accommodate a child. 2-night minimum in high season. Open mid-May through October.

Access *Kayaks and trailered boats:* Launch at the concrete public ramp 2/10 mile downhill from the inn; water at mid-tide and higher. *Sailboats:* The inn will arrange transportation for sailors from the Kollegewidgwok Yacht Club in Blue Hill (374-5581) or Buck's Harbor Marine (326-8829). *Walk to:* Restaurants, cafes, markets, food co-op, galleries, shops.

Address Union St., P.O. Box 403, Blue Hill, ME 04614. (207) 374-2844.

Surry Inn

#116, Chart 13316, Contention Cove, Surry.

The Surry Inn is so accustomed to welcoming boaters that they've placed a sign at the water's edge as well as along the road. The inn is noted for its dining room's fine French cuisine. Guest rooms are available in the main inn and in an annex nearer the water. Rooms are simply furnished with country oak antiques, chenille spreads, and stenciled walls. There are large stone hearths in both the water-view dining room and the living room. The games and puzzles set out in the living room invite you to settle into a comfortable sofa.

Meals A full breakfast with choice of entrees is included. Dinner is available and features French food prepared with local produce and seafood.

Rates 11 rooms with private baths, 2 with shared bath. $68-72 doubles from mid-July through August. 12% gratuity additional. Visa, MC, Discover. Children over 5 welcome. Open year round.

Access *Kayaks:* Easy carry 100 yards down a sloping lawn directly onto the beach; water at all tides. *Trailered boats:* Concrete town ramp 2 miles away in Surry. *Sailboats:* Innkeeper Peter Krinsky says sailors frequently anchor in the sheltered cove. *Other:* Canoe and rowboat for guests. *Walk to:* No groceries nearby.

Address Route 172, P.O. Box 25, Surry, ME 04684.
(207) 667-5091.

CAMPGROUND

The Gatherings Family Campground
#C17, Chart 13316, Contention Cove, East Surry

A family-oriented campground with mostly wooded, private sites. 1300-foot shoreline along Patten Bay. Swimming beach for the hardy. Playground. A quiet spot, but an easy drive to Ellsworth and on to Mount Desert Island.

Campsites 110 sites, of which 50 are suitable for tents. 23 waterfront. 25% tenters. Showers and flush toilets, wheelchair accessible. Large recreation room with pool tables and a few video games. Laundry. Groceries and snack bar.

Rates $13-25 tent sites. Visa, MC. Pets permitted. Open May 1 to October 15.

Access *Kayaks:* Launch at any tide from the beach, by climbing over a couple of rocks to reach the stone shore. *Trailered boats:* Launch at hard-surfaced ramps at Ellsworth or Surry. *Sailboats:* Rental moorings. *Walk to:* Surry Inn for dinner, 1/4 mile away.

Address Route 172, RFD#3 Box 69, Ellsworth, ME 04605.
(207) 667-8826.

Swan's Island

ON SHORE

Swan's is a large island of three separate communities: Atlantic on the north side, and the villages of Swan's Island and Minturn on either side of Burnt Coat Harbor on the south. Burnt Coat Harbor, lined with wharves and lobster gear, seems the epitome of down east Maine. The island's richly indented shoreline includes some marvelous sand and cobblestone beaches. You can observe the island's quiet beauty on foot or on a bicycle; some of the roads are paved. Island residents make you feel at home, waving as they drive by. Four hundred people call Swan's Island home year round.

There is frequent car ferry service to and from Bass Harbor on Mount Desert Island.

OFF SHORE

Small boaters should carefully assess their skills, equipment, and the weather before setting out across the open water to Swan's. The lodgings are on the southern end of the island, and the distance from mainland put-ins to Burnt Coat Harbor is at least 10 miles.

In addition to exploring the coves and harbors of Swan's itself, there is a little BP&L island to visit. Hen lies less than a half mile south of Buckle Island on the west side of Swan's. Watch your step; there is poison ivy.

REGIONAL ACCESS

Mainland launch areas with overnight parking

If you want to leave your vehicle on the mainland, options include the WoodenBoat School (see page 149), the town recreational dock in Stonington (see page 138), or the town dock and ferry parking lot at Bass Harbor. Of these three options, the WoodenBoat School is the only one with a ramp for trailered boats.

Ferry service

There is frequent car ferry service from Bass Harbor to the village of Atlantic on the north side of Swan's Island. The ferry will not take hand-carried kayaks. Call the Maine State Ferry Service at 624-7777 for general schedule information or 244-3254 for the Bass Harbor terminal.

LODGINGS

Jeannie's Place Bed & Breakfast
#117, Chart 13313, Burnt Coat Harbor, Swan's Island

Jeannie Joyce and her husband, Llewellyn, have been cheerfully welcoming boaters into their home for over ten years. Jeannie is an unabashed booster of their community and Llewellyn is a fifth generation Swan's Island lobsterman. Jeannie warned me that once you arrive and discover the island's peaceful nature, you won't want to leave.

Jeannie's "place" is a comfortable family home overlooking Burnt Coat Harbor's wharves and fleet of lobster boats. Inside, the rooms are simply and comfortably furnished, and guests are welcome to join their hosts in the living room or the kitchen. Outside, the deck provides a wonderful place to relax in the midday sun and admire the harbor.

Breakfast   A full breakfast, such as bacon and eggs or pancakes.
Rates   3 rooms with shared bath. $45 doubles, $35 singles. No credit cards. No drinking. Children welcome. Open year round.
Access   *Kayaks:* Kayakers can ask to launch and land their boats at the Fisherman's Co-op just south of Jeannie's house. The trip over from the mainland is for experienced paddlers only; less seasoned paddlers should come over on the ferry. *Sailboats:* Contact Kevin Staples at 526-4207 to rent a mooring. *Walk to:* Restaurant. There are groceries across the harbor in Minturn, accessible by boat or by getting a lift.
Address   P.O. Box 125, Swan's Island, ME 04685.
(207) 526-4116.

Harbor Watch Motel
#118, Chart 13313, Minturn, Swan's Island

On my trip to Swan's Island, I didn't get a chance to visit this motel, but I'm told it provides comfortable motel units in the village of Minturn. One unit is set up as an efficiency. Paul Stockbridge also manages cottages that are sometimes available as short-term rentals.

Breakfast   Not provided.
Rates   4 motel units. $50-70 doubles. No credit cards. Smoking permitted. Children welcome. Pets welcome. Open May through October.
Access   *Kayaks:* Kayakers can come in at the public float at Burnt Cove

Harbor across from Minturn or at the Mackerel Cove public float next to the ferry landing on the north side of the island. Paul can pick up boaters and give them a ride the 2 or 3 miles to the motel, as well as help kayakers find a place to store their boats. The trip over from the mainland is for experienced paddlers only; less seasoned paddlers should come over on the ferry. *Sailboats:* Call Kevin Staples on 526-4207 to rent a mooring in Burnt Cove Harbor, or anchor at Mackerel Cove. *Walk to:* General store close by for lunch or supplies. Boat or get a ride to the restaurant across the harbor or the one by the ferry landing.

Address   P.O. Box 114, Swan's Island, ME 04685.
(207) 526-4445.

THERE IS A SPECIAL DRAMA

to the ocean viewed from the top of a mountain, and to mountains viewed from the ocean. Visitors to Mount Desert Island get to experience this drama time and time again.

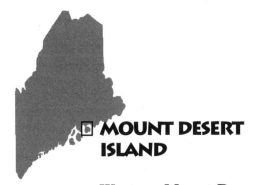

MOUNT DESERT ISLAND

Western Mount Desert Island: Bass Harbor, Southwest Harbor, and Somesville

ON SHORE

Mount Desert Island and Acadia National Park

There is a special drama to the ocean viewed from the top of a mountain, and to mountains viewed from the ocean. Visitors to Mount Desert Island get to experience this drama time and time again. They can thank the foresight of some wealthy Bar Harbor rusticators who donated large tracts of land to start Acadia National Park (288-3338). The park today covers nearly half the island. Hiking trails to summits and along water abound, and there are 50 miles of carriage trails. (The latter were built to provide the drivers of horse-drawn carriages a place to ride without interference from horseless ones. Today they are particularly well suited to biking.)

Mount Desert Island, which is attached to the mainland by a bridge, is essentially split into western and eastern segments. Somes Sound, the only fjord in the continental United States, acts as a magnificent divider. Communities on the western side include Bass Harbor, Southwest Harbor, and Somesville. On the eastern side are Bar Harbor and Northeast Harbor (see page 168). The Acadia National Park Hulls Cove Visitor Center (288-5262) is close to Bar Harbor.

Nearly three million people visit Acadia annually, and many of those visitors arrive in July and August. There is a tendency for people to focus on Bar Harbor and the Park Loop Road that starts nearby. If you are averse to crowds, visit in June or September, or favor the western side of the island. And if you come in midsummer, don't assume you're spending the night on the island if you haven't made reservations!

Bass Harbor

The village of Bass Harbor feels more like a working community than a summer retreat, with the boats in the harbor tending toward lobstering instead of sailing. There are a few restaurants though, so you won't go hungry if you visit. Just south of town is the pretty Bass Harbor Head Light, which can be reached on foot or by car.

Southwest Harbor

In the town of Southwest Harbor you can shop for mementos of your trip or go for something larger, such as a new yacht. The Hinckley Company and several other boatbuilders are located along the shore. Waterfront restaurants command some of the most spectacular views on the island, since diners can look up Somes Sound to the mountains.

Somesville

The village of Somesville is central to the island, but it's still waterfront thanks to its location on the shore of Somes Sound. It is an easy drive to nearly any town, trail head, or launch ramp from here. The historic district consists of attractive white clapboard houses. In the village is a popular bookstore accessible from the water, appropriately called Port in a Storm (244-4114).

OFF SHORE

The harbors of Bass Harbor and Southwest Harbor are interesting places to poke around. On a high tide those in small boats can explore the tidal region above Bass Harbor and Bernard. The photogenic Bass Harbor Head Light is south of town. Use caution around the Bass Harbor Bar and in the narrow passages between area offshore islands.

Enjoy boating along the sheer faces of Somes Sound, being mindful that the wind can sweep along the fjord's walls and make headway difficult.

While not strictly "off shore," the ponds and lakes in the park provide pleasant alternatives to the ocean for small boaters. Seal Cove Pond, Long Pond, and Echo Lake all have launch ramps.

REGIONAL ACCESS

Launch area with overnight parking

SOUTHWEST HARBOR: Kayakers can launch from the *upper town dock* floats on Clark Point Road, a few blocks from the center of town. There is 24-hour parking. For free multi-day parking, use the upper lot beyond the Southwest Harbor Municipal Offices (244-5404), a block behind Main Street. (The concrete launch ramp by the Coast Guard station, further east on Clark Point Road, has 3 and 8-hour parking spaces.)

Public moorings, slips

SOUTHWEST HARBOR: *Hinckley Great Harbor Marina* (244-0117) has slips at the head of the harbor. *The harbormaster* (244-7913) has moorings by the upper town dock in the northwestern section of the harbor.

LODGINGS

Bass Harbor Inn
#119, Charts 13313, 13316 & 13318, Bass Harbor

The innkeeping Graff family summers in Bass Harbor and makes time to get on the water by kayak, sailboat, or powerboat. They wheel their kayak across the road to paddle in the harbor and explore the tidal region to the north. Their family-style inn has an eclectic mix of casual furnishings. A studio that sleeps four includes a kitchenette. A wraparound porch offers a view of the harbor's large fleet of working boats.

Breakfast	Muffins and cereal.
Rates	3 rooms and 1 studio with private full baths, 4 rooms with private half baths and shared showers. $65-75 double occupancy in guest rooms, $110 for 4 people in studio, July to mid-September. Visa, MC. Children welcome. Dog and cat in residence. Open May through October.
Access	*Kayaks:* Launch 200 yards across the road, except at low tide. *Trailered boats:* Launch at paved and concrete ramp at Manset in Southwest Harbor. *Sailboats:* Boats often anchor in the harbor. *Walk to:* Restaurants, market.
Address	Shore Rd., P.O. Box 326, Bass Harbor, ME 04653. (207) 244-5157.

The Moorings Inn
#120, Chart 13318, Kings Point, Manset

If you've ever wanted to see a lot of Hinckleys in one place, here's your chance, since the yachts are built next door. Even without the Hinckleys, The Moorings Inn would have one of the most outstanding views of any lodgings on Mount Desert Island. From your lawn chair you can gaze across at Southwest Harbor, up Somes Sound, and over at the mountains of Mount Desert Island. If you're motivated to leave your chair, it's just a few steps to the stone beach that runs along the front of the grounds.

The Moorings has a decidedly old-fashioned and down-to-earth feel to it. There are comfortable rooms in the main inn, a motel annex, and a few cottages. The inn has been run for over 35 years by the extended King family; members work in various boating industries and enjoy recreational boating as well. Guests may use the inn's bikes, canoes, and kayak.

Breakfast   Continental breakfast included.

Rates   10 inn rooms, 3 motel units, 3 cottages, all with private baths. $55-100 doubles July to mid-September. Prefer checks to credit cards. Smoking permitted in some rooms. Children of any age welcome in cottages, over 5 in the inn. Pets may be permitted in cottages. Open May to October.

Access   *Kayaks:* Very easy launch at all tides from the stone beach. *Trailered boats:* Concrete public ramp nearby in Manset. *Sailboats:* Guest moorings. *Walk to:* Restaurant next door, groceries nearby.

Address   P.O. Box 744, Southwest Harbor, ME 04679. (207) 244-5523, (207) 244-3210.

The Kingsleigh Inn
#121, Chart 13318, Southwest Harbor

Visitors to this casually elegant inn seem to include a good number of sailors who are having boats built or repaired at one of the local yacht yards. The inn is very tastefully furnished with mid-19th-century antiques. To celebrate a special occasion, ask for the third-floor turret suite. It comes with a living room and a fireplace, and there's a telescope for surveying the harbor scene. The inn is located on Main Street, convenient to local restaurants and shops. Afternoon refreshments are served on the porch.

Breakfast   A full breakfast is served by candlelight. There are baked goods such as strawberry rhubarb crisp or cinnamon coffee rolls, and a hot entree such as eggs Florentine.

Rates   8 rooms with private baths. $90-125 double occupancy rooms, $175 for the turret suite, July to mid-October. Visa, MC. No smoking on the property. Children over 12 welcome. Dog in residence. Open year round.

Access   *Kayaks:* Launch from the public ramp at Manset or the lower town dock ramp at Clarks Point. *Sailboats:* Contact Hinckley Great Harbor Marina or the harbormaster. *Walk to:* Restaurants, groceries, shops, laundry, bicycle rentals.

Address   373 Main Street, P.O. Box 1426, Southwest Harbor, ME 04679. (207) 244-5302.

Lindenwood Inn
#122, Chart 13318, Southwest Harbor

There is something quite refreshing about the Lindenwood Inn. It could be the strikingly painted walls or the interesting artifacts from Australia and other distant places. Or perhaps it is the elegant decor of the common rooms, or the eclectic mix of old and new furnishings. Or maybe it's the small heated pool and outdoor spa. Whatever it is, guests are in for a sensory treat.

There are rooms in the main inn as well as in a newly acquired building across the street. The penthouse suite has a rooftop garden and its own hot tub.

Meals   A full breakfast is included and features muffins, cereal, and a hot dish. A "healthy natural dinner" is available at the inn, with an emphasis on organic ingredients.

Rates   24 rooms with private baths. $85-195 doubles July to Labor Day. Visa, MC, Amex. Wheelchair-accessible unit. No children. 3-night minimum in high season. Open April to January.

Access   *Kayaks:* Launch from the property at all tides, with a 200-foot carry down the lawn. *Trailered boats:* Use the concrete lower town dock ramp at Clark Point or the paved and concrete ramp in Manset. *Sailboats:* The inn is adjacent to the upper town dock; contact the harbormaster. *Walk to:* Restaurants, groceries, shops, laundry, bicycle rentals.

Address   118 Clark Point Rd., P.O. Box 1328, Southwest Harbor, ME 04679. (207) 244-5335, (800) 307-5335.

The Island House
#123, Chart 13318, Southwest Harbor

A stay at The Island House feels like a stay with relatives. Owner Ann Bradford raised her family here before opening the door to B&B guests. Interestingly, her home was part of the first summer hotel on Mount Desert Island in the mid-1800's (the other part was moved next door). Ask Ann to show you the photos from the inn's early years. Guest rooms are pleasantly homey, and you share the owners' living room. Ann's husband Charlie, a Southwest Harbor native, is a retired lobsterman who is happy to talk about boats and the water.

Breakfast   A "very full" breakfast might include fruit crepes, French toast, blueberry pancakes, souffles, or coffee cake.

Rates   4 rooms with shared baths, 1 loft efficiency apartment with private bath. $70 double occupancy guest rooms, $95 efficiency, June through October. Prefer checks but can accept Visa and MC.

Children over 5 welcome. $10 surcharge for 1-night stays in July and August. Open year round.

Access *Kayaks and trailered boats:* Launch from the concrete lower town dock ramp at Clark Point, 1/4 mile away, or from the paved and concrete ramp at Manset. *Sailboats:* The upper town dock is a few hundred yards away; contact the harbormaster. *Walk to:* Restaurants, groceries, shops, laundry, bicycle rentals.

Address Clark Point Rd., P.O. Box 1006, Southwest Harbor 04679. (207) 244-5180.

Harbour Cottage Inn
#124, Chart 13318, Southwest Harbor

Talk about "hot showers!" The Harbour Cottage Inn offers wet, grubby boaters the luxury of a steam shower, steam bath, or whirlpool bath with each room. Guest rooms are spacious and individually decorated. The common room offers plenty of diversions: a VCR with numerous movie titles, well-stocked bookshelves, and games. Glenda and Mike Sekulich, your energetic hosts, can fill you in on hiking opportunities in the national park.

Breakfast Glenda serves a hot "hikers' breakfast" on the porch or in the dining room.

Rates 8 rooms with private baths. $90-135 doubles July to Labor Day. Visa, MC, Amex, Discover. Children over 12 welcome. Open year round.

Access *Kayaks and trailered boats:* Launch from the concrete lower town dock ramp at Clark Point, 1/4 mile away, or from the paved and concrete ramp at Manset. *Sailboats:* The upper town dock is a few hundred yards away; contact the harbormaster. *Walk to:* Restaurants, groceries, shops, laundry, bicycle rentals.

Address 9 Dirigo Rd., P.O. Box 258, Southwest Harbor, ME 04679. (207) 244-5738.

The Claremont Hotel
#125, Chart 13318, Clark Point, Southwest Harbor

The Claremont Hotel is a grand old resort that has been in continuous operation longer than any other guest lodging on Mount Desert Island. For over 100 summers, guests have sat on the wraparound veranda and gazed at the entrance to magnificent Somes Sound. Now it's your turn to pull up a rocking chair and watch the Northeast Harbor yacht races, or stretch out in a hammock on the lawn running down to the water. If you arrive in early August you can participate in the

Claremont Croquet Classic, played on a lawn better groomed than a golf green. The hotel can provide you with a tennis racquet to use on its clay court, or a bicycle to ride into town.

Guest rooms are furnished in a Maine summer cottage style with antiques, white coverlets, and painted walls. Guest accommodations are found in the main building, the Phillips House, and several cottages on the grounds. Common rooms are fairly elegant yet inviting. Guests are welcome to sit down at the grand piano and play if the mood strikes them.

Gentlemen are expected to wear jackets and ties to dinner; the hotel can provide these if you didn't happen to pack them in your dry bag. Despite the jacket requirement, the Claremont doesn't have a "stuffy" feel to it. It welcomes the captains of any size craft as well as children.

> *Meals* Guests staying in the hotel itself or the Phillips House choose between a B&B or MAP room rate. Breakfast includes fresh fruit salad, waffles, pancakes, homemade bread, and the like. Those opting for dinner sit at water-view tables in the formal dining room. Lunch and beverages are available along the shore at the Boat House.
>
> *Rates* 24 rooms with private baths in the hotel, 6 rooms with private baths in Phillips House. From July to Labor Day, rates range from $120-195 for two, depending on room and whether the B&B rate (just breakfast) or the MAP rate (both breakfast and dinner) is selected. There is an additional 15% service charge. Cottages are $153-183 per day, excluding meals, plus a 10% service charge, from mid-June to mid-September. No credit cards. Smoking in common rooms and cottages only. Wheelchair-accessible rooms. Children welcome, asked to dine early. 3-night minimum stays in cottages. Open mid-June to mid-October.
>
> *Access* *Kayaks:* Carry down the gently sloping lawn 75 feet to the Boat House, then down 7 steps to a pebble beach good at all but low tide. *Trailered boats:* Launch around the bend at the Clark Point concrete public ramp. *Sailboats:* Several guest moorings for boats up to 50 feet. *Walk to:* Restaurants, groceries, shops, laundry.
>
> *Address* P.O. Box 137, Southwest Harbor, ME 04679.
> (207) 244-5036, (800) 244-5036.

MacDonalds Bed & Breakfast
#126, Chart 13318, Somes Harbor, Mt. Desert (Somesville)

Binnie and Stan MacDonald are sea kayakers with an interest in conservation issues. Their home, built in 1850, is elegantly furnished with family antiques from that period. Guests share the family's living room. The house is located in the historic district of Somesville. The village's white clapboard houses overlook Somes Sound, the only fjord in the continental United States. Port in a Storm, a waterfront bookstore, is just across the road from the B&B.

Breakfast   Fruit, muffins, and a hot entree such as eggs or pancakes.

Rates   3 rooms with private baths. $75-85 doubles mid-June to mid-October. Visa, MC. Children over 6 welcome. Resident cat. 2-night minimum in high season unless there is an opening. Open Memorial Day through November; other times by reservation.

Access   *Kayaks:* Launch just across the road on the top half of the tide. *Trailered boats:* Launch from the hard-surfaced ramps in Bar Harbor, Northeast Harbor, or Southwest Harbor. *Sailboats:* Sailors anchor in Somes Harbor and bring dinghies in to the Somesville Landing Corporation. *Walk to:* Deli, market.

Address   Route 102, P.O. Box 52, Somesville, ME 04660.
(207) 244-3316.

CAMPGROUNDS

Barcadia Campground
#C18, Charts 13316 & 13318, Oldhouse Cove, South of Trenton

Barcadia is the first campground you come upon after you drive across the causeway onto Mount Desert Island. It is just south of Thompson Island, facing scenic Western Bay. Many sites are arrayed along the 3500-foot shoreline; they overlook several islands. More open grassy sites than wooded ones. Basketball court and volleyball set.

Campsites   200 sites, with 28 specifically for tents. 87 waterfront. 33% tenters. Showers and flush toilets. Recreation hall, located away from campsites, has ping pong, pool, and arcade games. Laundry. Camp store.

Rates $16-24 tent sites late June to Labor Day. Visa, MC. Pets permitted. 3-night minimum on holiday weekends. Open mid-May to mid-October.

Access   *Kayaks:* Launch from designated spot on gravel beach at any tide, also from some sites. *Trailered boats:* Granite ramp in Trenton by the airport.

Address   RR#1 Box 2165, Bar Harbor, ME 04609.
(207) 288-3520.

Seawall Campground, Acadia National Park
#C19, Charts 13313 & 13318, Bennet Cove, Seawall

Attractive wooded sites are well spaced in this national park campground. A popple-stone beach is just across Route 102A at the Seawall Picnic Area. Sites are available on a first come, first served basis. (Reservations are taken for Acadia National Park's other campground on Mount Desert Island, Blackwoods, near Seal Harbor.)

Campsites	213 sites, most are suitable for tents. None on the water. 75% ten-ters. Cold running water, flush toilets, wheelchair accessible. Showers, laundry, and groceries available 1/2 mile away at a commercial facility.
Rates	$8 for walk-in tent sites, $13 for others. No credit cards, no personal checks. Pets permitted. Open May through September.
Access	*Kayaks:* A difficult launch from the Seawall Picnic Area, 1/2 mile from campsites. The carry is over tumbled rocks, best at half tide and higher. Launch is exposed to southerly winds and ocean swells, so it's recommended for experienced paddlers only. Easier, more sheltered launch in Manset. *Trailered boats:* Paved and concrete ramp in Manset.
Address	Route 102A, Southwest Harbor, ME 04679. (207) 244-3600.

Somes Sound View Campground
#C20, Chart 13318, Hall Quarry

At Somes Sound View, you may get to choose between a site overlooking a spectacular old granite quarry or one with a view of the continental United States' only fjord. The stone-cutting operation closed 40 years ago, and today children enjoy fishing in the quarry. Some tent platforms are tiered along the slope leading to Somes Sound, and a few sites are right on the water, for a great mountain-and-sea vista. Most sites are wooded and private. This is a quiet, tenter-oriented facility.

Campsites	60 sites, 50 of which are for tents. 6 waterfront. 85% tenters. Central showers and flush toilets. Pleasant campers' room with wood stove, tables and chairs, books.
Rates	$18-21 per site in July and August. No credit cards, no personal checks. Pets permitted. Open Memorial Day through September.
Access	*Kayaks:* Launch from the steep paved ramp at any tide; the ramp is a bit tricky to use because of its steepness. *Trailered boats:* Small boats can be launched from the paved ramp on the top half of the tide. *Other:* Dock.

Address   Hall Quarry Rd., Mount Desert, ME 04660.
(207) 244-3890.

Mt. Desert Campground
#C21, Chart 13318, Squantum Point, Mt. Desert (Somesville)

A quiet campground near Somes Sound Harbor designed for tenters. Sites are very wooded, shaded, and private; some sites are a short walk in from your car. A number of tent platforms are perched on the slope by the cove. A particularly nice camp store with fresh pastries, muffins, and cookies, plus Ben & Jerry's ice cream. Rental Keowee kayaks and canoes.

Campsites   150 sites, all suited to tents. 45 waterfront. 80% tenters. Showers and flush toilets. Camp store.
Rates $20-27 tent sites, late June to Labor Day. Visa, MC. No dogs in July and August; permitted other times. 3-night minimum reservations in July and August, though likely to be some same-day openings. Open Memorial Day to mid-September.
Access   *Kayaks:* Launch from shore at half tide and higher, or walk along 75 feet of floating rafts to 8-inch-high float to launch at low tide. *Trailered boats:* Launch maximum of 16-foot boat at high tide from paved ramp. *Sailboats:* Moorings for guests only.
Address   Route 198, Mount Desert, ME 04660.
(207) 244-3710.

Great Cranberry Island

ON SHORE

From the shore of Great Cranberry Island, there is a wonderful view north to the mountains of Mount Desert Island. The view reminds you that you're only a few miles from the high activity that characterizes parts of Mount Desert Island in summer. Yet Great Cranberry offers you the quiet pleasures: walking along the water at dusk and spotting deer, exploring the popplestone beaches on the island's southern side. There are only 100 year-round residents, and even in summer it's surprising when a car goes by.

OFF SHORE

It is a short trip over to inhabited Little Cranberry Island, where you can land at the town dock and visit the Islesford Historical Museum. Acadia National Park (288-3338) opens the museum from mid-June to September. Old property documents, household items, and fishing gear help illustrate the history of the Cranberry Islands.

Boaters are welcome to make day visits to spruce-covered Baker Island, most of which belongs to the national park. The best landing is just inside the bar. A path leads to the lighthouse at the center of the island and continues across to the exposed south side. No fires are permitted on the island.

Exercise caution going through narrow passages between these offshore islands. Potential trouble spots include The Gut between Great Cranberry and Little Cranberry, and where the bar forms between Little Cranberry and Baker.

REGIONAL ACCESS

Mainland launch ramp with overnight parking
The most convenient put-in for Great Cranberry is in Northeast Harbor (see page 169).

Ferry service
Beal & Bunker (244-3575) provides regular passenger ferry service between Great Cranberry and Northeast Harbor. The ferry can carry a few kayaks if the weather turns bad while you're staying on Great Cranberry.

LODGINGS

The Red House
#127, Chart 13318, The Pool, Great Cranberry Island

Dorothy and John Towns have been calling "The Red House" home every summer for over 50 years. The main house was built in 1769 and was one of the first on the island. Guests can select a room in the original section, with its wide floorboards and steep stairs testifying to its early construction, or one in the modern addition. The house is furnished in a country style, with hand-stenciled walls and curtains. There is a full guest kitchen and a living room stocked with board games and puzzles. You are invited into the Towns' living room to look over the collection of local writers' books on island living.

> *Meals* A full breakfast is included, with choices such as eggs prepared to your request and popovers. You can arrange to have Dorothy provide

dinner as well.

Rates   3 rooms with private baths, 3 with shared bath. $60-80 doubles from July to Labor Day. Visa, MC. Children over 5 welcome. Cat in residence. Open Memorial Day to Columbus Day.

Access   *Kayaks:* Land on the shore and walk 150 yards along a path through a meadow to the house. Access is on the top half of the tide, before the mud appears. *Sailboats:* Dorothy can arrange for a guest mooring and can pick up sailors at the ferry dock. *Walk to:* It's a little over a mile to the ferry dock, where you'll find a cafe offering take-out sandwiches and a general store for groceries.

Address   P.O. Box 164, Great Cranberry Island, ME 04625. (207) 244-5297.

Eastern Mount Desert Island: Northeast Harbor and Bar Harbor

ON SHORE

The towns of Northeast Harbor and Bar Harbor are located east of the Somes Sound fjord that divides Mount Desert Island. See page 157 for an overview of the island and Acadia National Park.

The park's classic attractions on this side include Cadillac Mountain, a rocky-topped spot that offers particularly impressive views when the sun is rising or setting. You can attain the summit the easy way, by car, or walk or cycle up. The Park Loop Road takes most of the park's visitors along to scenic natural wonders such as Thunder Hole and Sand Beach. The staff at the Hulls Cove Visitor Center (288-5262), northwest of Bar Harbor, can fill you in on hiking and biking opportunities that will carry you away from the crowds.

Northeast Harbor

This pretty town has a street of shops and restaurants just uphill from the water, but what often comes to mind when you hear "Northeast Harbor" is its yacht-filled harbor. The harbor is a destination for sailors from all over. The Asticou Terraces and Asticou Azalea Gardens, not far from town, are filled with lovely plantings.

Bar Harbor

Bar Harbor is the largest town on the island, with plenty of shops and restaurants. You can find anything from fine crafts to tacky tee shirts here; dining options are similarly diverse. The Shore Path takes you by some grand old summer mansions, survivors of the 1947 fire that destroyed many of Bar

Harbor's homes. June and September are better times to visit than midsummer, when the streets and sidewalks can get quite congested.

Guided activities departing from Bar Harbor include bus tours of the park, whalewatching cruises, and outfitted kayaking day trips. There are several places to rent bicycles suited to use on the carriage road network. The Bar Harbor Chamber of Commerce (288-5103) can help you sort out your options; it is located near the harbor, at 93 Cottage Street.

A pleasant walk at low tide takes you to Bar Island, most of which is part of the national park.

OFF SHORE

Boating destinations near Northeast Harbor include the Cranberry Islands and Baker Island (see pages 166-167) and Somes Sound (page 158).

The stretch between Northeast Harbor and Bar Harbor includes an area of exposed waters that can hammer into the shore; a trip between the two is not recommended for inexperienced small boaters.

Acadia National Park islands near Bar Harbor open to day use include Bald Porcupine, The Hop, and Bar Island. The Hop, barred to Long Porcupine at low tide, is a popular picnic stop. Avoid the home in the middle of Bar Island. No fires are permitted on the national park islands.

In the vicinity of Bar Harbor, keep an eye out for fast moving tour boats and the Nova Scotia ferry, which docks north of town.

On days when fog blankets the ocean, kayakers can enjoy paddling on Jordan Pond or Eagle Lake in the park.

REGIONAL ACCESS

Launch ramps with overnight parking

NORTHEAST HARBOR: *The Northeast Harbor Marina,* a town-owned facility, has a paved ramp with water at all tides; fee for trailered boats. Limited overnight parking available just uphill from the marina at the Northeast Harbor police station (276-5111) on Sea Street; pay for parking at the station.

BAR HARBOR: There's a paved *public ramp* next to the town pier. Visit the harbormaster's office (288-5571) at the pier to obtain a recreational boater parking sticker and instructions for all day or overnight parking.

Public moorings, dock space

NORTHEAST HARBOR: *The Northeast Harbor Marina* (276-5737) has moorings and dock space. Moorings are on a first come, first served basis; some dock space can be reserved.

BAR HARBOR: *The harbormaster* (288-5571) has moorings and dock space. Moorings are on a first come, first served basis; dock space can be reserved.

LODGINGS

Kimball Terrace Inn

#128, Chart 13318, Northeast Harbor

The Kimball Terrace Inn is actually a motel, built on the site of an earlier inn. It provides the closest accommodations to the Northeast Harbor Marina, which is 300 yards away. Most of the motel rooms open onto patios or decks with views of the marina. There is a pool on site; public tennis courts are available at the marina. Laundry pick-up can be arranged.

Meals	None included in room rate. Three meals available daily at the Main Sail Restaurant on site.
Rates	70 motel rooms. $112-130 doubles July and August. Visa, MC, Amex, Discover. Designated rooms for smokers. Wheelchair-accessible unit. Children welcome. Open April through October.
Access	*Kayaks and trailered boats:* Launch at the paved ramp at the marina; water at all tides. *Sailboats:* Contact the harbormaster. *Walk to:* Restaurants, groceries, shops, laundry, bicycle rentals.
Address	Huntington Rd., P.O. Box 1030, Northeast Harbor, ME 04662. (207) 276-3383, (800) 454-6225.

The Maison Suisse Inn

#129, Chart 13318, Northeast Harbor

The Maison Suisse Inn was built as a New England Shingle-style summer "cottage" in the late 1800's. Its warm interior is furnished with antiques and there is wall-to-wall carpeting for good sound attenuation. The inn provides easy access to the shops of Main Street, yet thanks to a beautiful terraced garden, it feels removed from the shoppers. Clusters of seats are tucked into sheltered spots in the garden, inviting you to linger.

Breakfast	Guests receive a voucher to eat at a restaurant with bakery just across the street.
Rates	6 rooms and 4 suites, all with private baths. $115-215 doubles in July and August. Visa, MC. Children welcome "under caring adult supervision." Single-night stays can sometimes be arranged. Open mid-May to mid-October.
Access	*Kayaks and trailered boats:* Launch at the paved ramp at the Northeast Harbor Marina; water at all tides. *Sailboats:* Contact the harbormaster. *Walk to:* Restaurants, groceries, shops, laundry, bicycle rentals.

Address Main St., P.O. Box 1090, Northeast Harbor, ME 04662.
(207) 276-5223, (800) 624-7668.

Harbourside Inn
#130, Chart 13318, Northeast Harbor

The Harbourside Inn was truer to its name when it was built over 100 years ago, but trees have had time to grow and obscure the view. It is a delightful place nonetheless, with its Shingle architecture and grounds full of gardens and tall trees. Inside, the rooms are spacious and comfortably furnished with canopy beds, clawfoot tubs, and original marble sinks. Some rooms provide kitchen facilities.

Your hosts, the Sweet family, are longtime residents of the area. They have operated the inn for 20 years and count boating, camping, and hiking among their interests. You can tie into the Acadia National Park trail network easily from here.

Breakfast Blueberry muffins are served on the sun porch.
Rates 11 rooms and 3 suites, all with private baths. In August, $90-125 for guest room doubles, $150-175 for suites. No credit cards. No smoking anywhere on premises. Children over 10 welcome. 2-night minimum. Open mid-June to mid-September.
Access *Kayaks and trailered boats:* Launch at the paved ramp at the Northeast Harbor Marina 1/2 mile away; water at all tides. *Sailboats:* Contact the harbormaster. *Walk to:* Restaurants, groceries, shops, laundry, bicycle rentals.
Address Route 198, Northeast Harbor, ME 04662.
(207) 276-3272.

Nannau Seaside Bed & Breakfast
#131, Chart 13318, Compass Harbor, Bar Harbor

Just a mile from downtown Bar Harbor, Ron and Vikki Evers have created a quiet haven on their heavily wooded property. They worked hard to restore this 1904 Shingle-style summer cottage accurately, using period furnishings and William Morris curtains and wallpapers. Deep sofas and beds with down comforters contribute to guests' comfort. Most bathrooms feature clawfoot tubs with handheld showers. There is a screened porch with wicker chairs. A path leads through the pines down to a secluded stone beach with a view of Bald Porcupine Island.

Breakfast A full breakfast is served in the formal dining room. The morning selection might be eggs Florentine or omelets with croissants.
Rates 4 rooms with private baths. $115-145 doubles. Visa, MC. Children

welcome "beyond the age of reason." Resident cat. 2-night minimum stays, 3-night minimum on holidays. Open Memorial Day through October.

Access   *Kayaks:* Carry boats 150 yards down a gently sloping path, with 4 steps to the beach, and access at all tides. *Trailered boats:* Paved public ramp in Bar Harbor. *Sailboats:* Sailors sometimes anchor in Compass Harbor, depending on the conditions. *Walk to:* 1 mile to restaurants, groceries, galleries, shops, laundry, bicycle rentals. A dairy bar is nearby.

Address   Lower Main St., P.O. Box 710, Bar Harbor, ME 04609. (207) 288-5575.

Ullikana Bed & Breakfast
#132, Chart 13318, Bar Harbor

This Tudor summer-cottage-turned-inn offers spacious rooms in the heart of Bar Harbor. You sense that innkeepers Helene Harton and Roy Kasindorf had fun decorating it: there are unusual and whimsical touches awaiting discovery amidst these casually elegant rooms. Some guest rooms have private terraces overlooking the harbor; others have fireplaces. The innkeepers enjoy helping guests find great hiking and biking trails.

Breakfast   Roy describes it as "a feast:" a full gourmet breakfast with muffins, a fruit dish, and an entree such as apple crepes or lemon souffle pancakes. You can take breakfast on the patio overlooking the harbor.

Rates   10 rooms with private baths. $110-190 doubles, mid-June through October. Visa, MC. Children over 8 welcome. Resident dog. Open May through October.

Access   *Kayaks and trailered boats:* A 2-minute walk to the paved public ramp; water at all tides. *Sailboats:* A 2-minute walk to the town pier. Contact the harbormaster. *Walk to:* Restaurants, grocery store, galleries, shops, laundry, bicycle rentals.

Address   16 The Field, Bar Harbor, ME 04609. (207) 288-9552.

Bass Cottage in The Field
#133, Chart 13318, Bar Harbor

The same Bar Harbor family has owned and operated this former summer estate since 1928. They "try to keep it like Bar Harbor used to be at the turn of the century." You will find original Victorian furnishings and wonderful stained-glass windows here. There is a large sun room filled with wicker. Most guest rooms are quite spacious. There were signs of wear when I visited, but the inn is a good option for the budget conscious who would like to stay in the heart of Bar Harbor. Bicycles can be stored on the porch.

Breakfast	Not provided.
Rates	6 rooms with private baths, 4 with shared baths. $55-90 doubles July to Labor Day. Singles start at $40. No credit cards. Quiet children over 3 are welcome "if they have well-behaved parents." Open Memorial Day to Columbus Day.
Access	*Kayaks:* A 3-minute walk to the paved public ramp; water at all tides. Off-street car parking in a commercial lot included for guests of the inn; kayakers might wish to use a cable lock on their boats. *Sailboats:* A 3-minute walk to the town pier. Contact the harbormaster. *Walk to:* Restaurants, grocery store, galleries, shops, laundry, bicycle rentals.
Address	14 The Field, Bar Harbor, ME 04609. (207) 288-3705.

Bar Harbor Inn
#134, Chart 13318, Bar Harbor

This full-service resort offers lodging and dining right next to the town dock and downtown shopping. The guest rooms in the main inn have reproduction traditional furnishings, while rooms in the newer oceanfront lodge and the motel are contemporary in design. Half of the inn rooms and all the oceanfront lodge rooms overlook the windjammer and tour boat activity in the harbor. There is room service, a jacuzzi, and a heated pool for those who desire some serious pampering.

Meals	A continental breakfast is included in the room rate. Full breakfast, lunch, and dinner are served in the Reading Room Restaurant, and lighter meals and refreshments are available at the Waterfront Terrace.
Rates	51 rooms in the inn, 64 in the oceanfront lodge, 38 in the motel, all with private baths. $115-310 doubles, late June to mid-October. Visa, MC, Amex, Discover. Smoking permitted in some guest rooms and part of the dining room. Wheelchair-accessible units. Children welcome in some rooms. Pets permitted in some rooms. Open year round.
Access	*Kayaks:* Can be carried down a set of stairs to the public beach right in front of the inn, or launched from the public ramp adjacent to the inn's property; water at all tides in either location. Since the shore

sees a good deal of foot traffic, store your kayaks on your car. The inn staff can help you find a place to store your kayaks if you arrive by sea. *Trailered boats:* Launch from the adjacent paved ramp. *Sailboats:* Contact the harbormaster. *Walk to:* Restaurants, grocery store, galleries, shops, laundry, bicycle rentals.

Address   Newport Dr., Bar Harbor, ME 04609.
(207) 288-3351, (800) 248-3351.

Manor House Inn
#135, Chart 13318, Bar Harbor

This elegant inn sits on an acre of land in a quiet neighborhood convenient to downtown Bar Harbor and the Bridge Street kayak launch area. Romantic Victorian furnishings include floral wallpapers and fabrics, carved wooden headboards, and large bureaus and armoires. There are guest rooms and suites in the inn itself and in the Chauffeur's Cottage, plus two cottages by the gardens. Five rooms have fireplaces. Guests can play the piano or sit in front of the fireplace in the living room. There is a lovely veranda with rattan furniture and a porch swing.

Breakfast   A full breakfast with muffins or bread, fruit, and entrees such as egg frittata with sweet pepper sauce or blueberry French toast. It's served buffet style, so guests can eat in the dining room or carry their silver trays to the living room or veranda.

Rates   14 rooms, suites, and cottages with private baths. $89-175 doubles late June to mid-October. Visa, MC. Children over 10 welcome. 2-night minimum unless there is a hole in the schedule. Open April into November.

Access   *Kayaks:* Kayakers can drop their boats off at the bottom of Bridge Street where the bar forms to Bar Island; access is at all tides but can be tricky before the bar is exposed. Kayakers should drive their cars back to the inn, as the dirt lot on Bridge Street is private; it's less than a 5-minute walk. Other options are the town ramp and the public beach next to it. *Trailered boats:* Can be parked in front of the inn on the street. Launch at paved town ramp. *Sailboats:* Contact the harbormaster; the harbor is a 5-minute walk away. *Walk to:* Restaurants, grocery store, galleries, shops, laundry, bicycle rentals.

Address   106 West St., Bar Harbor, ME 04609.
(207) 288-3759, (800) 437-0088.

Black Friar Inn

#136, Chart 13318, Bar Harbor

The Black Friar Inn has been hosting sea kayaking clinics for several years and even has a kayak rack on the back of the house. The inn has many interesting architectural elements salvaged from old area churches and mansions: stained glass, tin walls for the sun room, dark wood paneling for the pub room. Guest rooms are papered in attractive florals. A good selection of VCR tapes includes a few on kayaking and sailing, reflecting hosts Perry and Sharon Risley's interests in boating.

Perhaps due to the inn's in-town location near the Chamber of Commerce, there is air conditioning in all of the guest rooms, a rare feature in Maine inns.

Breakfast   Choices such as banana or gingerbread waffles, Scotch eggs, lemon chive eggs, and fruit parfaits. The innkeepers are happy to accommodate dietary restrictions.

Rates   7 rooms with private baths. $90-140 doubles mid-June to mid-October. Visa, MC, Discover. Children over 12 welcome. Resident Brittany spaniel. 2-night minimum in high season unless there is an opening in the schedule. Open May through November.

Access   *Kayaks:* Kayakers can drop their boats off at the bottom of Bridge Street where the bar forms to Bar Island; access is at all tides but can be tricky before the bar is exposed. Kayakers should drive their cars back to the inn, as the dirt lot on Bridge Street is private; it's just a couple of blocks away. Other options are the town ramp or the public beach next to it. *Sailboats:* Contact the harbormaster; the harbor is a 5-minute walk away. *Walk to:* Restaurants, grocery store, galleries, shops, laundry, bicycle rentals.

Address   10 Summer St., Bar Harbor, ME 04609.
(207) 288-5091.

The Tides

#137, Chart 13318, Bar Harbor

Surprisingly, this grand waterfront Greek Revival house has just three spacious guest suites and one guest room. If your hosts or the few other guests aren't nearby, you might be tempted to feel like a baron or baroness with this estate to call home. The luxurious guest suites each have a water-view bedroom and private sitting room, and two have fireplaces. Outside, there is a wonderful unscreened veranda complete with large fireplace. (The fireplace used to warm the turn-of-the-century ladies taking tea and admiring the sweeping ocean view.) An amble down the lawn brings you to a set of Adirondack chairs at the water's edge, where you can sit and watch the bar to Bar Island being revealed by the outgoing tide.

Breakfast Entrees such as quiche, omelets, or French toast.

Rates 3 suites and 1 guest room with private baths. $225-265 for two in the suites, $125 for two in the guest room, Memorial Day weekend and mid-June to mid-October. Visa, MC, Discover. Smoking prohibited on the veranda as well as in the house. Children over 12 welcome. Cat occasionally in the inn. 2-night minimum in high season. Open year round.

Access *Kayaks:* Can be launched at any tide from the gravel beach in front of the inn. Walk 200 yards down the gradually sloping lawn and down a few granite steps to the beach. The Bridge Street put-in is a few hundred yards away. *Sailboats:* Contact the harbormaster; the harbor is 1/4 mile away. *Walk to:* Restaurants, grocery store, galleries, shops, laundry, bicycle rentals.

Address 119 West St., Bar Harbor, ME 04609.
(207) 288-4968.

Bar Harbor Hotel and Marina
#138, Chart 13318, West of Bar Harbor

This full-service hotel, a Holiday Inn SunSpree Resort, is located just north of the Nova Scotia ferry dock. Amenities include a heated outdoor pool by the ocean, a hot tub, putting green, room service, and laundry service. Children's programs are offered during the day. Rooms are furnished in a Queen Anne style.

Meals None included. On-site restaurant offers three meals daily; poolside lunches and refreshments are available.

Rates 221 hotel rooms. $149-189 doubles mid-July to mid-August. Visa, MC, Amex, Discover. Smoking permitted. Wheelchair accessible. Children welcome. Open year round.

Access *Kayaks:* Can launch from a marina slip. *Trailered boats:* Paved ramp in downtown Bar Harbor. *Sailboats:* Slips available for rent in the marina. *Walk to:* 1.5 miles into Bar Harbor for groceries.

Address 123 Eden Street (Route 3), Bar Harbor, ME 04609.
(207) 288-9723.

Inn at Canoe Point
#139, Chart 13318, Canoe Point, Bar Harbor

When staying at this Tudor-style inn you're right above the water; it is rather like being in your boat without needing to navigate. Oceanfront seating choices include couches in the bright and casual "Ocean Room" or chairs on the deck that perches over the high tide line. Guest rooms are pleasant and comfortably furnished, but what really sets this inn apart is its spectacular location. There are paths to groups of chairs scattered along the wooded bluff, and stairs down to a secluded pocket beach.

The innkeepers, Tom and Nancy Cervelli, escaped from New York several years ago and enjoy biking, hiking, and sailing in the area.

Breakfast	A full breakfast is served on the deck or in the Ocean Room. It might include fruit, baked goods, and an entree such as eggs Benedict, blueberry pancakes, or omelets.
Rates	5 rooms with private baths. $135-245 doubles mid-May through October. Visa, MC, Discover. Smoke-free premises, including deck. Children over 12 welcome. Open year round.
Access	*Kayaks:* Easy access to the water at any tide; simply carry kayaks from your car, across the deck, and down a set of stairs to the stone beach. *Sailboats:* May be able to obtain a guest mooring from the Bar Harbor Yacht Club (288-3275), which is next door to the inn. *Walk to:* Groceries. Bar Harbor restaurants are 3 miles away; the innkeepers can give you a ride or call a taxi for you.
Address	Route 3, P.O. Box 216, Bar Harbor, ME 04609. (207) 288-9511.

Park Entrance Oceanfront Motel
#140, Chart 13318, Hulls Cove, Bar Harbor

All the rooms in this family-oriented motel have ocean views. Rooms come in three sizes, and some have kitchenettes. There is 1/4 mile of shore frontage, with plenty of room for children to play on the lawn or shoreline. On the grounds are a heated pool, hot tub, picnic tables and grills, and bike lockers.

Breakfast	Not provided.
Rates	58 motel rooms that sleep 2-6. Rates are per room and vary with the season; highest rates are $129-299 in early August. Visa, MC. Smoking in designated rooms. Children welcome. Open May through October.
Access	*Kayaks:* Kayakers can drive their cars right down to the shoreline to

unload, with an easy launch from the beach at any tide. *Trailered boats:* Launch from the property's pebble beach. *Sailboats:* Three guest moorings and dock. *Walk to:* Restaurant, groceries.

Address Route 3, RR#1 Box 180B, Bar Harbor, ME 04609.
(207) 288-9703, (800) 288-9703.

Emery's Cottages on the Shore
#141, Chart 13318, Sand Point, Bar Harbor

Here's a chance to stay in a classic motor court cottage. The cottages have been nicely refurbished, and include refrigerators, cable television, and electric heat. Many also have kitchen facilities. The cottages are set on a lawn that slopes to a pebble beach on Eastern Bay. Picnic tables and lawn chairs dot the lawn, and barbecue grills and a stove for cooking lobsters are provided. There is a coin-operated laundry on the premises.

Breakfast Not provided.

Rates 21 cottages with private baths. They are usually booked by the week in July and August. 3-night reservations available May, June, and September, with $36-60 per night doubles in May, $46-70 in June, and $56-85 in September. Visa, MC, Amex. Smoking permitted. Children welcome. Open May through October.

Access *Kayaks:* Easy launch from the beach at any tide. *Trailered boats:* Closest ramps are the paved and granite one in Trenton by the airport and the paved one in downtown Bar Harbor. *Walk to:* Restaurant and convenience store 1 mile away.

Address Sand Point Rd., P.O. Box 172, Bar Harbor, ME 04609.
(207) 288-3432.

THE ISLANDS

of Maine's coast are special places for locals and visitors alike. We are inspired by their beauty, and we relish the solitude we can find on an island. See pages 19-23 for information on Maine's wild islands, how to care for them, and how to determine which ones you may visit.

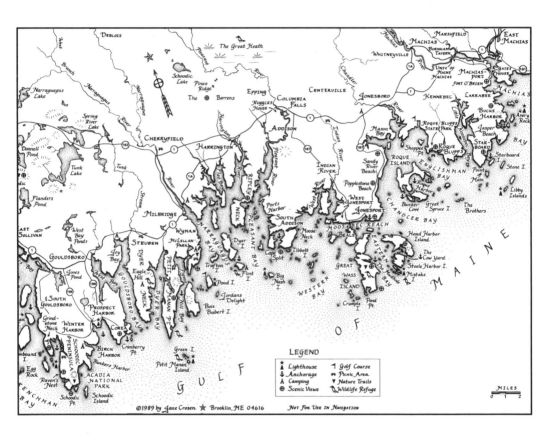

LEGEND

★ ▲ Lighthouse	⌐ Golf Course
↓ Anchorage	✻ Picnic Area
⋀ Camping	▼ Nature Trails
⊕ Scenic Views	⋏ Wildlife Refuge

MILES
0 1 2

©1989 by Jane Crosen ★ Brooklin, ME 04616   Not For Use In Navigation

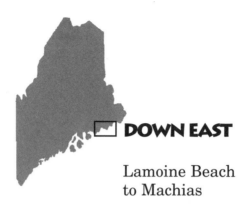

DOWN EAST

Lamoine Beach
to Machias

The Down East region is well worth exploring. The coast is bolder, the tides higher, the eagles and other wildlife more plentiful than in other parts of the coast. You'll be boating among some magnificent islands with very little company. Villages whose residents still rely heavily on fishing are scattered along the coast wherever there is a snug harbor.

ON SHORE

"Down east" can refer to a way of life, a landscape, a seascape, or a specific geographic region. Let's define it here as the coastal communities north and east of Frenchman Bay. (There are certainly places west of Frenchman Bay that, by their traditional ties to the sea and their rural nature, bring "down east" to mind: Friendship, Vinalhaven, Stonington, and Swan's Island being among them.)

It is a region well worth exploring, and not just because the summer crowds seem to visit Mount Desert Island and then pull a U-turn back south. The coast gets bolder, the tides higher, the eagles and other wildlife more plentiful. You'll be boating among some magnificent islands with very little company. Villages whose residents still rely heavily on fishing are scattered along the coast wherever there is a snug harbor. If you can time your visit for an Independence Day celebration or one of the local lobster boat races, so much the better.

Schoodic Peninsula

Visitors with cars can tour a striking, less-visited section of Acadia National Park (288-3338) on the Schoodic Peninsula. A one-way driving loop offers numerous spots along the shore to view the mountains of Mount Desert Island beyond Frenchman Bay. Schoodic Point is an especially good vantage point for watching surf crash against rocks.

Prospect Harbor and Corea are among the quiet fishing villages with guest lodgings near Schoodic Point. Neither caters to tourists, which is part of their charm.

Milbridge

Shops in the town of Milbridge line up along Route 1 and the Narraguagus River. It is a good place to stop for groceries, get a bite to eat, or take in a movie. You can drive to McClellan Park to enjoy a picnic on a rocky bluff above Narraguagus Bay.

Jonesport

Jonesport stretches along Moosabec Reach and has a busy fishing fleet. This is a good-sized town with restaurants, groceries, and other supplies. Captain Barna Norton (497-5933) departs from Jonesport for Machias Seal Island, where his passengers have the opportunity to view puffins. Great Wass Island, connected by bridges to Jonesport, is home to a wonderful Nature Conservancy preserve with hiking trails along the shoreline.

Machias

The large town of Machias lies up the Machias River from the open water, and provides a convenient place to get supplies or find a meal. Helen's Restaurant (255-8423) is renowned for its blueberry pies.

OFF SHORE

Some of the best gunkholing on the coast of Maine lies in the Down East region, assuming the fog doesn't keep you ashore. (The mythical "fog-maker" is reputed to be located in the vicinity of Jonesport.) You can spend days exploring rivers, remote coves, and quiet harbors. Keep in mind that the tidal range increases the further east you go, that there are dangerous points such as Schoodic, and long stretches with no shelter from the wind and waves. Should you get into trouble, there aren't a lot of other boaters around to lend a hand. (Because of the bold coast between Machias and Lubec, no coastal lodgings are listed east of Machias.)

Besides the Acadia National Park islands described on page 169, there are other islands in Frenchman Bay open to visitors. Preble and Dram, just off shore from the Sorrento town dock, are protected by The Nature Conservancy and open to day use. Steer clear of any nesting osprey. To protect wildlife, no pets are permitted ashore. Fires are discouraged and must be built below the high tide line. Little Crow, a tiny stretch-your-legs island unsuitable for camping, is a Bureau of Parks and Lands (BP&L) island just west of Crow Island and Grindstone Neck. Pond Island, northwest of Schoodic Point, is a part of Acadia open to day use; no fires are permitted.

Not far from Corea, in Gouldsboro Bay, is a grassy BP&L island called Dry. Dry is not a good place to pitch a tent. East of Petit Manan Point lies wooded Bois Bubert Island, managed by the U.S. Fish and Wildlife Service. Visits are restricted to daytime use of the Seal Cove area; there are nesting eagles and private property on other sections of the island. Fires are discouraged but can be built below the high tide line. No pets are permitted on Bois Bubert.

West of Jonesport is Daniels Island, which provides a pleasant view of Wohoa Bay. It's a BP&L island with water access on the top half of the tide. Also west of Jonesport, and a half mile south of the village of Indian River, is BP&L's Indian River Island. Watch that you're not stranded by the tide.

East of Great Wass Island is spectacular Eastern Bay. The Nature Conservancy welcomes day visitors to its beautiful Mistake Island preserve, where there is a boardwalk leading to the Moose Peak lighthouse. Keep to the boardwalk or shoreline to avoid disturbing the subarctic vegetation found there. Adjacent Knight Island, also a Nature Conservancy preserve, provides a good view of the Moose Peak light. No pets are permitted and fires are discouraged on Nature Conservancy islands. (If you feel a fire is necessary, it must be built below the high tide line.) A mostly ledge BP&L island, Little Water, is less than a half mile northwest of Mistake Island.

Other Nature Conservancy island preserves in the Great Wass archipelago open to day visitors are Crumple, Black, and the Mans. Crumple is south of Great Wass Island. The treeless Man Islands are east of Steele Harbor Island, and Black is north of it, near The Cows Yard.

A handsome island on the eastern side of the Roque Island archipelago open to day use is Halifax. The U.S. Fish and Wildlife Service requests that visitors stay to high ground and away from sensitive bog vegetation. (Note that Roque Island itself is privately owned.) Another U.S. Fish and Wildlife Service day-use island is Cross, located in Machias Bay. Fires are discouraged on these islands, but they can be built below the high tide line. No pets are permitted.

REGIONAL ACCESS

Launch ramps with overnight parking

LAMOINE BEACH: *Lamoine State Park* (667-4778) has a paved ramp with water at all tides. Overnight parking can be arranged with park management.

JONESPORT: *Jonesport Shipyard* (497-2701) has a ramp with water on the top 2/3 of the tide.

Public moorings

JONESPORT: *Jonesport Shipyard* (497-2701), east of the Jonesport Marina, has moorings.

LODGINGS

The Crocker House Country Inn
#142, Chart 13318, Hancock Point

This country inn offers guests both pleasant lodgings and fine dining on quiet Hancock Point. Hosts Richard and Elizabeth Malaby can accommodate children of any age, and have cribs and rollaways available. Somewhat formal guest rooms are available in the main inn, and country-style furnishings are used in the spacious rooms of the carriage house. Common spaces include a television/reading room and an indoor sauna in the carriage house, as well as a sitting room in the inn.

Guests may use the clay tennis courts and library of the Hancock Point Village Improvement Society. The inn has bicycles for guests to borrow.

Meals A full breakfast is included in the room rate. In the evening the dining room opens to the public, and Richard might serve filet mignon, salmon Florentine, scallops, or a rack of lamb. There is a jazz piano player on Thursday, Friday, and Saturday evenings.

Rates 9 rooms in the inn and 2 in the carriage house, all with private baths. $100-130 doubles in August. Visa, MC, Amex, Discover. Smoking permitted in one common room and limited guest rooms. Children welcome. Pets welcome. Open late April through October, then weekends until New Year's.

Access   *Kayaks:* Easy launch at any tide from the Hancock Point Village Improvement Society dock and launch ramp, 1/4 mile from the inn. If you arrive by kayak, the Malabys can arrange help in moving your boats to the inn. *Trailered boats:* The local launch is gravel and rock, so four wheel drive is preferable. *Sailboats:* One mooring available for a boat up to 35 feet at no charge. Rental moorings can be arranged through the Society; contact Willis Fields at 422-3126. The float is out Memorial Day to the third week of September. *Walk to:* No groceries nearby.

Address   Hancock Point, ME 04640.
(207) 422-6806.

Island View Inn
#143, Chart 13318, Sullivan

When this inn was created from a traditional turn-of-the-century summer cottage, many of the original country furnishings were available. These were restored and placed throughout the house. There are spectacular views of the Mount Desert Island mountains from the dining room and the wraparound porch. Most of the spacious guest rooms have their own balconies. Visitors may have trouble choosing between the porch swing, the rocking chairs, the lawn chairs, or the pebble beach for their afternoon lounging.

Breakfast   Eggs any style, French toast, and cereal.

Rates   6 rooms with private baths. $60-90 doubles, July to mid-September. Visa, MC, Discover. Smoking permitted in living room. Children welcome. Cats in the inn. Well-behaved pets welcome. Open Memorial Day to Columbus Day.

Access   *Kayaks:* Carry boats down the lawn and a set of stairs to the water. There is access at all tides except one hour either side of low. *Trailered boats:* A granite town ramp is located a few hundred yards away. *Sailboats:* The innkeepers have one mooring in use, and suggest sailors tie off a small boat or anchor near the cove. *Other:* Experienced sailors may rent a Rhodes 18 keel sloop. *Walk to:* Market half mile up the road; nearest restaurant 2 miles away.

Address   Route 1, HCR32 Box 24, Sullivan Harbor, ME 04664.
(207) 422-3031.

Sullivan Harbor Farm

#144, Chart 13318, Sullivan

Innkeeper Leslie Harlow is an enthusiastic sea kayaker who enjoys giving guests paddling route recommendations. She is quite knowledgeable about down east sailing as well. Her husband, Joel Frantzman, runs a salmon smokehouse on the premises. Guest rooms in their rambling 1820 shipbuilder's home are simply furnished with antiques and original art. Guests have their own living room with extensive library. Two cottages, which can accommodate groups of boaters, may be available.

Breakfast	Leslie serves a full breakfast that includes some of their prize-winning smoked salmon.
Rates	2 inn rooms with private baths, 1 with shared bath. $60-70 doubles May through October. Visa, MC. A designated smoking area indoors. Children welcome. Dog, cat, and hamster in residence. Guest pets permitted. If cottages haven't been rented by the week, they are available for 2-night minimum stays. Open year round.
Access	*Kayaks:* Carry boats across road, down a 50-yard right-of-way to a stone beach; water at all tides. *Trailered boats:* Launch from the nearby granite town ramp. *Sailboats:* Leslie can arrange for a mooring and transportation if sailors call ahead. *Other:* Guests can use the canoe or the sit-on-top kayaks. *Walk to:* Market half mile up the road; nearest restaurant 2 miles away.
Address	Route 1, Sullivan Harbor, ME 04664. (207) 422-3735.

The Sunset House

#145, Chart 13318, Jones Cove, West Gouldsboro

The Johnson family raises alpine dairy goats, turkeys, and chickens on their small farm, and guests are welcome to visit the animals, or pitch in and help with chores. The Sunset House borders on a three-mile-long freshwater pond, which offers paddling opportunities when the tide is out in Jones Cove. Cozy rooms are furnished in a Victorian style, and there is a guest kitchen.

Meals	A country breakfast is included and might feature smoked salmon, sourdough waffles, or omelets with homemade fresh herb goat cheese. Dinner with the family can be arranged.
Rates	3 rooms with private baths, 3 with shared bath. $59-79 doubles July to mid-September. Visa, MC, Amex, Discover. Children over 5 welcome. Dog and cat in residence. Open year round.

Access   *Kayaks:* You can drive your car down a right-of-way 500 feet from the house and drop off kayaks; water at mid-tide and higher. Easy access to Jones Pond behind house. *Trailered boats:* Concrete ramp at Bunker Cove, South Gouldsboro. *Walk to:* No restaurants or groceries nearby.

Address   Route 186, HCR60 Box 62, Gouldsboro, ME 04607. (207) 963-7156, (800) 233-7156.

Albee's Ocean View Cottages
#146, Chart 13324, Inner Harbor, Prospect Harbor

These ten rustic cottages have commanded a grand view of the harbor for at least 70 years. There's a 450-foot shorefront, and high tide comes to within 10 feet of half the cottages. Most cottages have kitchens, so you can prepare your dinner and then bring it out to a picnic table by the water. Linens are furnished.

Breakfast   Not provided.

Rates   10 cottages that can sleep 2-4 people. $44-67 doubles, $5 additional guests. No credit cards. Children welcome. Pets permitted on a very limited basis. 1-week minimum reservations in July and August; there may be shorter openings. Open Memorial Day to mid-October.

Access   *Kayaks:* Easy carry from your doorstep to the stone beach; launch at all but low tide. *Trailered boats:* Paved ramp in Winter Harbor. *Walk to:* Deli for take-out meals and groceries.

Address   Main St., P.O. Box 70, Prospect Harbor, ME 04669. (207) 963-2336, (800) 963-2336.

Oceanside Meadows Inn
#147, Chart 13324, Sand Cove, Prospect Harbor

Sand beaches are few and far between in Maine, so the lovely wide one in front of the Oceanside Meadows Inn is a real find. It is exposed to the south, so expect some interesting surf when the wind's up. There are guest rooms in the main inn, and multi-room suites with kitchens and living rooms in an adjacent building. Bicycle rentals can be arranged with notice.

Breakfast   Three-course hearty gourmet. Vegetarian and other dietary needs can be accommodated.

Rates   7 inn rooms and 3 multi-room suites, all with private baths. $85-95 for inn doubles, $143-190 per day for suites. Visa, MC, Amex, Discover. Well-behaved children welcome. Well-behaved pets permitted. Open

May through October; other times by reservation.

Access   *Kayaks:* Sand beach 200 yards from the inn; water at all tides. You can drive to within 50 yards of the water to drop off kayaks. *Trailered boats:* Paved ramp at Winter Harbor. *Walk to:* Deli 1 mile away.

Address   Route 195, Corea Rd., P.O. Box 90, Prospect Harbor, ME 04669. (207) 963-5557.

The Black Duck Inn on Corea Harbor
#148, Chart 13324, Corea Harbor

As I was researching coastal accommodations, innkeepers kept suggesting I visit The Black Duck. Once I did, I understood why: it's a particularly charming B&B. Innkeepers Barry Canner and Robert Travers have filled the inn with some fascinating collections of paintings, photographs, and other artwork. A chain-saw-carved American Indian chief presides over the large living room, and delightful animal sculptures pop up in unexpected places in the attractive gardens.

Barry describes a stay in the small fishing village of Corea as "restorative." It is a quiet spot where you can enjoy a stroll through the village without the usual shopping distractions.

Breakfast The entree might be baked orange French toast with pears and orange sauce, or Eggs Black Duck with popovers. The hosts are happy to cater to dietary restrictions.

Rates   2 rooms with private baths, 2 with shared bath. $65-85 doubles Memorial Day to Columbus Day. There is a waterfront cottage for $95 per night. Visa, MC. Children "pre-crawling" or over 8 welcome. Dogs and cats in residence. 3-night minimum in cottage. Open year round.

Access   *Kayaks:* There is somewhat difficult kayak access on the property 100 yards from the house, by carrying boats down over rocks; water at all but dead low tide. An easier option is Sand Cove, less than 1/2 mile away, with a beach that kayakers can use at any tide. *Trailered boats:* The hosts can arrange for a spot to launch boats into the harbor. *Sailboats:* Barry recommends checking at the lobster co-op by the channel entrance before 2 p.m. for a mooring. *Walk to:* There are no restaurants or groceries within walking distance; hosts can pick up food for guests with notice.

Address   Crowley Island Rd., P.O. Box 39, Corea, ME 04624. (207) 963-2689.

Moonraker Bed and Breakfast
#149, Chart 13324, Milbridge

The Moonraker was built in 1939 and is furnished as it might have been then, with formal mahogany pieces. While the furnishings tend toward the elegant, there is a make-yourself-at-home feeling to this in-town B&B. The enclosed porch facing Main Street is fitted with stained-glass windows.

Breakfast	The full breakfast might include fruit, eggs, and sausage.
Rates	1 room with private bath, 4 with shared baths. $50-60 doubles. Visa, MC. Children welcome. Open year round.
Access	*Kayaks:* 1 mile to concrete public ramp; water at most tides. *Walk to:* Restaurants, groceries, laundry.
Address	Route 1, Main St., Milbridge, ME 04658. (207) 546-2191.

Pleasant Bay Bed and Breakfast
#150, Chart 13324, Whites Point, Addison

If you approach by car, you'll be surprised by the unusual animals grazing in the meadows near this riverside B&B. Hosts Joan and Leon Yeaton raise 35 llamas, as well as chickens and goats. Guests are welcome to take the gentle llamas hiking along the property's 7000-foot shoreline and 4 miles of trails. They can also feed the animals and collect chicken eggs.

The Yeatons' house was built on an airy open plan to showcase the views of meadows on one side and the Pleasant River on the other. It is attractively furnished with Shaker and country antiques. It's easy to settle into comfortable couches in the large family room; there is also a spacious reading room. From the big deck you can keep an eye out for eagles and osprey fishing in the river.

There is a guest refrigerator, and guests may use the kitchen to prepare simple meals when the hosts are not using it.

Breakfast	The country breakfast might include blueberry-stuffed French toast, popovers, or very fresh eggs.
Rates	1 room with private bath, 2 with shared bath. $45-70 doubles. Visa, MC, Discover. Children welcome. Dog and cat in residence. Open year round.
Access	*Kayaks:* Launch at all but full moon low tide 150 feet down the lawn. *Trailered boats:* Concrete ramp in Addison. *Sailboats:* Guest mooring. Sailors can use the Yeatons' canoe to come ashore. *Walk to:* No restaurants or groceries within walking distance.
Address	West Side Rd., Box 222, Addison, ME 04606. (207) 483-4490.

Tootsie's Bed and Breakfast

#151, Chart 13326, West Jonesport

Charlotte Beal ("Tootsie" to her grandchildren) converted her home into Washington County's first B&B 15 years ago. While her house is not on the water, Charlotte's warm hospitality and reasonable rates are two good reasons to stay here while in the Jonesport area. She welcomes you to the comfortable home where she and her late husband, a lobsterman, raised their children. As a native of Jonesport, she can fill you in on local events or the area's history.

Breakfast	Full breakfast with your choice of eggs, French toast, or pancakes.
Rates	3 rooms with shared bath. $40 doubles, $25 singles, including tax. No credit cards. Children welcome. Guest pets may be accepted; inquire. Open year round.
Access	*Kayaks:* Closest kayak launching spot is Hopkins (or Dan Watt) Beach, just east of the Coast Guard station and less than 1/2 mile away. Another option is the paved public ramp at Jonesport Marina on Sawyer Square; water at all tides. *Trailered boats:* Launch at Jonesport Marina. *Sailboats:* Moorings available 2 miles away at Jonesport Shipyard. *Walk to:* Restaurants, markets.
Address	RR#1 Box 575, Jonesport, ME 04649. (207) 497-5414.

Raspberry Shores B&B

#152, Chart 13326, Jonesport

There is a pleasant view of Moosabec Reach and Beals Island from the deck and gardens of Raspberry Shores. Host Geri Taylor has an antiques shop on the property, and has furnished her B&B with Victorian pieces.

Breakfast	A big country breakfast. Omelets with home fries, waffles and bacon, or quiche are among the possibilities.
Rates	3 rooms with shared bath. $50 doubles. Visa, MC. Children welcome. Cat in residence. Open April through October.
Access	*Kayaks:* An easy 50-foot carry to 24 shallow stair steps that lead to a sand and rock beach; water at all tides. *Sailboats:* Moorings available 1 mile away at Jonesport Shipyard. *Walk to:* Restaurants, markets, laundry at shipyard.
Address	Main St., Jonesport, ME 04649. (207) 497-2463.

Harbor House on Sawyer Cove
#153, Chart 13326, Jonesport

Harbor House is just one building east of the Jonesport Marina and public ramp, and commands a good view of Jonesport's waterfront activity. When I visited, the owners had finished renovating the first floor of this 150-year-old former telegraph office. At street level is an antiques shop with the original shopkeeper's desk; there are plans for a cafe that will serve cappuccino as well as lobsters. Two large second-floor B&B rooms are scheduled to be available by July 1997.

Meals   A full breakfast will be included and will be served to guests only, in the cafe or on the deck. Dinner will be available to the public May through September.

Rates   2 rooms with private baths. Rates in the $65-85 range for doubles. Visa, MC. Older children welcome. Open year round.

Access   *Kayaks:* Easy 75-foot carry to the stone beach in front of the B&B, or carry over to the public ramp 200 feet away; water at all tides. *Trailered boats:* Adjacent paved public ramp. *Sailboats:* Moorings 1/4 mile away at Jonesport Shipyard. *Walk to:* Restaurants, markets, laundry at shipyard.

Address   Sawyer Square, P.O. Box 468, Jonesport, ME 04649. (207) 497-5417.

Machias Motor Inn
#154, Chart 13326, Machias

The Machias Motor Inn provides a convenient place to begin or end a coastal trip. Comfortable motel rooms have decks overlooking the Machias River. There is an indoor heated pool.

Meals   None included, but you can walk next door to Helen's Restaurant for meals all day.

Rates   35 motel rooms. $60-65 from June to mid-September. Visa, MC, Amex, Discover. No personal checks. Some non-smoking rooms. Wheelchair-accessible units. Children welcome. Dogs permitted. Open year round.

Access   *Kayaks:* There is access at high tide for kayaks from a point of land on the property 25 feet from the parking lot, and easier access at any tide from the public ramp 100 yards away. *Trailered boats:* Launch from the adjacent paved ramp. *Walk to:* Restaurants, groceries, shops.

Address   Route 1, East Main St., Machias, ME 04654. (207) 255-4861.

CAMPGROUNDS

Lamoine State Park
#C22, Chart 13318, Lamoine Beach

A rustic state park that provides access to Eastern Bay. Pleasant views of Mount Desert Island's mountains from the picnic area. Most campsites are uphill 1/4 mile from the water. Playground and volleyball. Sandy Lamoine Beach is a mile east.

Campsites	61 sites, all suitable for tents. A few waterfront. 50% tenters. Privies.
Rates	$12 tent sites for Maine residents, $16 for non-residents, including lodging tax. No credit cards. Pets permitted. 2-night minimum reservation, single-night stays available at check-in. For state park reservations, dial (800) 332-1501 from Maine phones, (207) 287-3824 from outside the state. Open mid-May to mid-October.
Access	*Kayaks and trailered boats:* Launch from gravel ramp; water at all tides. *Other:* Overnight parking can be arranged with ranger.
Address	Route 184, Lamoine Beach, ME. Mail: RR#2 Box 194, Ellsworth, ME 04605. (207) 667-4778.

Ocean Wood Campground
#C23, Chart 13324, Birch Harbor

This beautiful wooded campground, adjacent to a dramatic rocky shore, caters to quiet campers. The shoreline is covered with large rumbling popplestones. Campsites are well spaced, with plenty of privacy. Campers carry in their gear a short distance to one set of waterfront sites. There is no office, but the manager or owner will find you once you've selected a spot.

Campers weary of their own cooking will enjoy the restaurant at the entrance to the campground. Despite the restaurant's white linens and harbor view, it welcomes those wearing hiking shoes.

Campsites	70 sites, with 50 for tents. 20 oceanfront. 60% tenters. Showers and flush toilets in central bathhouse, plus privies. Restaurant 1/2 mile from sites.
Rates	$14-20 for tent sites, including lodging tax, late June through August. No credit cards. Pets permitted. 2-night minimum reservations; single-night stays available at check-in. Open early May through October.
Access	*Kayaks:* Only experienced kayakers should launch from the cobble

beach, which is exposed to southeast winds and ocean swells. It is a difficult 75-yard carry over large popplestones to the water, with water at any tide. Another launch option is near the restaurant, with a 25-yard carry over grass; mid-tide or higher avoids the mud. Although this is quieter water, it quickly leads to exposed seas. *Trailered boats:* Paved ramp in Winter Harbor. *Walk to:* Groceries and phone 1.5 miles.

Address P.O. Box 111, Birch Harbor, ME 04613.
(207) 963-7194.

Mainayr Campground
#C24, Chart 13324, Joy Cove, Steuben

Mainayr, a small, pleasant campground, offers quiet tidal estuary boating on Joy Cove and Joy Bay. South of Joy Bay are the more open waters of Gouldsboro Bay. Campsites are mostly wooded and private. The friendly folks in the office can fix you up with live or cooked lobsters in the evening, and coffee and donuts in the morning. Rental canoes.

Campsites 32 sites, most suitable for tents. 24 waterfront. Showers and flush toilets. Laundry. Basic groceries and lobsters.
Rates $15.75 tent sites. No credit cards. Pets permitted. Open Memorial Day to mid-October.
Access *Kayaks:* Launch from the boat ramp or directly from any of a half dozen sites (such as #27 and #29), best at 1/2 tide and higher. *Trailered boats:* Launch from grassy ramp. *Sailboats:* Reported to be good holding ground for anchoring.
Address RR Box 69, Steuben, ME 04680.
(207) 546-2690.

Bayview Campground
#C25, Chart 13324, Fish Point, Milbridge

Bayview offers open sites looking over the Narraguagus River to the town of Milbridge. It provides a good jumping-off point for exploring Pleasant Bay. A gas grill and lobster cooker are available to campers, along with two attractive shingled screen houses.

Campsites 30 sites total, 12 suitable for tents. 14 waterfront. 20% tenters. Showers and flush toilets.
Rates $12 tent sites. No credit cards. Pets permitted. Open May 15 to October 15.

Access *Kayaks:* Carry boats down a 75-foot path for easy launching at half tide and higher. Water access at most tides at town marina. *Trailered boats:* Concrete ramp at nearby town marina. *Walk to:* Restaurants, groceries, and laundry in town, 1 mile away.

Address Route 1A, P.O. Box 243, Milbridge, ME 04658.
(207) 546-2946.

Sunset Point Campground
#C26, Chart 13324, Mill Creek, Harrington

Sunset Point has open sites overlooking the Harrington River. There are a few wooded sites down near the water.

Campsites 30 sites, of which 10 are for tents. None waterfront. 50% tenters. Showers and flush toilets.

Rates $12 tent sites. No credit cards. Pets permitted. Open mid-May to mid-October.

Access *Kayaks:* Launch into Mill Creek with a 25-yard carry; water at all but low tide. *Trailered boats:* Concrete ramp in Addison.

Address Marshville Rd., Harrington, ME 04643.
(207) 483-4412.

Henry Point Campground
#C27, Chart 13326, Sawyer Cove, Jonesport

This municipal campground offers basic open sites along scenic Moosabec Reach, for convenient access to the Great Wass archipelago. Campers can walk into town for meals or groceries.

Campsites 40 sites; any can be used by tenters. Most sites waterfront. 30% tenters. Chemical toilets. Showers and laundry machines available nearby at the Jonesport Shipyard.

Rates $7 tent sites. No credit cards. Pets permitted. Open May 1 to November 1.

Access *Kayaks:* Easy launch from harbor side of campground at any tide. *Trailered boats:* Paved public ramp at Jonesport Marina. *Sailboats:* Moorings at Jonesport Shipyard. *Walk to:* Restaurants, groceries.

Address Kelley Point Rd., Jonesport, ME 04649.
(207) 497-2804.

Cobscook Bay Side Trip

ON SHORE

Boating in Cobscook Bay is listed as a side trip because the voyage from Machias would require travelling beside a long stretch of bold coast. Cobscook Bay State Park and nearby lodgings make good destinations for boaters who would like to day-trip in the bay. This is an area especially rich in wildlife; bald eagles are sighted frequently.

It's a short drive to West Quoddy Head, the easternmost point in the United States. There is a red and white-striped lighthouse and a hiking trail, and you can see Grand Manan Island on a clear day. Another tour takes you across the border at Lubec to visit Campobello Island in New Brunswick. Beautiful old summer cottages and hiking trails are on the grounds of the Roosevelt Campobello International Park (506-752-2922) created around Franklin D. Roosevelt's summer home.

OFF SHORE

A boating trip on Cobscook Bay will put you into a remote area with few other boaters and extreme tides. You may not recognize a tiny island you passed at high tide on your return six hours later, when it has become quite large and surrounded with impressive mudflats. "Cobscook" means "boiling tides," and there are dangerous reversing falls where Whiting and Dennys Bays meet Cobscook Bay.

Read boating guidebooks (such as Venn's *Sea Kayaking along the New England Coast* or *A Cruising Guide to the Maine Coast* by Taft, Taft and Rindlaub) and seek local knowledge about the tides and strong currents of this region before venturing out. Tides in the bay are on the order of 15 to 20 feet. Low tide occurs significantly later in the far reaches, such as near the state park.

LODGING

Yellow Birch Farm
#155, Chart 13394 (1:50:000), Young's Cove, West Pembroke

Yellow Birch Farm provides accommodations near Dennys Bay, which is one of the more sheltered sections of the Cobscook Bay region. It's a 5-minute walk through a parcel belonging to the Moosehorn National Wildlife Refuge to reach the water. Innkeepers Gretchen Gordon and Bunny Richards raise organic vegetables and chickens next to their 200-year-old farmhouse. I did not have an opportunity to visit, but Gretchen reports that they offer a spacious room with 2 skylights and 3 west-facing windows in the farmhouse, and a cabin with a kitchen and wood stove. Guests can borrow bicycles to ride to the park by the reversing falls.

Breakfast	Likely to feature vegetables or berries from the property, and just-collected eggs. House favorites include homemade bread or muffins, crepes with berries, and 7-grain hot cereal.
Rates	1 room with private bath; 1 cabin with outdoor hot shower and privy. $45 doubles. No credit cards. Inquire before bringing children. Cabin tends to be rented by the week. Open year round.
Access	*Kayaks*: Drive down to the water on a right-of-way through the wildlife refuge and launch into Young's Cove on the top half of the tide. Access to Dennys Bay at all tides 2 miles away at a dirt ramp. *Trailered boats*: Two nearby dirt launch ramps. *Other:* Rental canoe. *Walk to*: No restaurants or groceries within walking distance.
Address	Young's Cove Rd., Pembroke, ME 04666. (207) 726-5807.

CAMPGROUND

Cobscook Bay State Park
#C28, Chart 13394 (1:50:000), Broad Cove, Dennysville

The state park provides mostly wooded, well-spaced campsites on beautiful Whiting Bay. There are hiking trails to help you with your wildlife spotting. Based on my visit a few years ago, I'd suggest bringing plenty of insect repellent.

Campsites	106 sites, of which 79 are for tents. Half the sites are waterfront. 80% tenters. Showers and privies, wheelchair accessible.
Rates	$12 tent sites for Maine residents, $16 for non-residents, including lodging tax. Visa, MC. Personal checks drawn on Maine banks only. Pets permitted. 2-night minimum reservations, single-night stays available at check-in. For state park reservations, dial (800) 332-1501 from Maine phones, (207) 287-3824 from outside the state. Open mid-May to mid-October.
Access	*Kayaks:* Paddlers can launch from the park ramp or a few campsites on the top 2/3 of the tide. *Trailered boats:* Concrete ramp at park.
Address	Route 1, Dennysville, ME 04628. (207) 726-4412.

APPENDIX A
Emergency Numbers

Coast Guard Search and Rescue

VHF radio	Channel 16
Cellular phone	*CG
Portland	207-799-1680
Boothbay Harbor	207-633-2644
Rockland	207-596-6667
Southwest Harbor	207-244-5121
Jonesport	207-497-2134
Eastport	207-853-2845

State Police

Cellular phone	*77
Portland – Brunswick	800-482-0730
Brunswick – Belfast	800-452-4664
Belfast – Machias	800-432-7381

Local Emergency Services   911

Northeast Marine Animal Lifeline 207-851-6625
Marine mammal strandings hotline

Department of Marine Resources 800-232-4733
Hotline for red tide closures

APPENDIX B
Inn-to-Inn Options for Kayakers and Sailors

Inn-to-inn options for kayakers
Considerations for planning inn-to-inn kayaking trips were offered earlier, starting on page 12. The following are some sample itineraries. Other combinations are certainly possible and you are encouraged to devise your own.

It is your responsibility to review your skills, equipment, the weather, and nautical charts to determine if the distances and crossings required to travel between lodgings are appropriate for you and all members of your party. Remember that fog can settle in when you least expect it, making navigation difficult and spotting landmarks almost impossible. Have back-up plans and enough emergency food, water, clothing, and shelter in your kayaks to get through a cold night at an emergency landing spot.

If you have doubts about the appropriateness of inn-to-inn travel for you and those accompanying you, consider driving between a few different waterfront lodgings for a "coastal sampler" trip instead (see page 18).

The starting locations listed below provide your accommodations for your first one or two nights. Stops after that may warrant a visit of two or three days, so take your time and explore. You can day trip from your lodgings and still have time to enjoy your onshore surroundings.

See descriptions of lodgings, launches, and overnight parking for planning details, such as minimum stay requirements for reservations and tide restrictions. The "On Shore" and "Off Shore" sections will point out some of the places you may wish to visit. Mileages given for boating are in nautical miles (which are longer than statute miles, with one nautical mile equal to 1.15 statute miles). At some of the lodgings, the access to shore is via a float, which some kayakers are unaccustomed to using; check the lodging entries for this information.

In cases where starting-point lodgings are listed without a separate note on parking, the lodging hosts indicated that they might be able to store a car for a few days; this is sometimes dependent on whether it is high season. Ask the hosts when you are making reservations if they can help you with a parking spot while you're away.

Casco Bay
Trip A
- *Start:* Yarmouth. Stay at lodgings in Portland, South Freeport, or Freeport. Park at any of the boatyards on the Royal River in Yarmouth.
- *2nd stop:* Chebeague Island: Any lodging.
- *3rd stop:* Peaks Island: Keller's B&B.

- *Return:* Yarmouth.

Notes: Peaks Island back to Yarmouth is the longest paddle, 12 miles.

Trip B
- *Start:* Stay at lodgings in South Freeport or Freeport. Park at Brewer's South Freeport Marine or Winslow Memorial Park.
- *2nd stop:* Chebeague Island: Any lodging.
- *3rd stop:* Harpswell: Harpswell Inn.
- *Return:* South Freeport.

Notes: Direct inn-to-inn distances no more than 7 miles.

Trip C
- *Start:* Stay at Bethel Point: Bethel Point B&B or Harpswell: Hazel-Bea. Park at Bethel Point Boatyard.
- *2nd stop:* Sebasco Estates: Sebasco Lodge or Rock Gardens; or Bailey Island: Bailey Island Motel.
- *Return:* Bethel Point.

Notes: Direct inn-to-inn distances no more than 7 miles.

Rivers and Boothbay Harbor

Trip A
- *Start:* Southport: Lawnmeer Inn or Trevett: Hodgdon Island Inn.
- *2nd stop:* Southport: Albonegan Inn or Ship Ahoy Motel.
- *3rd stop:* Boothbay Harbor: Spruce Point Inn or one of the inner harbor accommodations with floats.
- *4th stop:* East Boothbay: Any lodging.
- *Return:* Southport or Trevett.

Notes: Longest paddle is 9 miles, assuming passage through Townsend Gut. Some of the lodgings on East Boothbay can store your car, if you'd like to start at the eastern side of the loop; no restaurants within walking distance of the Hodgdon Island Inn though.

Trip B
- *Start:* Rutherford Island: Coveside.
- *2nd stop:* Pemaquid Beach: Any lodging.
- *Return:* Rutherford Island.

Notes: Ye Old Fort Cabins are on the beach, but tend to be week-long rentals. Apple Tree Inn and Pemaquid Beach House are 250-300 yards from a public beach, so kayak wheels would be helpful. A 5-mile paddle through the scenic Gut.

Muscongus Bay
- *Start:* Medomak. Stay at The Briar Rose B&B in Round Pond, park at Broad Cove Marine. Or start at Friendship: Cap'n Am's.
- *2nd stop:* Friendship: Harbor Hill B&B.
- *3rd stop:* Port Clyde: Ocean House.
- *Return:* Medomak or Friendship.

Notes: Port Clyde to Medomak is 10 miles, some stretches exposed to wind. For an easier trip, go from Medomak to Friendship and back.

Western Penobscot Bay
Trip A
- *Start:* Tenants Harbor: Harbor View Guest House or East Wind Inn, park at Cod End Marina or town lot.
- *2nd stop:* Clark Island: Craignair Inn.
- *3rd stop:* Waterman Beach: Blue Lupin.
- *4th stop:* South Thomaston: Weskeag Inn.
- *Return:* Tenants Harbor.

Notes: 10-mile paddle from South Thomaston to Tenants Harbor can be broken up with another stop at Waterman Beach or Clark Island.

Trip B
- *Start:* Lincolnville: Spouter Inn, park at ferry lot.
- *2nd stop:* Camden: Owl and Turtle or Hawthorn Inn (in town), or High Tide Inn (north of town).
- *3rd stop:* Rockland: The Old Granite Inn or Rockport: Oakland Seashore Motel and Cabins (south of town).
- *4th stop:* Camden: Owl and Turtle or Hawthorn Inn (in town), or High Tide Inn (north of town).
- *Return:* Lincolnville.

Notes: A fairly straight section of coast, open to wind, with up to 10 miles between lodgings. Rockland and Camden are busy harbors. Kayakers staying at the Hawthorn Inn and Granite Inn would want kayak wheels. The trip can originate in Rockland (park at Knight Marine Service) or Rockport's Oakland Seashore Motel and Cabins; head to Camden and Lincolnville, and then return via Camden.

Eastern Penobscot and Blue Hill Bays
Trip A
- *Start:* West Brooksville: By-the-Sea B&B.
- *2nd stop:* Castine: Holiday House.
- *Return:* West Brooksville.

Notes: A short trip in mostly sheltered waters; leaves time to explore Smith Cove or the Bagaduce River.

Trip B
- *Start:* Buck's Harbor: Stay at Buck's Harbor Inn, park at Buck's Harbor Marine.
- *2nd stop:* Brooksville: Oakland House – Shore Oaks Seaside Inn.
- *3rd stop:* North Deer Isle: Inn at Ferry Landing.
- *Return:* Buck's Harbor.

Notes: 6 miles from Inn at Ferry Landing back to Buck's Harbor along Eggemoggin Reach. The innkeepers at Inn at Ferry Landing or Oakland House might be able to help you with parking if you'd like to start at one of those inns. The closest restaurant to Inn at Ferry Landing is a 2-mile walk, or you can paddle up to its beach.

Trip C
- *Start:* Oceanville: Oceanville Seaside B&B.
- *2nd stop:* Stonington: Ocean View House, Inn on the Harbor, Boyce's Motel, or Pres du Port (in town).
- *3rd stop:* West Stonington: Burnt Cove B&B or Sunset: Goose Cove Lodge.
- *Return:* Oceanville.

Notes: 8 miles from 3rd stop lodgings to Oceanville. Downtown Stonington lodgings would be easier to reach using kayak wheels; to reach the first three listed you would come in on the town recreational dock, the fourth on a right-of-way. Limited kayak storage at Inn on the Harbor.

Trip D
- *Start:* Stonington: Any lodging. Park at Isle au Haut ferry parking, the town lot, or Steve's Parking.
- *2nd stop:* Isle au Haut: Keeper's House.
- *3rd stop:* Oceanville: Oceanville Seaside B&B or West Stonington: Burnt Cove B&B or Sunset: Goose Cove Lodge.
- *Return:* Stonington.

Notes: Trip legs of up to 9 miles. Sea conditions out by Isle au Haut can get quite rough. This trip is for experienced paddlers only. The ferry can transport kayaks if necessary.

Trip E
- *Start:* North Deer Isle: Inn at Ferry Landing.
- *2nd stop:* Town of Deer Isle: Pilgrim's Inn or Deer Isle Village Inn.
- *3rd stop:* Sunset: Goose Cove Lodge or West Stonington: Burnt Cove B&B.
- *4th stop:* Oceanville: Oceanville Seaside B&B.
- *Return:* North Deer Isle.

Notes: This trip around Deer Isle is for strong paddlers only, as the paddling legs average 10 miles each day, and there are exposed stretches. Depending on the tide, you can portage over the Little Deer Isle causeway on the first leg and the causeway east of Greenlaw Neck on the last leg. You might start the trip at the Deer Isle Village Inn, Goose Cove Lodge, or Oceanville Seaside B&B.

Trip F
- *Start:* North Deer Isle: Inn at Ferry Landing.
- *2nd stop:* North Brooklin: The Lookout.
- *3rd stop:* Oceanville: Oceanville Seaside B&B.
- *Return:* North Deer Isle.

Notes: 12-mile paddle from Oceanville back to start. Can start in Oceanville, paddle to North Brooklin, then North Deer Isle, then return.

Mount Desert Island
- *Start:* Northeast Harbor: Stay at any lodging, park at police station.
- *2nd stop:* Cranberry Island: The Red House.
- *3rd stop:* Southwest Harbor: Moorings Inn, Lindenwood Inn, or Claremont Hotel.
- *Return:* Northeast Harbor.

Notes: 5-mile trip out to Cranberry Island. Arrive at lodging on top half of the tide. Passenger ferry available. Strong paddlers can head up Somes Sound to MacDonalds B&B before returning to Northeast Harbor.

Mount Desert Island and Down East
- *Start:* Sullivan: Island View Inn or Sullivan Harbor Farm; or Hancock: Crocker House Country Inn.
- *2nd stop:* North of Bar Harbor: Inn at Canoe Point, Park Entrance Oceanfront Motel, or Emery's Cottages on the Shore.
- *3rd stop:* Bar Harbor: Ullikana B&B, Bar Harbor Inn, or The Tides.
- *4th stop:* South of Bar Harbor: Nannau Seaside B&B
- *5th stop:* North of Bar Harbor: Inn at Canoe Point, Park Entrance Oceanfront Motel, or Emery's Cottages on the Shore.
- *Return:* Sullivan or Hancock.

Notes: Longest paddling leg 8 miles, Sullivan over to Mount Desert Island; the trip from Hancock to Mount Desert is shorter. Stronger paddlers can eliminate one or two of the intermediate stops.

Down East

Trip A
- *Start:* Corea: Black Duck Inn.
- *2nd stop:* Prospect Harbor: Albee's Ocean View Cottages or Oceanside Meadows Inn.
- *Return:* Corea.

Notes: Corea to Prospect Harbor is 5 miles with an exposed stretch.

Trip B
- *Start:* Addison: Pleasant Bay B&B.
- *2nd stop:* Jonesport: Raspberry Shores B&B or Harbor House on Sawyer Cove.
- *Return:* Addison.

Notes: 15-mile trip for experienced paddlers. Open stretch in middle of trip.

Inn-to-inn options for sailors

The distances that sailors can cover in a day vary tremendously depending on boat size and equipment as well as the weather. Many of the lodgings that can accommodate cruising sailors are shown below. They are listed from southwest to northeast, to help you plan suitable inn-to-inn trips. (This list can also be used as a reference by sailors who have been staying aboard their boats, and who would like to come ashore for a night or two.)

It's assumed that you are sailing from your home base, so the availability of long-term parking is not a consideration. Where a "guest mooring" is indicated, your host may have a mooring available for you to use, free of charge. Where a "rental mooring/slip/float/dock" is indicated, it will generally be at a nearby boatyard; check lodging listings for details on the closest places to tie up. You will need to check with the hosts or boatyards to see if they can accommodate your boat.

It is your responsibility to review your skills, equipment, the weather, and nautical charts to determine if the crossings and distances required to travel between lodgings are appropriate for you. Remember that fog can settle in when you least expect it, making navigation difficult and spotting landmarks almost impossible. Have back-up plans and enough emergency food, water, and clothing to get through a cold night aboard your boat.

Most of the lodgings will allow a single night's stay, but take your time and explore your onshore surroundings. Most lodgings have restaurants within walking distance if they don't serve dinner themselves, but you may need to sail to dinner in a few cases. This will be noted in the lodging listings. The "On Shore" and "Off Shore" sections will point out some of the places you may wish to visit.

Lodgings with minimum stay requirements for reservations may be flexible about filling holes in their schedule on short-notice requests.

Casco Bay

- Portland: Any lodging, rental moorings or slips.
- Peaks Island: Keller's B&B, rental moorings or slips.
- Chebeague Island: Any lodging, guest moorings.
- South Freeport: Atlantic Seal B&B or Porter's Landing B&B, rental moorings.
- Bailey Island: Bailey Island Motel, rental slips.
- Sebasco Estates: Any lodging, rental moorings at Sebasco Lodge.

Rivers and Boothbay Harbor

- Georgetown: Grey Havens Inn, guest mooring.
- Southport: Newagen Seaside Inn, rental moorings or Ship Ahoy Motel, guest mooring.
- Boothbay Harbor: All the lodgings listed have either guest or rental moorings, dock space, or slips at the property or close by.
- East Boothbay: Five Gables Inn, LeeWard Village Motel and Cottages, and Smuggler's Cove Inn have guest moorings.
- Rutherford Island: Coveside, guest moorings and slips.
- Pemaquid Beach: Any lodging, guest or rental moorings.

Muscongus Bay

- New Harbor: Gosnold Arms, guest moorings.
- Port Clyde: Ocean House, rental moorings.
- Monhegan: Any lodging, Shining Sails Guesthouse rents a mooring, Island Inn has a small boat mooring for their guests.

Western Penobscot Bay

- Tenants Harbor: Any lodging, rental moorings.
- Rockland: Any lodging, rental moorings and dock space.
- Vinalhaven: Old Harbor Inn can arrange for a mooring or dock space. Other lodgings, use rental moorings.
- Rockport: Samoset Resort, guest moorings. Sign of the Unicorn, small boat guest mooring, or rental moorings and dock space.
- Camden: All lodgings listed except High Tide Inn have rental moorings, floats, or dock space nearby.
- Islesboro: Dark Harbor House, guest mooring.
- Belfast: Jeweled Turret Inn and Thomas Pitcher House, rental moorings.
- Searsport: All lodgings, rental moorings.

Eastern Penobscot and Blue Hill Bays

- Castine: Holiday House has guest moorings; others, use rental moorings.
- Buck's Harbor: Buck's Harbor Inn, rental moorings.
- Brooksville: Eggemoggin Reach B&B and Oakland House have guest moorings.
- Sunset: Goose Cove Lodge, guest moorings.

- West Stonington: Burnt Cove B&B has guest moorings.
- Stonington: Any lodging, rental moorings, except Inn on the Harbor has a guest mooring.
- Isle au Haut: The Keeper's House, rental moorings.
- Oceanville: Oceanville Seaside B&B, guest mooring.
- Swan's Island: Jeannie's Place B&B and Harbor Watch Motel, rental moorings.

Mount Desert Island
- Southwest Harbor: Any lodging, either guest moorings or rental moorings or slips.
- Great Cranberry Island: The Red House, arrange guest mooring.
- Northeast Harbor: Any lodging, rental moorings and dock space.
- Bar Harbor (in town): Any lodging, rental moorings and dock space.
- Bar Harbor (north of town): Bar Harbor Hotel and Marina rents slips. Inn at Canoe Point, possible guest mooring. Park Entrance Hotel, guest moorings.

Down East
- Hancock Point: Crocker House Country Inn, guest mooring.
- Sullivan Harbor: Sullivan Harbor Farm can arrange for a mooring.
- Corea: Black Duck Inn, check for vacant mooring.
- Addison: Pleasant Bay B&B, guest mooring.
- Jonesport: Any lodging (Harbor House on Sawyer Cove is closest to boatyard), rental moorings.

APPENDIX C
Public Transportation along the Maine Coast

Boaters using folding kayaks or meeting friends on sailboats may be able to do without a car. Those planning an inn-to-inn trip that doesn't form a loop may be able to use local transportation to get back to their car. While Maine is not noted for its public transportation, there are more options than many realize. These choices include planes, buses, shuttles, and taxis today, with the hope of rail service from Boston in the future.

For information on ferries serving island communities, refer to the Regional Access sections covering those islands.

Airlines
Three coastal locations are served by national or regional commercial airlines. The Portland International Jetport is within five miles of Portland Harbor or the East End Beach public launch ramp. Several major airlines fly into the Jetport. The Knox County Regional Airport (listed as Rockland) is four miles from the South Thomaston launch ramp or Rockland Harbor. The Hancock County – Bar Harbor Airport has what may be the biggest public launch ramp in the state adjacent to it, one wide enough to accommodate sea planes. Although it is listed as "Bar Harbor," the airport is actually located across the Mount Desert Narrows in Trenton, 11 miles from the harbor. A regional carrier, Colgan Air (800-272-5488), flies from Boston to these latter two airports.

Buses and shuttles
Bus service is available from Boston to Portland on either Concord Trailways (800-639-3317) or Greyhound (800-231-2222). Concord offers a coastal route between Portland and Searsport. Intermediate stops include Brunswick, Bath, Wiscasset, Damariscotta, Waldoboro, Rockland, Camden/Rockport, Lincolnville, and Belfast. Greyhound has a daily trip between Portland and Bar Harbor in summer.

Local transportation options include buses and taxis in larger communities. Portland has good local bus service, and shuttles operate in Rockland and Camden. Coastal Trans provides limited service to small coastal communities from eastern Casco Bay to southwestern Penobscot Bay. For information on service in Sagadahoc County for eastern Casco Bay towns, call 443-6207. For Lincoln County towns in the Boothbay Harbor to Muscongus Bay region, call 563-6244. For Knox County towns near western Penobscot Bay, such as Port Clyde and South Thomaston, call 596-6605.

Public transportation options, including taxis, are quite limited in the Blue Hill peninsula, Deer Isle, and Down East regions.

APPENDIX D
Wheelchair-accessible Accommodations

Lodgings
The number of lodgings in this guide with facilities accessible to wheelchair users and meeting the Americans with Disabilities Act codes is fairly small. This is due, in part, to the fact that many of the lodgings were built over 100 years ago. The hosts of the following accommodations indicated that they have wheelchair-accessible rooms:

Casco Bay
Portland: Portland Regency Hotel
Sebasco Estates: Sebasco Lodge

Rivers and Boothbay Harbor
Southport: Newagen Seaside Inn, Ship Ahoy Motel
Boothbay Harbor: Tugboat Inn, Rocktide Inn, Cap'n Fish's Motel, Brown's
    Wharf Motel, Spruce Point Inn
East Boothbay: LeeWard Village Motel and Cottages
South Bristol: Coveside

Western Penobscot Bay
Rockland: Trade Winds Motor Inn, Capt. Lindsey House Inn, The Old Granite
    Inn
Rockport: Samoset Resort
Camden: Camden Harbour Inn, Highland Mill Inn, The Camden Riverhouse
    Hotel
Belfast: Belfast Bay Meadows Inn

Eastern Penobscot and Blue Hill Bays
Stonington: Island House, Inn on the Harbor

Mount Desert Island
Southwest Harbor: Lindenwood Inn, The Claremont Hotel
Northeast Harbor: Kimball Terrace Inn
Bar Harbor: Bar Harbor Inn, Bar Harbor Hotel and Marina

Down East
Machias: Machias Motor Inn

Campgrounds

Campgrounds often have ramps leading into their rest room facilities, although the shower and toilet stalls themselves may not be to current wheelchair use standards. The hosts of the following campgrounds indicated that their facilities are wheelchair accessible:

Casco Bay
Freeport: Winslow Memorial Park

Rivers and Boothbay Harbor
Boothbay: Little Ponderosa Campground

Western Penobscot Bay
Warren Island: Warren Island State Park
Belfast: The Moorings
Searsport: Searsport Shores Camping Resort

Eastern Penobscot and Blue Hill Bays
East Surry: The Gatherings Family Campground

Mount Desert Island
Southwest Harbor: Seawall Campground, Acadia National Park

Down East
Dennysville: Cobscook Bay State Park

APPENDIX E
Chart Excerpts

The following chart excerpts have been taken from 1:40,000 NOAA charts, except the last two, which are from a 1:50,000 chart. *They are not to be used for naviga-tion, but instead should be used in conjunction with full size NOAA nautical charts.* Each chart excerpt includes a latitude and longitude reference. The latitudes given are north, and the longitudes given are west; all are rounded to the nearest minute. The excerpts will help you see where the lodgings and campgrounds list-ed in this guide are located. This should help you with day trip, inn-to-inn, or campground-to-campground planning.

Lodging and campground numbers run in a southwest to northeast manner. Campgrounds carry a "C" prefix. Number placements are approximations only.

If you are launching from the shore of your accommodations, confirm your loca-tion before launching by making your own observations and checking with your hosts or local boaters. If you will be arriving by sea, check first with the hosts for information on landmarks and approaches. You might ask them to place identify-ing markers at the shore for you. If it's feasible, you might wish to drive to lodg-ings that you'll approach later by sea, to scout out the waterfront approaches. Refer to the section on "Locating your accommodations from the water" on page 16 for more details.

Fog is quite common on the Maine coast. Visibility may be so restricted that you will be unable to see the shoreline, let alone any landmarks. Have back-up plans and enough emergency food, water, clothing, and shelter to get through a cold night aboard your boat or at an isolated emergency landing spot.

Lodging and campground numbers by region

Casco Bay	#1-21, C1-C5
Rivers and Boothbay Harbor	#22-44, C6-C9
Muscongus Bay	#45-56, C10
Western Penobscot Bay	#57-93, C11-C14
Eastern Penobscot and Blue Hill Bays	#94-118, C15-C17
Mount Desert Island	#119-141, C18-C21
Down East	#142-155, C22-C28

Lat. 43°40' Long. 70°15'

Lat. 43°39' Long. 70°12'

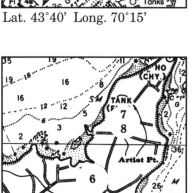

Lat. 43°45' Long. 70°06'

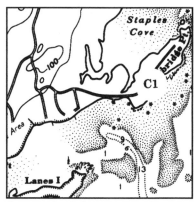

Lat. 43°48' Long. 70°07'

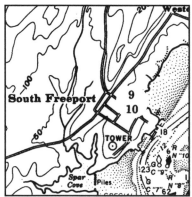

Lat. 43°49' Long. 70°07'

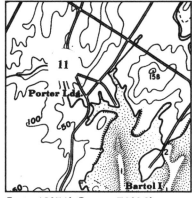

Lat. 43°51' Long. 70°06'

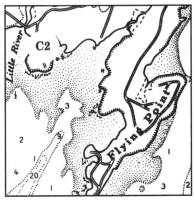

Lat. 43°50' Long. 70°04'

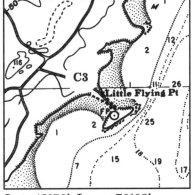

Lat. 43°50' Long. 70°03'

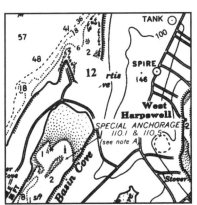

Lat. 43°46' Long. 70°01'

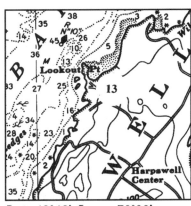

Lat. 43°48' Long. 70°00'

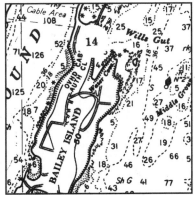

Lat. 43°45' Long. 70°00'

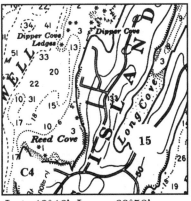

Lat. 43°46' Long. 69°58'

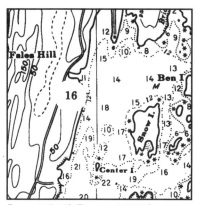

Lat. 43°49' Long. 69°55'

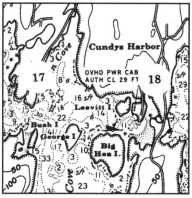

Lat. 43°48' Long. 69°54'

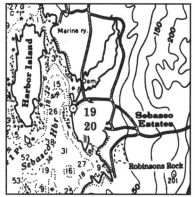

Lat. 43°46' Long. 69°52'

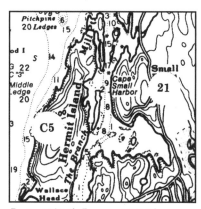

Lat. 43°44' Long. 69°51'

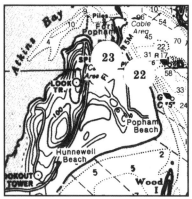

Lat. 43°45' Long. 69°47'

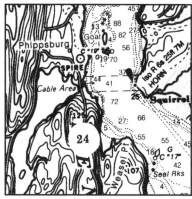

Lat. 43°49' Long. 69°49'

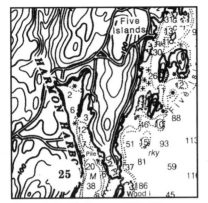

Lat. 43°49' Long. 69°43'

Lat. 43°57' Long. 69°43'

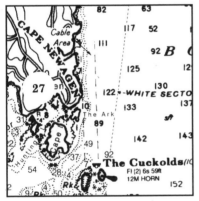

Lat. 43°47' Long. 69°40'

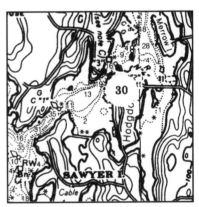

Lat. 43°53' Long. 69°40'

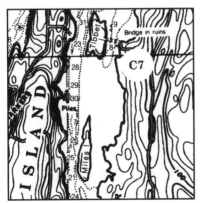

Lat. 43°55' Long. 69°39'

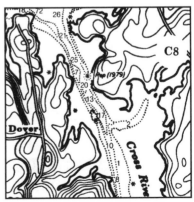

Lat. 43°56' Long. 69°37'

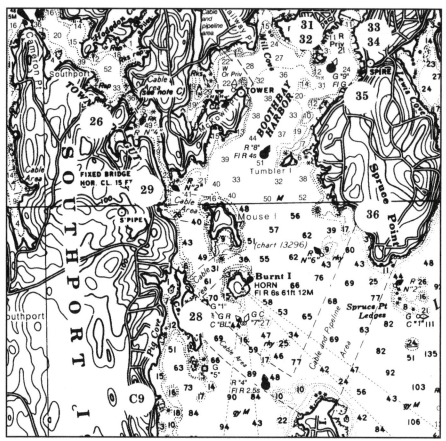

Lat. 43°50' Long. 69°38'

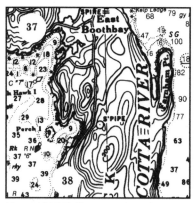

Lat. 43°51' Long. 69°36'

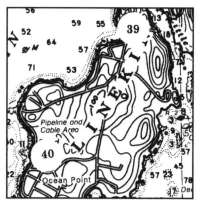

Lat. 43°49' Long. 69°36'

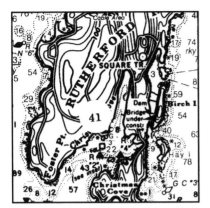

Lat. 43°51' Long. 69°33'

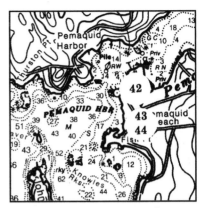

Lat. 43°52' Long. 69°31'

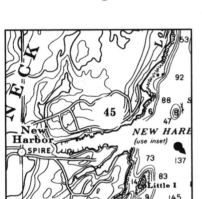

Lat. 43°52' Long. 69°29'

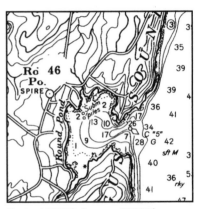

Lat. 43°57' Long. 69°28'

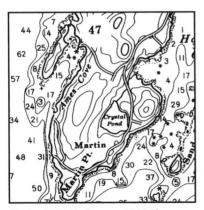

Lat. 43°59' Long. 69°22'

Lat. 43°59' Long. 69°20'

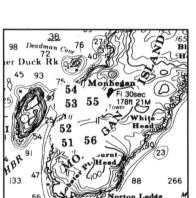

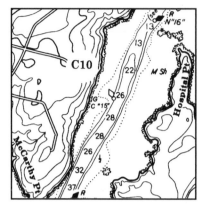

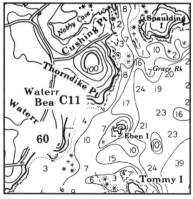

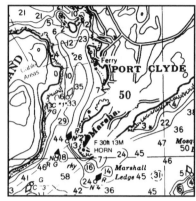

Lat. 44°03' Long. 69°12'

Lat. 43°55' Long. 69°15'

Lat. 43°46' Long. 69°19'

Lat. 43°58' Long. 69°13'

Lat. 43°59' Long. 69°11'

Lat. 44°01' Long. 69°08'

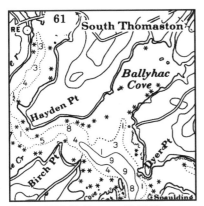

Lat. 44°03' Long. 69°08'

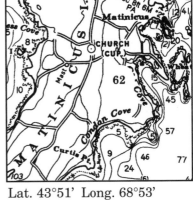

Lat. 43°51' Long. 68°53'

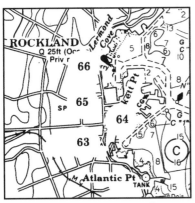

Lat. 44°06' Long. 69°07'

Lat. 44°03' Long. 68°51'

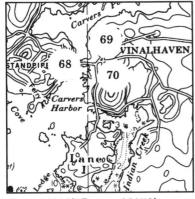

Lat. 44°03' Long. 68°50'

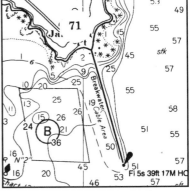

Lat. 44°07' Long. 69°05'

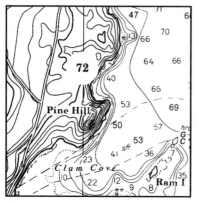

Lat. 44°09' Long. 69°05'

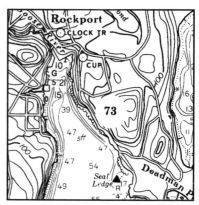

Lat. 44°11' Long. 69°04'

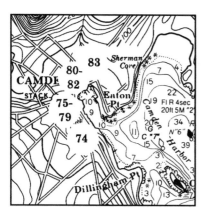

Lat. 44°13' Long. 69°04'

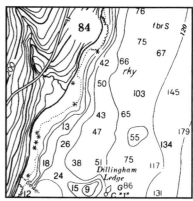

Lat. 44°15' Long. 69°02'

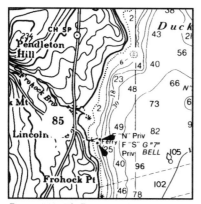

Lat. 44°17' Long. 69°01'

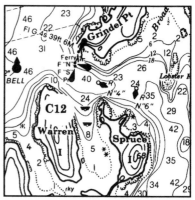

Lat. 44°16' Long. 68°57'

Lat. 44°15' Long. 68°55'

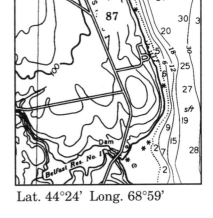

Lat. 44°24' Long. 68°59'

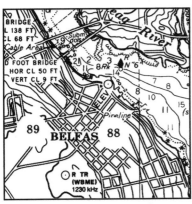

Lat. 44°25' Long. 69°00'

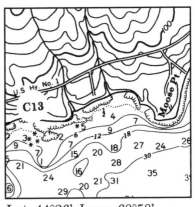

Lat. 44°26' Long. 68°58'

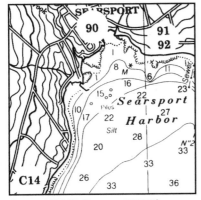

Lat. 44°27' Long. 68°55'

Lat. 44°29' Long. 68°52'

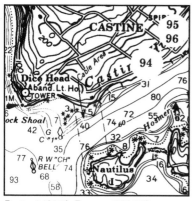

Lat. 44°23' Long. 68°48'

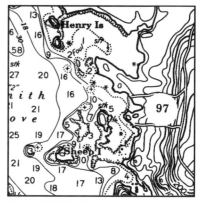

Lat. 44°22' Long. 68°45'

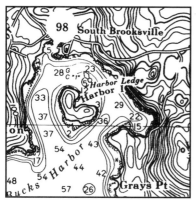

Lat. 44°20' Long. 68°44'

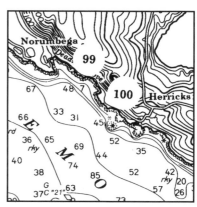

Lat. 44°19' Long. 68°43'

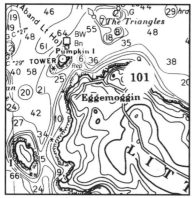

Lat. 44°18' Long. 68°44'

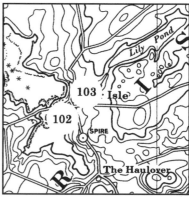

Lat. 44°13' Long. 68°41'

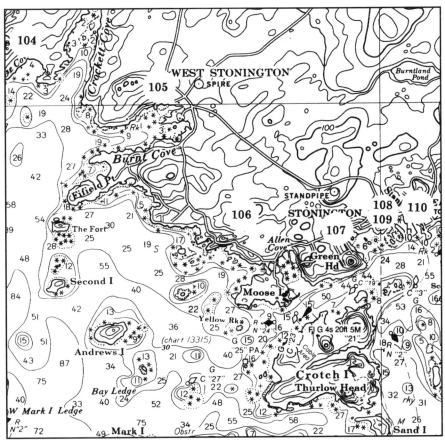

Lat. 44°10' Long. 68°41'

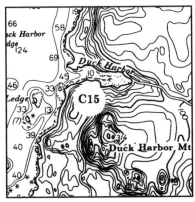

Lat. 44°02' Long. 68°39'

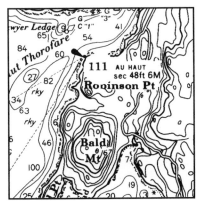

Lat. 44°04' Long. 68°39'

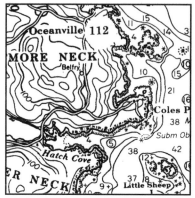

Lat. 44°11' Long. 68°37'

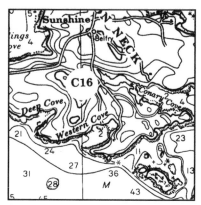

Lat. 44°12' Long. 68°35'

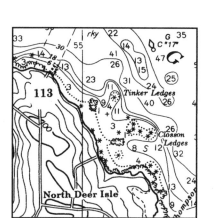

Lat. 44°17' Long. 68°40'

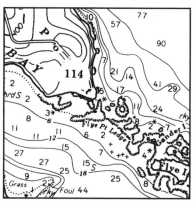

Lat. 44°16' Long. 68°31'

Lat. 44°25' Long. 68°35'

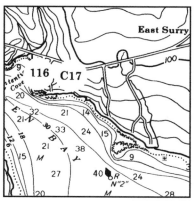

Lat. 44°30' Long. 68°28'

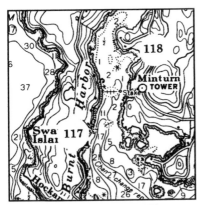

Lat. 44°09' Long. 68°27'

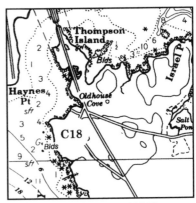

Lat. 44°25' Long. 68°22'

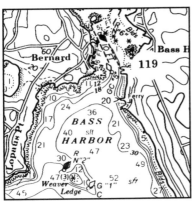

Lat. 44°14' Long. 68°21'

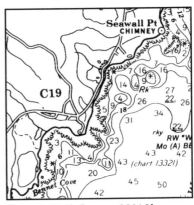

Lat. 44°14' Long. 68°18'

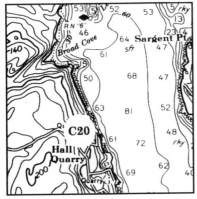

Lat. 44°20' Long. 68°19'

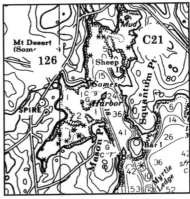

Lat. 44°22' Long. 68°20'

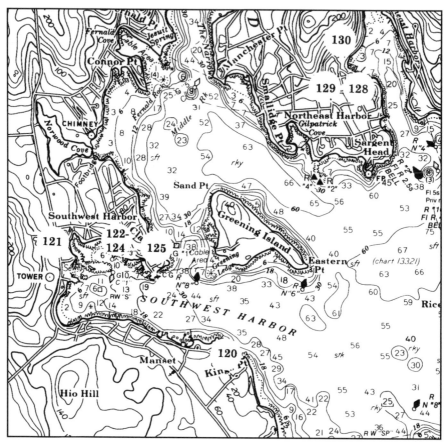

Lat. 44°17' Long. 68°18'

Lat. 44°15' Long. 68°16'

Lat. 44°23' Long. 68°12'

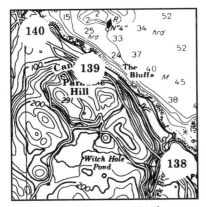

Lat. 44°24' Long. 68°15'

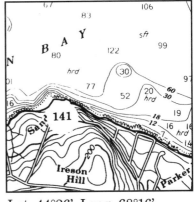

Lat. 44°26' Long. 68°16'

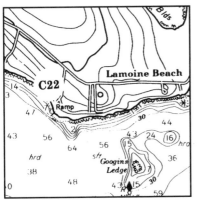

Lat. 44°27' Long. 68°18'

Lat. 44°28' Long. 68°14'

Lat. 44°31' Long. 68°12'

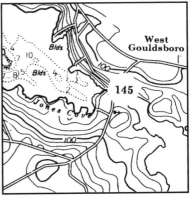

Lat. 44°28' Long. 68°06'

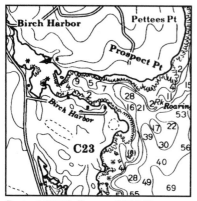

Lat. 44°23' Long. 68°02'

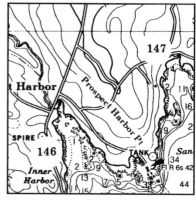

Lat. 44°25' Long. 68°01'

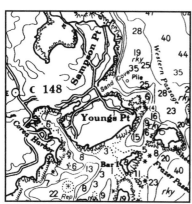

Lat. 44°23' Long. 67°58'

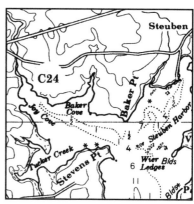

Lat. 44°30' Long. 67°59'

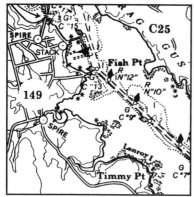

Lat. 44°32' Long. 67°52'

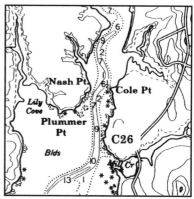

Lat. 44°35' Long. 67°47'

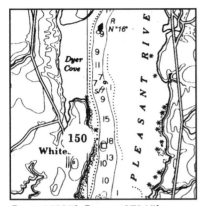

Lat. 44°35' Long. 67°45'

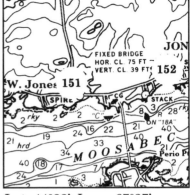

Lat. 44°32' Long. 67°37'

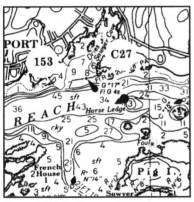

Lat. 44°32' Long. 67°35'

Lat. 44°43' Long. 67°27'

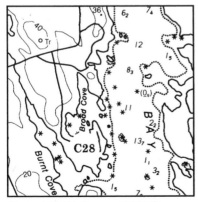

Lat. 44°45' Long. 67°10'

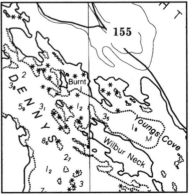

Lat. 44°50' Long. 67°09'

BIBLIOGRAPHY

Boating Guides

Brechlin, Earl D. *Paddling the Waters of Mount Desert Island*. Camden, Maine: Down East Books, 1996.
> Six saltwater trips as well as paddles on the lakes and ponds of Mount Desert Island. Tips on local paddling conditions.

Duncan, Roger F., et al. *The Cruising Guide to the New England Coast*. New York: W. W. Norton & Co., 1995.
> Geared to helping sailors navigate the coast and find services ashore. Interesting historical anecdotes.

Taft, Hank, Jan Taft, and Curtis Rindlaub. *A Cruising Guide to the Maine Coast*. Peaks Island, Maine: Diamond Pass Publishing, Inc., 1996.
> Richly detailed guide to boating in Maine. Includes information on harbor services, navigation, weather, islands, and coastal communities. Valuable for boaters in any size craft.

Venn, Tamsin. *Sea Kayaking along the New England Coast*. Boston: Appalachian Mountain Club Books, 1991.
> Several Maine coast paddling trips are carefully described. Venn also provides tips on paddling Maine waters.

General Reference

Ackermann, Rick and Kathryn Buxton. *The Coast of Maine Book: A Complete Guide*. Lee, Massachusetts: Berkshire House, 1996.
> A guide to events, attractions, dining, and lodgings on the coast of Maine.

Chesler, Bernice. *Bed & Breakfast in New England*. San Francisco: Chronicle Books, 1996.
> In-depth coverage includes detailed descriptions of guest rooms.

Conkling, Philip W. *Islands in Time*. Camden, Maine: Down East Books, 1981.
> A natural history and human history of Maine's islands.

Curtis, Wayne. *Maine: Off the Beaten Path*. Old Saybrook, Connecticut: Globe Pequot Press, 1995.
> A guide to interesting and overlooked places far from Route 1.

DeLorme Mapping Co. *The Maine Atlas and Gazetteer.* Yarmouth, Maine: DeLorme Mapping Co., 1997
> Detailed road maps for Maine, produced at a scale of 1/2" to the mile. Valuable for finding boat launching sites, hiking trails, campgrounds, historic sites, and the smallest of coastal villages.

Hill, Ruth Ann (ed.). *Maine Forever: A Guide to Nature Conservancy Preserves in Maine.* Topsham, Maine: Maine Chapter, The Nature Conservancy, 1989.
> An illustrated guide to preserves open to the public for day visits.

Maine Island Trail Association. *The Maine Island Trail Guidebook.* Rockland, Maine: The Maine Island Trail Association, 1996.
> The annual guide for association members covers low-impact techniques for visiting islands, boating safety, and a network of islands appropriate for recreational use. (Contact the association at 207-596-6456 for membership information.)

McLane, Charles B. *Islands of the Mid-Maine Coast. Pemaquid Point to the Kennebec River.* Rockland, Maine: Island Institute and Gardiner, Maine: Tilbury House, 1994.
> Fourth volume of a series on the histories of individual islands. Old photographs and maps accompany descriptions of early settlements. Earlier books in the series cover Penobscot and Blue Hill Bays, Mount Desert to Machias Bay, and Muscongus Bay and Monhegan Island.

Tree, Christina, and Kimberly Grant. *Best Places to Stay in New England.* Boston: Houghton Mifflin Co., 1996.
> Bed and breakfasts, inns, and other accommodations are described in detail.

Tree, Christina, and Elizabeth Roundy. *Maine: An Explorer's Guide.* Woodstock, Vermont: Countryman Press, 1997.
> A thorough guide to attractions, activities, dining, and lodgings throughout the state. Good coverage of the less-visited coastal communities.

Periodicals

Atlantic Coastal Kayaker, P.O. Box 520, Ipswich, MA 01938. (508) 356-6112.
Cruising the Maine Coast Magazine, RR1, Box 1769, Troy, ME 04987. (207) 948-2200.
Maine Boats and Harbors, P.O. Box 758, Camden, ME 04843. (800) 710-9368.

INDEX

General

Lodgings

Campgrounds

HOT SHOWERS!
MAINE COAST LODGINGS
FOR KAYAKERS AND SAILORS

A great gift for a boating friend or anyone who enjoys an ocean view from their guest room or tent site!

Toll-free phone orders: Call Audenreed Press at: 888-315-0582 (orders only) 9 AM - 5 PM Eastern time
To order by mail:

___ copies of Hot Showers! Maine Coast Lodgings for Kayakers
     and Sailors, $17.95 each: _____

6% sales tax for deliveries within Maine, $1.07 per book: _____

Shipping: $2.00 first copy to each address, $.50 each
additional copy: (Priority shipping $4.00 for first book)   _____

                                                Total: _____

Send check to:
     Audenreed Press
     P.O. Box 1305 #103
     Brunswick, Maine 04011

Your name   _____

Address   _____

    _____

Phone   _____

Gift recipient's name   _____

Address   _____

    _____

Gift message   _____